This book must be returned by the date specified at the time of issue as the DATE DUE FOR RETURN.
The loan may be extended (personally, by post, telephone or online) for a further period if the book is not required by another reader, by quoting the above number / author / title.

Enquiries: 01709 336774

www.rotherham.gov.uk/libraries

MANCHESTER
CITY
RUINED MY LIFE

MANCHESTER
CITY
RUINED MY LIFE

COLIN SHINDLER

headline

First published in 2012
by HEADLINE PUBLISHING GROUP

1

Cataloguing in Publication Data is available from the British Library

Hardback ISBN 978 0 7553 6360 5

Typeset in Bliss by Avon DataSet Ltd,
Bidford-on-Avon, Warwickshire

Printed and bound in Great Britain by
Clays Ltd, St Ives plc

Headline's policy is to use papers that are natural, renewable and
recyclable products and made from wood grown in sustainable forests.
The logging and manufacturing processes are expected to conform to the
environmental regulations of the country of origin.

HEADLINE PUBLISHING GROUP
An Hachette UK Company
338 Euston Road
London NW1 3BH

www.headline.co.uk
www.hachette.co.uk

DEDICATION

This book is dedicated to Amy and David,
my two wonderfully supportive and City-supporting children,
and to the memory of our friend Jack Rosenthal.

Acknowledgements

In any autobiography the list of people to thank can feel rather like a roll call if the author were to acknowledge his friends and family who helped him with his life in general, rather than those who helped specifically in the compilation of the following pages. Therefore at the risk of upsetting a great many friends and family who belong in the former category I would specifically like to thank my daughter Amy Shindler, a highly talented writer herself, whose ability to view the content of this book dispassionately was a lesson in objectivity for her father. Others who read the book in part or in whole to whom I am particularly grateful are Geoff Watts, with whom I have been going to City matches since before the start of the Premier League; Amy Rosenthal, whose abundant writing talents would have delighted but not surprised her father; and David Bernstein, friend and chairman in that order.

I am also grateful to Howard Davies, whose nostalgic recollections of Chris Glennon have sustained our friendship over forty years; to Michael Henderson for endless agonising discussions about Manchester City, Lancashire CCC, Mozart, Schubert and Beethoven. Thanks also to my brother Geoffrey Shindler, to ace photographer Graham Parkinson, to Maureen Lipman and above all to Katherine Fisher for providing the happy ending without which this book, to say nothing of life, would have been a considerably darker work.

Jonathan Taylor, my esteemed editor at Headline and long-suffering QPR supporter, knew exactly what this book was about the moment he heard my first sentence. Luigi Bonomi my agent provided his much valued support in both personal and professional capacities. The attitudes revealed in this book have been shaped by interaction with a great many people but at the end of the day and in the final analysis and after the last cliché has sounded the views contained herein, mistaken or otherwise, are those of the author alone.

Foreword

MANCHESTER UNITED RUINED MY LIFE WAS A MEMOIR OF my early life and a love story about my undying affection for Manchester City Football Club. It was written at a time in my life when I felt optimistic and even though I included the details of my mother's early death it didn't cloud the essentially sunny tone of that first book. The warmth of the response to it was probably caused by a general feeling of goodwill that was widely displayed towards Manchester City in 1998 because its publication coincided with the club's relegation to the third tier of English football.

In writing this sequel I would have liked nothing better than to have replicated the tone of the first book. I believe there is plenty of comedy to be found in the pages that follow but an auto-biography by its very nature is subject to the events of a particular life. What happened to me at the start of the twenty-first century encouraged only the blackest of comedy so the tone of this book has to be different from the first one.

What has happened to Manchester City in the intervening years has been extraordinary. As a Blue since before I started at primary school I thought I had experienced the entire spectrum of the emotions that can engulf a City supporter. As I have been about much else in life, I was wrong about that. In writing about

Manchester City I cannot ignore what has happened to me off the field as it were because to me, sport only makes sense as part of life and not as a thing apart. My feelings therefore about City may well have been significantly influenced by events unrelated to football.

This book is the cry of a frustrated romantic. Despite what you may hear and read I love my club still. Love, we are told, means never having to say you're sorry. I therefore make no apology for the following story which might surprise and possibly shock you. It begins back in the days when bankers were to be trusted, the World Trade Center stood proudly above Lower Manhattan and Manchester City were in the Football League Second Division. In other words, once upon a time, a long long time ago . . .

Chapter One

'You watch. They'll score now. Just to annoy us.'

THERE IS SOME DISPUTE IN THE FAMILY AS TO WHO PRECISELY uttered those fateful words. My daughter Amy claims she spoke them, whereas I am reluctant to cede ownership of such a prescient line. My son, David, the child of an extremely diplomatic mother, pleads the Arsene Wenger defence. On this occasion, 'I did not see it' becomes 'I did not hear it'. Parental pride, I suppose, is its own form of egocentricity, so I am happy officially to credit Amy with the line. What is indisputable is that the words were articulated in the ninetieth minute of the League Two play-off final at Wembley on Sunday 30 May 1999 and Manchester City were losing 2–0 to Gillingham. On the previous Wednesday night Manchester United had scored twice to win in the last moments of the Champions League final. Now, to watch City, two leagues below the despised local rivals, stumble in such an inept fashion on such an occasion, was going to be difficult to bear even for those of us who have borne so much over a lifetime of supporting Manchester City. A few seconds later, Shaun Goater was through on goal. His progress was blocked by the diving goalkeeper and the ball rebounded to Kevin Horlock, who sent a low left-footed shot from the edge of the area into the Gillingham net and, just as Amy had predicted, we were about to lose 2–1 rather than 2–0. 'I told you' muttered at least one of us.

The 'City till I die' supporters who had been streaming towards the exits stopped. I suppose, to be honest, if I hadn't been commissioned to write a piece for a newspaper for the following day's edition which had to be phoned in half an hour after the final whistle, my children and I might well have joined the disappointed throngs heading back up Wembley Way. The goal itself, as Amy's line makes clear, did not greatly change our mood. Losing 2–1 was, if anything, going to be even more frustrating than losing 2–0 and Kevin Horlock would have the honour of scoring the most irrelevant goal in the club's history. What changed our mood was the decision by the match referee Mark Halsey as to the amount of time to be added on to the now expired forty-five minutes of the second half. When it was revealed to thunderous cheers, Mark Halsey instantly became my favourite referee and I found myself greatly concerned by the news that he was suffering from cancer and genuinely delighted when he survived and made a welcome and admirably courageous return to that most widely despised of tasks – refereeing in the Premier League. Halsey communicated the magic number and there followed the ceremonial raising of the board by the fourth official.

The number 5 has never stood out or shined as brightly as it did at that moment. Five minutes seemed to us to represent Hope in a way only an audience at a mediaeval morality play could truly appreciate. For Gillingham fans it must have been as if the natural laws had been suspended. How could five minutes represent an Eternity? It is on occasions like this, when sport simply transports its congregation to a place of religious certainty. Rarely can one referee have been taken so warmly into the hearts of the supporters of a club that was losing a Wembley final.

The five minutes of stoppage time were almost consumed but the faith that had been rekindled refused to die. With less than sixty seconds left, the ball was still in the City half but Gerard Wiekens collected a throw-in and hoofed it upfield where it was headed on to Shaun Goater. His progress was impeded but the ball ran into the path of Paul Dickov, who from ten yards sent a right-foot shot high into the Gillingham net past the goalkeeper Bartram, who, we were thereafter told on numerous occasions, had been the best man at his wedding. It was a goal whose import-ance for City it is impossible to overstate. The crowds had held up well during the club's first ever sojourn in the third tier of English football but condemned to another season in that division one couldn't help but be fearful that City's long-term as well as its short-term future would be bleak indeed. With United the current European champions what little boy would risk a school lifetime of merciless humiliation by choosing to belong to the blue half of Manchester?

After the Miracle of the Dickov, we all expected City to roll over Gillingham in the thirty minutes of extra time. Psychologically Gillingham must have been devastated by that last late goal but, to their credit, they gave as good as they got and there was no further score. It was only when we began the penalty shoot-out that we saw the psychological nature of the two teams laid bare. Horlock scored calmly from the first penalty and Gillingham's first effort, hit tamely along the ground in the centre of the goal, was saved by Nicky Weaver with his legs. Up stepped the hero Dickov, the one man in the ground who couldn't miss. Or so we all thought. He thumped the ball decisively against the right-hand post, from where it sped along the goal line to clip the left-hand post and came out. Surely not, we all groaned, not at this supreme moment . . . The next Gillingham player sent the ball so wide it seemed he was aiming at the City supporters who had left after eighty-nine minutes and were still queuing to get into Wembley Park station. He was followed by the diminutive former Manchester United winger Terry Cooke, whose trickery had helped to transform City's season and led to the club paying United £600,000 they couldn't really afford. As soon as the cheque was cashed Cooke's performances dropped off alarmingly. He had had yet another poor game at Wembley but at least he scored from the spot, though Gillingham immediately replied so the score stood at 2–1 after six penalties.

Richard Edghill, who had suffered years of abuse from his own fans for reasons that weren't exactly obvious and who had never scored a goal for the first team, broke his duck at this most opportune moment with a shot that went in off the underside of the bar and left poor fall guy Guy Butters, the Gillingham centre-back, as the proud inheritor of the title bestowed successively on Stuart Pearce, Chris Waddle, Gareth Southgate and (at that time) David Batty. Weaver was in a mood that brooked no interference with his (and our) manifest destiny. Predictably he saved Butters's feeble attempt and it was all over. We'd won and we were up. United could keep their European Cup; what cared we for such baubles when the League Two play-off trophy was at stake?

It was a moment when the club and its supporters were as one, a moment when not just my own family but the wider City Family reached a peak of happiness together. To have been there with my children was a very special moment in the history of our family, a moment that would become even more poignant in the years to come. Behind me I could see the happy smiling faces of David Bernstein, the chairman, and Bernard Halford, the long-serving secretary; no doubt they must have been only too aware of the financial implications of defeat and victory but at that moment I have no doubt they were caught up in exactly the same exhilaration as the rest of us. Near them were the two ageing heroes of my youth, Francis Lee and Mike Summerbee, remembering no doubt what it had felt like to win at Wembley. In front of me were the celebrating players waving frantically at their delirious supporters. In such moments as these are the memories of a lifetime created. No City supporter who was there will ever forget it. It remains an imperishable memory of the triumph of the Just and Righteous (with apologies to the otherwise blameless Gillingham fans).

Does that win compare with Newcastle '68, Wembley '69, '70 and '76 or Vienna '70, those fabled triumphs of thirty years and more previously? Admittedly those victories, lovingly burnished in the memory of all who saw them, had produced a title as well as a tin pot, first place and not a still-faintly-embarrassing third place permitting us only to compete the following season in what had traditionally been called the Second Division. I maintain that it does. Those 35,000 or so City fans who were at Wembley in May 1999 had stuck with the club through thick (not much of that around in the 1980s and 1990s) and thin (plenty of that laid on with a trowel by Peter Swales). This was their moment of redemption and it really didn't matter that it was only the League Two play-off final.

Undoubtedly some of that deep satisfaction had much to do with the manner of the victory. If it had been a comfortable 3–1 win with the result rarely in doubt after the first City goal, we would have taken pleasure in seeing the world grudgingly begin to right a terrible wrong but it would not have had the impact that the Miracle of the Dickov made on us. This was City at their most seductive, teasing their faithful supporters by showing them the abyss to which they were going to consign them before pulling

COLIN SHINDLER

back and dragging them by the scruff of the neck to the summit, almost choking them to death on the journey.

The manager on that day was Joe Royle and he called this manner of behaviour 'City-itis', which he had sworn to stamp out. Poor old Joe. He never understood that City-itis is not a bacterial infection that can be cured by the antibiotics of running the club in a professional manner with a 'winning mentality'. City-itis is a vitamin deficiency that we are born with. We can take vitamin supplements to build up our immune system but they are not strong enough to deal with diseases like Thaksin Shinawatra or signing Jamie Pollock from Bolton Wanderers. The latter, a combative midfielder, was one of Royle's so-called 'dogs of war', imported to save our Division One status in 1998. We could only stare in amazement at him as, in the last home game of the season, a game we simply had to win to stand any chance of staying up, he brilliantly flicked a cross from the right wing up in the air, rather like Gazza against Scotland in the 1996 European Championships, and then very carefully and successfully headed the ball over Margetson into the net. The only slight miscalculation was that Martyn Margetson was the City goalkeeper and this outstanding piece of football trickery by Pollock gifted Queens Park Rangers a goal that contributed significantly to our relegation. Joe should have known better before castigating us for our 'City-itis'.

After the spectacular implosion against QPR, there was one game left in that 1997–8 season, an away game at the old Victoria Ground against Stoke City who were going down with us if results from elsewhere went against us – which they did. It was a bright sunny Sunday in May and I was playing cricket. Helpful teammates fed the score to me as I categorically refused to listen to the radio. 'You're winning,' they crowed. The goals flew in from all

6

angles and the game finished 5–2 to City, an entirely pointless three points. On the back of that 5–2 victory, City were relegated to what my United-supporting brother enjoyed calling 'Division Three (North)'. That's City-itis, Joe. There's no point in complaining about it and shouting 'unclean' at us. You had it then as badly as we've had it all these years.

You can only understand the Miracle of the Dickov if you understand how we got there. We had started that relegation season full of hope and optimism like every supporter of every club in the land but with slightly more reason than many others. Peter Swales had, to the rejoicing of the multitudes, been deposed by Francis Lee. We had in Frank Clark a manager who had seemed in his six months in charge to be organised and competent where his predecessors, the comically inept Alan Ball, the suddenly-taken-very-ill Steve Coppell and the utterly hapless Phil Neal had simply embarrassed us as well as the club and themselves. It was just before the start of the season that the club proudly announced that they had signed a new centre-forward who, the implication was, would score the goals that would take us back to the Premier League whence we had been ejected in 1996. His name was Lee Bradbury and City had paid Portsmouth a club record £3 million for his services.

Early in the season we played at the City Ground, Nottingham, and I went up to see the new star for the first time. I was sitting very close to the front of the stand behind the goal City were attacking in the first half. A cross came over from the left towards the near post. Bradbury and his marker both shaped as if to go for it but Bradbury decided discretion was the better part of valour and he appeared to shrink from the possibility of physical contact, not really what you want to see in your new centre-forward. He pulled back and allowed the Forest defender to head the ball clear, hoping no doubt that the ball might fortuitously rebound to him. It didn't and my heart sank. We actually won that night, an impressive 3–1 win that marked us out immediately as candidates for promotion but all the way home I was thinking that we had just blown £3 million and our goal-scoring problems were not solved. We all knew as well as City's bankers that there wasn't another £3 million where that had come from. In October the following year Bradbury (wittily renamed Badbuy by City supporters) made the last of his forty appearances for the club before being moved on to Crystal Palace. Sorry, Lee, if you're reading this. It's not personal, well I suppose it is from your point of view, it's just that your story is so helpfully symptomatic of the time you spent with us that telling it enables the rest of the world to see more clearly the clinging, chest-deep mud in which we were mired.

Nevertheless, it took a while before it became apparent that installing City as promotion favourites was a significant miscalculation. In the Georgian midfielder Kinkladze, signed from Dinamo Tbilisi in 1995, City had the most skilful player in the division. Kinky, as inevitably he became known, was a great favourite with the crowd who sighed like a lover at the rich display of skills he slowly unfurled. We had finished the previous season under Clark strongly. That we would get out of the division few supporters doubted. And of course we did get out of the division. The only marginal negative was that we went down instead of up.

By the time Pollock scored his wonder own goal, the manager Frank Clark had been replaced by Royle who had absolutely no time for the fabled tricks of the over-indulged Kinkladze. The Georgian was earning £12,000 a week, which sounds insignificant in comparison to the sums earned by current Manchester City players but at the time it was, according to Dennis Tueart, vastly more than anyone else in the dressing room. One of the first matches Royle oversaw was an away match at Vale Park on a foul day on a mud heap of a pitch against a Port Vale side that revelled in the chance to send the *galácticos* of Maine Road back to Manchester with bruises to the body and the ego. Even if Royle were later to over-emphasise the need for physical aggression, he was right to insist on total commitment in such a confrontation. Vale put a defender on Kinkladze to mark him at all times and that was enough for the Georgian, who showed more interest in the Ferrari he had recently bought and crashed than in the opportunity to win three vital points for the club that was paying his wages and the supporters who worshipped him. It was no surprise that he left for Ajax at the end of the season, where he failed to make an impact and returned to England where he had a similar limited effect at Derby County. His gifts were prodigious but his application was woeful.

Francis Lee had been the man who had brought Kinkladze to Maine Road as well as two other members of the Dinamo Tbilisi side. They outnumbered the players who had arrived through the City youth system, which was clearly in a state of disrepair since the brutal and short-sighted sacking of Glyn Pardoe as youth team coach. Lee had indulged Kinkladze because he had mistakenly seen in the Georgian a way of re-ingratiating himself into the hearts of the fans who had started to make their feelings of disenchantment abundantly clear, in the same way they had displayed them towards Peter Swales for so many years. Swales, however, had never been the idol of the terraces in the way Lee had been and I found the chairman's fall from grace tragic in the most classical sense of the term. Francis Lee was certainly a true hero to me but the goals he had scored and the unstinting efforts he had put in for the team during his seven seasons with us were of no value to him now.

To an extent he had brought his downfall on himself by encouraging the supporters' expectations and then failing to meet that level of expectation (which was certainly pitched a lot higher than another relegation, this time to the third tier of English football). He had taken over amid widespread adulation and had promised to walk away within three years if he had not achieved his and our ambitions. This struck me at the time as slightly ambiguous as we wanted him there for the long haul but, of course, I suppose he was trying to tell us that he would not hang on to power in the wake of failure in the outrageous way Peter Swales had done. Clark and Lee went within days of each other in March 1998. Clark was dismissed in the most unfortunate manner, hearing on the radio that the club was speaking to Joe Royle. In this toxic atmosphere of fear and loathing, Lee was forced to resign as chairman of the club but, unlike his manager, he was permitted to depart with his dignity intact which was ensured by his successor, David Bernstein. In the midst of disaster the club had stumbled upon its greatest chairman. If ever there was a real hero at Manchester City who has never kicked a ball in anger it was David Bernstein.

It was Bernstein and Royle who presided over the recovery, which was both spectacular and was achieved with very little money. Despite the unfortunate rancorous circumstances of the final collapse of their professional relationship, they were as much a credit to the club as the thousands of supporters who stayed loyal despite the humiliation we all felt at hosting the likes of Lincoln City and Chesterfield. There is no disrespect intended to the supporters of these clubs but they will acknowledge that for us it was a reminder of how far we had fallen and, of course, we were a prize scalp to these teams.

On Christmas Day 1998 City were mid-table having just lost 2–1 at York City but on Boxing Day they won away at Wrexham with a goal from central defender Gerard Wiekens and then two days later, during the 2–1 win over Stoke City, something magical started to happen. Goals from Dickov and Gareth Taylor turned round a one-goal first-half deficit and somewhere from deep within the Kippax a rumbling started. It shook the ground, enveloped the players and carried the team to the end of the season on a run spoiled only by two careless defeats. City were on the march again and our great expectations would not be denied. There were still plenty of classic City moments – a 6–0 win at Turf Moor against Burnley was followed the very next match by a 1–2 defeat at home to Oldham Athletic. Eventually, a tense play-off semi-final against a fierce Wigan Athletic team was settled in the second leg at Maine Road by a scrambled goal which ran in off Goater's outstretched shin. It was enough to take us to Wembley and our Rendezvous with Destiny, as Franklin D. Roosevelt would have called it, had he not previously used the phrase in his acceptance speech at the Democratic National Convention in 1936 and, of course, had he not already been dead for fifty-four years.

That victory over Gillingham in such dramatic, not to say hysterical, circumstances was quite typical of life for a Manchester City supporter of over forty years. When I was busily engaged in attempting to acquire tickets for the play-off final I had to report to my friend Howard Davies, who had deputed me to get hold of tickets for him and his boys, too, that I was in Manchester and I was not achieving much in the way of success. At the time Howard was in charge of the Financial Services Authority and I did think that perhaps from his lofty vantage point he could prise tickets that I couldn't. 'Listen,' he said with the sort of fine outrage that made hardened bankers shake in their shoes before they were about to be disciplined and punitively fined by him, 'we've been supporting those bastards for over forty years. They owe us.' With

11

that the phone went down and the Financial Services Authority were regulated even more severely until tickets were eventually secured. 'They' came through and with trembling hands I wrote out as large a cheque as I have ever written to gain admittance to a football match – particularly, as my brother would have reminded me, a match in the Third Division (North).

Howard has been a close friend since our teenage years. Recently, in clearing out the loft, Amy discovered a letter written by him the day after her birth and which had been kept by her mother in a box containing birthday cards, Get Well Soon cards and envelopes in her name sent as First Day Covers. It reveals very clearly the essence of our friendship.

> I can't of course say too much about your offspring as yet since I know very little about it. I understand that it is of a different genetic persuasion to, say, Colin Bell but I have not even been told if it came out American or British, Jew or Gentile, Red or Blue (football-wise), Conservative or Labour (that should be easy at least – though the question of whether or not to join the Tribune Group in due course will be a tough one) . . . Looked at calmly I think it is on the whole a good thing that it turned out to be a lady because with it being born just after the League Cup a boy would have to be called Ron after Ron Saunders . . .

Seeing Manchester City relegated, seeing them in financial turmoil, seeing the revolving door in the manager's office and the chairman's office spinning furiously was like seeing your children being bullied at school. It made you feel wretched because you were helpless; you just had to be outwardly calm whatever the inner torments and show that you had kept faith with them and that you believed they would find the way to the sunlit uplands again and you would accompany them every step of the way, offering belief when they were despondent, offering hosannas of praise at their ultimate triumph.

On 27 September 2011 Carlos Tévez refused to come on to the field in a group match in the Champions League away at Bayern Munich. Whether he refused to play as the manager Roberto Mancini alleged or he refused to warm up, which is what he claimed, is not really the point. His actions caused outrage and the club launched an official investigation which, like all such investigations, merely confirmed a few weeks later what everybody already knew at the time. Tévez's actions, or rather his lack of action, became a significant talking point not just in Manchester but throughout the world of football. Although I thought Tévez's behaviour to be despicable, I thought it was a natural consequence of the way in which this wonderful new winning culture at the club, which we were all told repeatedly we had to admire, was simply indulging brattish players who, like children when they are spoiled, will never thank you for it and behave even worse having been given licence to do so, or so they believe. The club's poor behaviour was as culpable as the player's inexcusable behaviour. My honest reaction to them both was a shrug of the shoulders. 'A plague on both their houses,' I thought (and still think). How could the man who cried when his team played its last match at Maine Road react with such a lack of concern? Did he not care? Had he lost the passion that had sustained him for over half a century? How on earth did he get to this place from that place?

Chapter Two

IS HAPPINESS ANYTHING MORE THAN A FLEETING MOMENT of pleasure, a warm memory of something now only dimly remembered, glimpsed from the depths of a new trough of despair? Happiness is, maybe, just something we see in the rear view mirror.

I had many reasons to be happy in 1999, although I am only too aware that I appreciated very few of them at the time. City's remarkable propensity for self-dramatising heroics so in evidence in the Gillingham game was certainly one of them. I had been married for over twenty-five years; I had two wonderful children and a reasonable standard of living. It wasn't anything to make me give thanks to God on a daily basis for the profusion of gifts He had bestowed on me. It was just life as I had got used to it over the past twenty years or so – a few ups, a few downs, pleasurable times with friends and family, a few disagreements with friends and family.

I was busy and as content in my work as I had been for some years. I had made a reasonably successful transition from my freelance work as a television drama producer and writer to the status of a part-time university lecturer and an author of books. My childhood memoir, *Manchester United Ruined My Life*, conveniently emerged for the first time the week of the 1998 relegation and the Gillingham game coincided with the paperback publication.

It was extremely thoughtful of City to ensure that they were newsworthy for good or ill at exactly the time that best suited the publishers. On the back of that fortunate success I wrote a novel called *High on a Cliff*, based partly on the real story of a twelve-year-old boy who borrowed his father's credit card and flew halfway round the world. It was inspired by John Gilbert's dying line at the end of *Queen Christina* in which he wishes he could have taken his lover, played by his former lover in real life, Greta Garbo, to see his home in Spain, high on a cliff.

I had recently started lecturing at Cambridge University on film and American history which had been a passion since I had begun my Ph.D. there on that subject a few weeks after Manchester City had won the European Cup Winners' Cup by beating Górnik 2–1 in 1970. Now I was back in the same faculty building which had been much loathed by the students because it was too hot to work in when the sun shone and too wet when it rained because the water got into the library at inconvenient places. Needless to say the building had won architectural prizes and is still loathed by students and staff alike forty years later. It couldn't be knocked down because it was now a listed building but listing in the gale force winds that batter Cambridge remorselessly at all times of the year was about the only thing the building never did.

I had been toying with the prospect of some sort of return to academic life for a few years and in 1996 had revised my Ph.D. thesis to take account of recent research which was then published under the title *Hollywood in Crisis 1929–41* in the *Cinema and Society* series of monographs. I wanted to be ready with the right sort of qualification if I could create the right opening for myself but I had decided not to do anything about it as long as my children were undergraduates in Cambridge. Amy went up to read History in 1994 and David who, unlike his sister, did not want to take a gap year after leaving school, followed the next October, joining the Social and Political Sciences department. That meant that Amy left in 1997 and went on to Webber Douglas drama school where she took a one-year postgraduate course in acting before emerging to clinch the part of Brenda Tucker in *The Archers* to the amazement of her parents. She made her career choice against the advice but with the willing complicity of her parents, one of whom at least knew only too well the rocky shoals towards which she had set sail with the blithe insouciance of the young.

David, who had probably enjoyed Cambridge more, had a tougher time on graduation in 1998. He played Cambridge exactly the way it should be played, doing enough work to keep his parents and Director of Studies off his back but otherwise exploiting its opportunities for pleasure to the full. One of his achievements was to play for the college at as many sports as he was capable, which included in due course Women's Hockey. He had done remarkably well to get there in the first place having triumphed over the dyslexia that had cruelly tormented his childhood. It meant that reading was always difficult for him (and still is) so he had to think laterally and find ways of coping with his handicap. One of them was to get his friend Chris to tell him what the books he should have read were about. On one now infamous occasion he managed to get Chris to give him an excellent summary of the main points of the book that formed the central point of the week's work and which, of course, he had not read. On the way over to their joint tutorial David absorbed every word of his friend's excellent analysis. When their supervisor opened the discussion by asking David what he made of the book, David was able to respond fluently and accurately, clearly to the satisfaction of the tutor who then turned to the hapless Chris and asked, 'And what did you make of it?' Poor Chris could only point at David and stammer, 'I agree with him.' The two are still good friends.

David has had plenty of tough times in his life but somehow he has always managed to retain his sense of humour and a sense of perspective. However, when he left Cambridge it was to join a political lobbying firm which nearly destroyed his confidence for all time with its toxic mixture of bullying and crass incompetence. He lasted just four miserable months, hating the poisonous office politics, and finally left in January 1999. He then applied for all sorts of jobs, many of which did not give him as much as a reply let alone an interview, until at the end of January he was invited to recruit at a management consultancy firm called Bain & Company in The Strand.

He returned in dreadful spirits, having lost his wallet and walked the seven miles back to Muswell Hill in the rain. He was in despair, a state of utter hopelessness which I had never seen in this essentially sunny boy ever before. I scarcely knew where to start to pick him up and tell him this wasn't the end of the world. Clearly to him, at that moment, that was exactly what it must have felt like. The phone call which would tell him if he'd got the job (which sounded both extremely attractive and highly unlikely) was due to be made around 5.30pm. As each heart-stopping minute passed, the prospect of the call being positive receded. When the phone eventually rang at nearly 7pm that fateful Friday evening we both supposed it was a polite acknowledgement conveying a message of sympathy and disappointment.

I was upstairs working and David was downstairs in the lounge. I couldn't hear the 'ping' from the extension phone on my desk that would tell me the call was finished so I stuck my head out of my room and listened. David was doing a lot of grunting which didn't tell me anything. I returned to work but couldn't write a word. After a further twenty minutes of this agony, my hopes started cautiously to rise. Nobody spends this amount of time telling someone they haven't got the job. Finally I heard a bellow from the bottom of the stairs; a guttural roar that sounded like an animal in pain. I dashed out and there was David, his face contorted in what looked like agony but was in fact ecstasy. Eventually the roar was transmuted into the words, 'I got it!' That job, working ridiculous internee hours, frequently getting home in a mini-cab after midnight and getting up again the next day at 6.30am to go back to work on the tube, was to be the making of him. The family was whole again.

My family and my football club (and to be fair Lancashire CCC, which has also been the recipient of much genuine emotion over the years) are somehow locked together. I care about them both passionately and, although I am not stupid enough to confuse the one with the other or to pretend that they even equate on any real level, I do acknowledge the power of each to cause me extremes of emotion. I wrote in my previous works on this subject that Manchester City became an emotional prop in the years after my mother's premature death from an aneurysm. Her unexpected death filled me with fear of the unexpected absence, of being abandoned by the one person in the world I trusted to look after me and to be there constantly for me. Manchester City were to be found at Maine Road every other Saturday from the end of August until the end of April. Somehow in that club, with those players, inside the Maine Road ground, I found another home with an entity I could love for ever. Admittedly there would be days when rain or ice or fog would cause the postponement of matches and leave me aching with loneliness but they were few and far between and my trip every other Saturday from Grand Lodge near the entrance to Heaton Park with my three closest school friends became the bedrock of my slow emotional recovery.

It didn't matter that in that first 1962–3 season when I started going to every home game, City were a poor side. It didn't matter that they got relegated at the end of it, even though that relegation, like all the subsequent ones, was painful and somehow unfair. The point was there was always another game, always another season. Manchester City, I knew, would never leave me and that was all I needed from them. Success was to be desired and striven for and celebrated when it came but above all City were to be my other family; a faith as certain as a religious conviction with which I was not blessed.

Faith plays a large part in this story and I would like to have explained clearly the relationship I have with my religion but I find to my frustration that I don't think I can explain my religious feelings to my own satisfaction let alone anyone else's. I can't quite empathise with Jonathan Miller's rather limited description in *Beyond the Fringe*: 'I'm not a Jew, I'm just Jew-ish; it's not the same thing at all.' On the other hand, on my Sunday morning drive into Golders Green to buy the bagels – I can thoroughly recommend the rye by the way – I regularly pass the black coats, black hats and long hair of the profoundly religious Jews with bad eyesight and large Volvos. If I say I am a Jew, which I am quite happy to own up to, why does this sight not feel like I am among my own tribe?

My parents named my brother and me Geoffrey and Colin and not Moishe and Mordechai because, though I don't remember having this conversation, I feel pretty sure they wanted us to assimilate into the native British culture. We didn't go to the Jewish day school; we went to Park View County Primary School, both of them a ten-minute walk from our house. We didn't go to the King David School for our secondary education; we went to Bury Grammar School. I have never had the slightest reason to doubt that they made the right decision. I'm perfectly aware of where I came from both emotionally and geographically, and I am quite happy to acknowledge it, but for many Jews this is not enough. A 'pick and mix' Jew, as I was once contemptuously termed, is no Jew at all for them. The fact is I have lived no further than a couple of miles from a Jewish delicatessen in Manchester, London and Los Angeles. I resent the term a 'pick and mix' Jew but I will happily confess to being an eating Jew, if that's what they mean. It's a religion rooted in food as well as family values and on those occasions I feel entirely Jewish. What I have never claimed to be is a religious Jew because most intellectual orthodoxies permit little deviation and that kind of claustrophobia makes me feel uncomfortable.

Manchester City always used to be a broad church, an open synagogue. Nobody cared what you did on Saturday morning if you were at Maine Road on Saturday afternoon and that is how it should be in a free society. I made a free choice of supporting Manchester City and I have never regretted it but I do not believe that my support of Manchester City is in any way more or less passionate than that of any other fan of any other club. A 'pick and mix Jew' I may be to that Orthodox critic but my Jewishness means as much to me as it does to him even if I do not openly display it as such. Similarly, my football team is not 'better' than yours. It's just mine. I might beat your team 6–1 at your ground in front of your supporters causing you grief, heartache and humiliation, but my team is only better than yours on the football field on that particular day. Where then does the hatred that disfigures the game come from?

I don't remember hatred being an intrinsic part of the life of a football supporter in the 1960s. I remember not caring for Manchester United and hoping that they would lose every game but I had plenty of friends who supported United and I thought no less of them for holding that allegiance. The idea of hating them because they were Reds would have been absurd. In her wonderful historical detective story *The Daughter of Time*, Josephine Tey tries to convey to her readers in 1951, the year it was first published, what it was like to be a Lancastrian or a Yorkist at the time of the Wars of the Roses.

> *You would have a family row over the result [of a battle] because your wife was probably Lancaster and you were perhaps York but it was all rather like following rival football teams. No one persecuted you for being a Lancastrian or being a Yorkist any more than you would be persecuted for being an Arsenal fan or a Chelsea follower.*

This tolerance is not necessarily the case now although it depends where you are when you express your allegiance. Outside the ground a shared love of football can help supporters band together perfectly affably. Inside the ground it is a different matter entirely.

A couple of years ago I was invited by Tottenham-supporting friends to watch a match with them at White Hart Lane. I have a soft spot for Spurs because of the pleasure given to me by their 1961 double-winning side, whose eleven I can still name on demand. Sometimes it's a pleasant relaxation to watch a match in which City are not involved because I can enjoy it whoever wins since I don't particularly care about the outcome, something that has, until recently, never been true when City are playing. Our seats were level with the opposition penalty area and ten minutes or so had passed unremarkably so there was no score when on the far side two players tussled fairly for possession of the ball which eventually rolled out of play and the linesman raised his flag to indicate a throw to the opposition. The crowd behind the official went berserk. I watched in fascination. Would that have been me if City were playing? I didn't think so and, to be honest, it was frightening to watch the crowd reach such a peak of incensed outrage.

Across the narrow width of the pitch I could see their faces contorted with hatred. This was the mob at work, the unfettered violence of which previous centuries had learned to deal with by punitive legislation and zero tolerance punishment. Why would you give these people the vote, asked the Founding Fathers of the United States of America? Accordingly they invented the Electoral College in order to keep the popular vote away from the legislative assembly they were inventing to help govern the newly independent country. Football is obviously not responsible for mob violence and certainly that linesman who had given a throw-in against the home team was not responsible for the uncontrolled reaction to his decision. This is where blind faith in any religion gets you in the end, whether belief in a football team or belief in a God. At one level religion is a great comfort and source of moral inspiration. At the opposite end of the spectrum it is a breeding ground for the hatred and violence that has besmirched society down the ages and certainly long before 9/11.

Mention of the destruction of the World Trade Center makes me realise that starting this chapter in the 1999–2000 season reminds us it was not only another century it was another age and, secure in my belief in Manchester City, I did not think anything could ever shake it. Similarly, of course, thinking back to the Western world before 9/11, before Afghanistan and Iraq, before we had to take our shoes off when we checked in at the airport, it just reinforces the understanding that City's team in 1999, including such stalwart names as Danny Allsopp and Richard Jobson, was a long way removed from the splendours that have been lavished upon us in recent times.

It was the season after the Miracle of the Dickov and Manchester City were on the rise again, curiously with little contribution from Dickov himself. He played only twenty-two games, made twelve appearances as a substitute and scored just five goals, whereas Shaun Goater, his strike partner during that year in the lower division, missed only six league games and scored twenty-three goals. Goater was a City hero not just for his goal-scoring record but perhaps more for his large smiling face and his whole-hearted efforts which endeared him to us.

There are players like Shaun Goater who seem to 'belong' to City in a way that their more talented brethren do not. Trevor Francis, for example, was one of the most skilful and exciting players who came to Maine Road during John Bond's time there and he took us, briefly, to the top of the old First Division. Maybe it was because he stayed scarcely more than a season and after he left we began a descent of terrifying swiftness but I don't think he ever really 'belonged' to us in the way that, say, Uwe Rösler, the German forward who played for us in the mid-1990s, did. Rösler made it quite clear (and has done in the interviews he has given since he returned to English football as the manager of League One side Brentford at the start of the 2011 season) that he fully reciprocated the Maine Road crowd's love, which of course strengthened those bonds of affection even more. Indeed, Rösler eventually became the subject of one of the City crowd's wittiest songs when they gave full voice to:

> Who bombed Old Trafford?
> Who bombed Old Trafford?
> Uwe, Uwe's granddad did
> Uwe, Uwe's granddad did . . . etc.

It was sung to the tune of 'Knees Up, Mother Brown' and that lyric contains a knowledgeable historical reference to the time during the Second World War when Old Trafford was bombed by the Luftwaffe who had been sent to destroy the nearby Salford dockyard and surrounding industry. Indeed, Manchester United spent the early post-war years playing at Maine Road while Old Trafford was being slowly rebuilt. You couldn't conceive of such a situation occurring today in almost any two-team city across the land but the 1940s was a decade of consensus and cooperation. British people struggled with rationing and a poor standard of living but they had a much clearer sense of moral values. Maybe that is why in 1951 it was possible for Josephine Tey to observe that nobody persecuted you for being an Arsenal supporter or a Chelsea follower.

In 1949 Manchester City supporters also took the former Nazi paratrooper Bert Trautmann to their hearts. The idea that Trautmann's fellow countryman Uwe Rösler was a hero to Manchester City supporters because of his goals and his putative grandfather even more so because he loathed Manchester United so much he dropped his payload on their ground, strikes me as perfectly harmless and a lot of fun. I don't see in it any of the loathing of those idiots who make references to the Munich air disaster and I wish whoever created that marvellous Uwe Rösler lyric was still around because as the club has become more successful it has become a lot less humorous. I suspect there might well be a causal relationship between success and loss of humour. There is certainly one between success and loss of perspective.

In May 1998, after the 5–2 win at Stoke and the relegation to Division Two that followed, a photograph appeared in the next day's newspapers of a tearful young fan, aged maybe about twelve years old. David Bernstein spotted the photograph, had it enlarged, framed and hung in the boardroom. It was a poignant reminder of what the club's failure can do to its supporters and it served as a constant reminder to the other directors that they had an urgent and important job to do to bring back the smiles to the faces of fans like that youngster. Two years later the club was celebrating promotion back to the Premier League.

In March 2012, Manchester City lost 1–0 at Swansea City in a Premier League match, a result which, combined with United's 2–0 victory at home to West Bromwich Albion, caused City to drop into second place in the league table for the first time since October 2011. On the television highlights of the match that night a City fan, quite unaccountably, was shown crying at the devastation of the hurt he was feeling. It was a ludicrous over-reaction to a defeat by a goal seven minutes from time, although the fan later attributed his response to the amount of beer he had consumed. While, understandably, the fan was the target of mild mockery on television, the response on the internet and the anti-social networks was overwhelming. This absurdly melodramatic individual was not teased but unmercifully abused for 'bringing the club into disrepute', his telephone number was displayed for all to see and he was subjected to constant unpleasant harassment in his own home.

What a contrast this was to the reaction to the crying child photographed after the Stoke match in 1998. I hate to sound old-fogeyish about this but how can it be explained except in terms of the way in which standards of social behaviour have declined in the first few years of the twenty-first century? If I describe how I have found my faith in Manchester City under threat does this mean I am deliberately inviting this sort of martyrdom? It most certainly does not. I doubt that the fans who sang so wittily and attractively about Uwe Rösler's granddad are the same fans who left obscene messages on the telephone of the young man who had travelled to South Wales and certainly did not ask to appear on television.

Back in the 1999–2000 season, when the fans still retained their sense of humour and perspective, the goals of Shaun Goater and the meanest defence in the division, excellently marshalled by Richard Jobson and including some outstanding performances from young Nicky Weaver in goal, took City to the fringe of a second successive promotion. The idea that we could be back in the Premiership again, less than eighteen months after that defeat at York City had left us seemingly marooned in the middle of the Third Division (North), was truly wonderful. On Easter Monday, with three games to go and hotly pursued by Ipswich for the second automatic promotion spot, David and I met up with Howard at Fratton Park. Goals from Spencer Prior and 'Fat Bob' Taylor, who had been signed from Gillingham just before Christmas 1999, put us 2–1 ahead but, instead of sealing victory, we conceded an equaliser and only a desperate scramble in the City goal mouth prevented Lee Bradbury, of all the appropriate opponents, from scoring what would have been a devastating winner.

As it was, I drove to Manchester from London the next Friday afternoon to watch 'Fat Bob' score the only goal of the game against Birmingham, which took us to the brink. As it was the last home game of the season, the crowd did what the crowd was expected to do and invaded the pitch at the end of the game, waiting patiently on the grass as the players went off and then came out again to salute their supporters. It was an odd moment. Ipswich could still pip us to that final promotion spot consigning us to the lottery of the play-offs for the second season in a row, and the Suffolk club was not enchanted by the sight of City supporters celebrating so enthusiastically with promotion as yet unconfirmed. We would need at least a point at Blackburn on the following Sunday, nine days away, to be sure of success, but then it had been an odd season all round, as if our feet hadn't quite touched the ground after the Wembley play-off eleven months before. We were celebrating a little prematurely, given our lovingly preserved penchant for screwing everything up at the last moment, and it was to come back to haunt us a year later but at the time it was worth it to stand applauding with the 30,000 and feel part of the whole experience. It felt like a kind of naughty party at your own house when your parents have gone out for the night. We weren't supposed to be there but we were having such a good time we weren't going home any time soon.

The number of tickets on offer for the match at Ewood Park was limited and for the first time in my life I watched a promotion match on television but even that experience was better than Howard's who was at some conference saving the world economy in Switzerland. Blackburn took a deserved lead just before half-time and then in the space of three minutes Ward hit Weaver's crossbar, Jansen hit Weaver's post, Howard rang from Switzerland, City went up the other end, Kevin Horlock sent a wicked cross from the left wing and the ball evaded the entire Blackburn defence, finding Goater at the far post who equalised. All Howard had done was to ask, 'What's the score?' to be told 'We're losing 1–0', and then he heard shrieks and cries of ecstasy as the living room erupted into noise. It was probably time for him to go back and tell Gordon Brown the really important news.

I know I told Howard that God had decided we were going up despite being a goal down at the time. Nobody watches the ball fly off the woodwork into the grateful arms of the well-beaten goalkeeper twice in a minute without realising you are playing in a game controlled by some kind of superior force. Soon enough,

Dailly put through his own goal, and Mark Kennedy, a talented winger who gave us excellent service that year and then virtually disappeared the following season, made it 3–1 before Dickov, a second-half substitute, appropriately scored the last goal of the season. It had been another 'typically City' performance but it was almost as emotionally satisfying as the previous year's spectacular climax. I drove David into town to meet his friends and took a detour trying to find a pub with celebrating City supporters but my radar for pubs has never worked particularly well and it failed yet again.

So, we've reached the dawn of a new millennium and so far life seems to be fine. David is now fully employed by Bain & Company, after McKinsey perhaps the largest and most prestigious of global management consultants. Amy has moved out of the family house and is living in west London with her boyfriend Matt whom she met at university and whose star is rapidly rising in the City. The kids were OK. It was the first ingredient in the recipe for happiness.

My wife, Lynn, was working successfully as a teacher of dyslexic children. Because she had spotted David's dyslexia when he was six and worked long, patiently and successfully with him to help him deal with his difficulty, she had always been interested in dyslexic children. In 2000 she was working part time as a Special Needs teacher at St Anthony's, David's old school, and also saw private pupils at the house. Each year she spent the months of January and February in Santa Barbara, California, living with her parents who were just about to enter their eighties. There, she could learn about the latest techniques in the teaching of dyslexic children, which she brought back to St Anthony's, while spending time with her parents who were inevitably starting to slow down. To her great relief she could also absorb the sunshine that she missed greatly when she was in England because she suffered from Seasonal Affective Disorder.

I might have been sceptical about SAD if I hadn't seen its effect at first hand. Growing up in Manchester there isn't much point complaining about the grey skies; they are a constant fact of life and they never really bothered me. However, when I saw Lynn lying on the bed from October to April watching endless episodes of *Oprah* I knew this was not the real Lynn.

As the seasons changeed, the hours of daylight lengthened, the flowers showed their delight in the restoration of decent living conditions and the sun appeared to offer as much heat as light, Lynn would change into another person. The pasty-faced listless woman who could barely get off the bed in the autumn and winter was transformed into the mad gardener who would be outside at first light hoeing and weeding and planting and watering. I had no idea what she did in the garden at 5am. I had another three hours of sleep to get through. She was a girl who grew up to the sound of the Beach Boys. Her natural habitat was the sunshine and beaches of Southern California. I grew up to the sound of the Mersey Beat (well, strictly speaking, to the sound of Gilbert and Sullivan but that doesn't offer the right contrast) and the sight of the umpires bringing the Lancashire batsmen off the field at Old Trafford as the light got worse. Nobody ever appealed against the light when they were 'Surfin' USA'.

I fell in love with Lynn at first sight in the grounds of a mansion in Beverly Hills where the American Film Institute had taken up residence in the late 1960s. We had been the only two people in a cinema showing the MGM weepie *Boys Town* starring Mickey Rooney and Spencer Tracy as Father Flanagan. She had barged in after the film had started as I was taking notes for my Ph.D. thesis and sat down in the seat next to mine in an otherwise deserted cinema. I don't know about you, but I loathe anyone heading inexorably towards me in that situation and I was astonished that the waves of hatred I was transmitting in her direction appeared to have no discernible effect.

When the lights went up she was clearly intrigued by the lunatic in the next seat who was crying his eyes out at the melodrama that had just finished. Instead of anger at the interloper I was now feeling only a sense of embarrassment at my lachrymose behaviour in the sight of the very obvious physical beauty of the woman who was observing it. After a short conversation we went our separate ways, she driving towards the exit I had already told her was closed and I to my car. Eventually, she returned as I knew she must, complained that the front entrance was shut and followed me, in my car, out of the grounds of the mansion and into the streets of Beverly Hills. We came to a crossroads. My mind was racing faster than the car's engine. She might turn the 'wrong' way and would be lost to me for ever. I pulled on the handbrake and went back to talk to her again. That was 22 May 1972. On the Fourth of July 1972 we became engaged, an appropriate day for an Anglo-American rapprochement, and on 23 September that same year we were married.

There followed thirty years of marriage, mostly up, sometimes down, but at the start of the twenty-first century this was a family in pretty good nick. I was now engaged in work on a second novel, a story of a woman who meets, after an interval of twenty years, the man who had been the first love of her life when they were students. Her marriage has already been compromised by the tragic death of her daughter while the family had been on holiday in Italy. I was also working on a biography of the Summerbee family called *Fathers, Sons and Football* which was a portrait of one family and three generations of footballers from George

Summerbee, Mike's father who was at Preston North End in the 1930s, to the present day because Nicky had, until recently, been playing well at Sunderland under Peter Reid.

None of us can see into the future and most of us would be well advised not to wish to be able to do so. Do you really think that the team that floated effortlessly through the First Division in 1999–2000 was ready for the demands of the Premiership? The first game back in the big time finished in a horrible 4–0 thrashing away at Charlton. Life was indeed about to get a lot tougher for all of us.

Chapter Three

I DON'T WANT YOU TO THINK THIS IS A REGULAR occurrence but Amy and I were at Glyndebourne when City played their first home match back in the Premiership since they had been relegated after a comically horrible 2–2 draw against Liverpool in May 1996. In fact, this was Amy's Glyndebourne debut and only the second time in my life I had been to the beautiful opera house deep in the heart of the Sussex countryside. The first time had been thirty years previously. The reason I draw attention to it is because it's a little like the famous question, 'Where were you when you heard that JFK had been made into a very weird film by Oliver Stone?' I remember that production of *Don Giovanni* largely for the constant worrying about what was happening at Maine Road.

Performances at Glyndebourne start at around 5.30pm and demand formal evening wear which means struggling uncom-fortably and complaining constantly while doing so in a dinner jacket on a hot summer's afternoon. The reason for the early kick-off is so that the audience can enjoy an open-air picnic in the picturesque grounds during the lengthy interval which lasts from around 7pm to 8pm. In other words, the interval ended just about the time the match started so there wasn't even the option of sitting in the car, eating a chicken leg and listening to the radio commentary. We were herded back into the opera house as City, buttressed by the new signings of Paulo Wanchope, George Weah, Alf-Inge Haaland, Steve Howey and Danny Tiatto, started their match against Sunderland. I suspect my thoughts wandered too easily from the seductions of Don Juan partly because it wasn't a particularly good production and partly because I was very conscious that I'd just laid out two hundred quid for the two tickets. In my defence I would say it's difficult to justify the excessive prices opera houses charge their patrons were it not for the fact that one of the great Mozart operas is always worth a hundred quid and Premiership football is rarely worth half of that amount. Mostly, however, I was worried that after the catastrophic opening day defeat at The Valley, City would be an embarrassment to their supporters for the rest of the season, paying the penalty for having risen so quickly back into the elite.

As things turned out, I had every reason to be worried but not that night. The Mozart magic eventually worked its miraculous charm, Don Giovanni descended into hell with a stirring baritone cry, Donna Anna decided it would take another year for her to think about marriage to Don Ottavio (don't do it, sweetheart, he's a twerp despite his two wonderful arias), Leporello went off to the pub to find a new master and we raced back to the car to discover that Wanchope had grabbed a hat-trick and Haaland had added the other in an impressive 4–2 demolition of the Mackems.

After two months of the season, City had won four, lost four and drawn two, an entirely satisfactory state of affairs. Mid-table anonymity would have been a very welcome position for us that whole season. 'We'll just play here, if you don't mind; you don't have to come and watch us, we'll be quite happy if you'll just leave us alone. We've had two promotions and two relegations in the last five seasons. That's quite enough excitement for us, thank you all the same.'

From the end of October, however, starting with a crushing 5–0 loss to Arsenal at Highbury, City embarked on a run of six consecutive defeats. Indeed, they won only two games between the end of October and the middle of April, one of which was a remarkable and entirely unprovoked 5–0 thrashing of Everton, who must have wondered what they had done to coax this performance out of a team who scored only forty-one goals all season. I went back for the derby match against United because somehow down the years, whatever the respective merits of the two sides in any given season, the derby has retained for me all its power to enthral and terrify. In the event, I was lugging some piece of camera equipment up the back of the Kippax, having filmed the opening ceremony and kick-off from the side of the pitch when Beckham scored what turned out to be the only goal of the game from a free kick.

The season continued to disappoint even as family circumstances started to change. Amy had been cast in a series of plays at the Swan Theatre in Worcester in April and her last day, which we'd promised to attend, coincided with a vital home game against West Ham. The plays were part of a continuing family saga so there were three plays on show that day, one in the morning, one in the afternoon and one that night. Never mind the pageant of English social history, if City lost to West Ham they would be down with two more games to go. As the curtain descended at 4.55pm and the applause rang out for the end of the second play, I turned my phone back on, willing Howard's text to be there. It was. An own goal from West Ham's Ian Pearce combined with some heroic goalkeeping from Carlo Nash had secured the three points. Amy was happy that night. We were all happy that night.

David had just left for America. The previous autumn he had met a girl from the Dallas branch of Bain & Company and whisked her off to Rome for the weekend where his knowledge of classical history had no doubt proved particularly useful. Within a few weeks they were a couple. Susie, a very bright and lovely young American woman, had been an instant hit with Lynn and me but when her six-month loan move to the London branch expired she had to return to her parent club, leaving the two of them devastated. They were so clearly unhappy at being apart that David decided to pack up and join her. The fact that he was the son of an American mother ensured that his working status over there was guaranteed but he was giving up a very good job with prospects in his home town for an uncertain life and a new relationship in Texas, a state which he had never visited before and which threatened the sort of culture shock that Cambridge provided for Lynn when she had arrived to be with me in 1972.

It was the knowledge that the original gamble had paid off that comforted me as I drove David down to Victoria station from where he would take the train to Gatwick and a plane to Dallas. 'Look,' I said, more trying to convince myself than him, 'you're not emigrating. You can always come back.' Even as I said the words I knew they weren't true. He *was* emigrating. He had fallen in love with Susie and they were going to make a life together. The strong likelihood was that they would make a life together in the United States. I was losing him in a way I had never lost him until that moment. We joked, of course, about the scene in *Airplane!*, one of his favourite films, when the departing war hero waves goodbye and his girlfriend, played by Julie Hagerty, races along with the train knocking over people and cases and station pillars as she endeavours unavailingly to keep pace with the train as it pulls away from the platform. It is a wonderful parody of the scene in

Since You Went Away in which Jennifer Jones bids a tearful farewell to the departing Robert Walker.

It was only when I got back home and went into his eerily quiet bedroom and sat down on his bed that the tears started to flow. It was just empty nest syndrome, hardly a unique condition, but I hadn't previously experienced that kind of aching longing for my children. When they both went off to university they went to my old college, Gonville & Caius, so although I didn't know what they would get up to, at least I knew where they would get up to it. I didn't know anything about Texas but I took a rather pointless comfort in the fact that David would be out of the country if results went against us in the next two matches. They did. After the temporary euphoria of the West Ham result we were faced with an awkward away trip to Ipswich who were riding high, looking to finish fifth and secure European football at Portman Road.

Howard, Geoff Watts, fellow ex-MGS and Oxonian, and I made the trip up the A12, Geoff remaining quite puzzled by the need Howard and I felt to listen *en route* to *The Archers* rather than the match preview on Radio 5 live. We tried to explain that Emma was going steady with the nice Will Grundy though clearly attracted to his ne'er-do-well younger brother Ed; a love triangle that Karenina, Anna and Vronsky could not approach for complexity and durability. Similarly, the scandal caused by Lydia Bennet running off with Mr Wickham in *Pride and Prejudice* would be like a minor confusion over a dance card compared to what would eventually hit Ambridge when Emma's true feelings were revealed after her marriage to Will. I fear that we never quite managed to communicate to Geoff our very real anxiety that this event might disrupt the superficial happiness of Borsetshire society. Geoff has been married for many years to Anne, who is a serious *Archers* addict, but he had travelled with us on the understanding we would be talking about why Royle had long since dispensed with the services of Weah and had seemingly fallen out with Wanchope at various times during the season, rather than being cowed into silence as the radio brought us news of momentous events in Ambridge.

It was a depressing evening in East Anglia, irrespective of the anxiety induced by *The Archers*. I looked at the team Royle put out and there were only five players who had started the season, which is not necessarily a bad thing if the replacements are significantly better than those whom they have replaced. More than thirty players had worn the blue shirt in that season which is at least ten more than is desirable. Either Royle didn't know what his best team was or his plans had been decimated by injuries. The truth was that all these players were much of a muchness, none of them capable of inspiring the team to heights of occasional brilliance and there were too many changes to induce a sense of continuity, which might have produced consistent performances. Nicky Weaver, who had been such a star during the two promotion years and as a young player appeared to have his best years ahead of him, gradually lost form and physical shape and succumbed to a succession of injuries, probably in reverse order.

Shaun Wright-Phillips offered some hope of future promise but Royle was clearly not yet convinced by him. Richard Dunne was to prove an outstanding buy but back then he just looked slow and ponderous; 'The Man with Three Buttocks' as he was termed by Michael Henderson. Wanchope was in and out of favour all season and neither he nor Goater reached double figures in the goals they scored. Weah, who had seemed the sort of prize foreign star that would demonstrate that City were back in the big time, played just five matches, scored just one goal and was on his way before the end of September. It was a rag bag of a team. Andrei Kanchelskis arrived in the January transfer window, made ten appearances and departed. Mark Kennedy, who had been such a prominent figure in the previous year's promotion, played half a season and was sent packing. The Royle–Bernstein partnership which had lifted the club from the floor by the scruff of its neck had lost its magic and was to end in a particularly unsightly legal mess.

There was a sour temper to the atmosphere at Portman Road that night, possibly related to the previous year when we had celebrated promotion after the Birmingham City game, even though Ipswich still stood a mathematical chance of taking the second automatic promotion slot. Too many City supporters for my liking spent the evening with their eyes averted from the pitch, more interested in chanting obscenities at the home fans, although God knows there wasn't a lot to celebrate, apart from Goater's goal in a lost cause. Ipswich under George Burley were going into Europe and we were going back to Division One and didn't they enjoy letting us know about it after the unwitting insult of the previous year? I suppose that kind of gloating must have happened in similar circumstances forty years or so earlier but it certainly felt strange and uncomfortable. The condescension from the home club, I was later given to understand, even extended to the boardroom where it would certainly not have happened under the benevolent reign of the much respected Cobbold family. For them, it was always said, a real tragedy for the club would have been running out of white wine.

On the mournful walk back to the car I was rung on the mobile by Radio 5 live who asked for my reaction to yet another relegation. I don't think I was rude but I was certainly short in my answer. This felt like an unwarranted intrusion on private grief, in which the media specialise these days, and I couldn't help observing that they hadn't rung me after the Blackburn match the previous year to wonder about my delight at promotion. Apparently, I had become the 'go to' man for defeat and disaster. When the phone rang again a few minutes later and the LCD failed to identify the caller, I was tempted to toss it on to the A12. In the event it turned out to be David in Texas who had followed the game on his computer and wanted to reach out across the ocean to make contact and feel he was sharing the misery. Naturally, as a father that immediately made me start on the cheerful paternal litany of 'we'll win so many games next year' and 'it'll be good to be free of this atmosphere of gloom' and 'all the mercenaries will go and we'll just have players who want to play for City'. By the end of the speech I had cheered myself up.

It didn't help that we went on to lose the last match at home to Chelsea and United won their third Premiership title in a row. In the end, we were eight points away from safety with a miserable thirty-four points; United finished ten points clear of Arsenal, who were in second place. It had been a thoroughly miserable season which had started with such high hopes and ended in despair and rancour. To nobody's surprise Royle was dismissed, a decision that he must have been expecting but it was one which he took very badly indeed. It was an unedifying spectacle to see the former manager claiming that because he had been dismissed before 30 June, which is when the football year officially ends, he had been a Premiership manager at the time of his sacking and was therefore entitled to a bigger pay-off than if he were to be considered the manager of a Division One club.

The fact that the whole world knew we had been relegated and would start the following season in the lower division did not affect his claim and, in a distasteful legal action which he won, Royle actually forced City to pay up. To add injury to insult this came at the time when the club was also having to write out a huge cheque to players like Laurent Charvet, an abysmal French full-back, in order to pay off their inflated contracts as we entered the netherworld of Division One. Fortunately, the wheels of justice would grind sufficiently long enough for the Court of Appeal to reverse the decision and Royle had to repay the money.

Within days of Royle's departure, City had signed perhaps the one manager who could make us look forward to life in Division One. Kevin Keegan had been 'at liberty' since his short spell in charge of the England national team had ended, as it always does, in misery and humiliation. According to reliable reports, he tendered his resignation in the toilets at Wembley Stadium shortly after which the wrecking ball knocked it down. It seemed an entirely appropriate place in which to offer his resignation.

Kevin Keegan has always aroused widely differing responses. As a player he was nothing short of admirable. He never let his lack of physical stature impede his game which was based on whole-hearted effort as well as considerable skill. Even the fisticuffs with the combative Leeds captain Billy Bremner which got them both sent off in the 1974 FA Charity Shield at Wembley demonstrated some kind of perverse refusal to back down. He was entirely committed to Liverpool for the six years he spent there and he left after the European Cup victory against Borussia Mönchengladbach in 1977 because he wanted to 'improve' himself by going to Germany at a time when few Englishmen would have dared to venture into such a foreign field.

As a manager he had returned to rescue Newcastle United eight years after helping them, as a player, to promotion to the old Division One. He saved them from the drop to the third tier of English football then took them up to the Premier League as champions of the new Division One where he fashioned a team of such attacking mien that Newcastle quickly became everyone's second favourite side. The Wrong but Wromantic cavalier Keegan was defeated at the end of the 1995–6 season by the Right and Repulsive roundhead Ferguson and, despite signing Alan Shearer for a record fee at the start of the 1996–7 season and beating Manchester United 5–0, by the beginning of January 1997 Keegan had had enough and walked out. He returned to manage Fulham successfully enough to be offered the England job, but despite the walkouts and the prickly nature of his reaction to perceived slights, he was still a firm favourite with football fans everywhere. His credit, therefore, was still good when he committed himself to taking City up after the desperately disappointing one-season sojourn in the Premiership.

The 2001–2 season turned into an undiluted triumph for Keegan and for the club, although it began with a typically chequered series of results. Goals flowed at each end of the pitch; a 3–0 win was followed by a 2–0 defeat, which was followed by a 5–2 win and then a 4–2 win and then a 0–4 loss at The Hawthorns. The crazy swings of the pendulum continued unabated and it took until the middle of October before we actually drew a match, by which time we had won six matches by large margins and lost four, scoring twenty-six goals and conceding twenty. It was breathtaking football and the crowd simply revelled in it.

Contrary to the traditional order of events over the previous twenty years, poor players went and good players came, particularly the combative Israeli Eyal Berkovic who could start an argument in a synagogue, probably while chanting Kaddish, the memorial prayer for the dead. I should add that this has not been verified by John Hartson, who once tried to remove Berkovic's head from his shoulders by kicking it during a training-ground fracas. In the middle of September, Keegan produced his greatest sleight of hand – the supremely talented Algerian-born midfielder Ali Benarbia, who had spent most of his professional career in the

French league. Nobody I knew had heard of him when City signed him but after his first match, which resulted in a 3–0 home win over Birmingham, Benarbia was awarded instant cult status by the crowd. I was enchanted by the man. He played football as it should be played, with the spirit of a child and the skill of a master, and he quickly joined my band of select City heroes which had started with Bert Trautmann.

Just as the infamous 1998–9 season turned round during the holiday festivities, so this season, too, took a turn for the better after Boxing Day. Keegan expressed considerable dissatisfaction with the performance during the 0–0 home draw against West Bromwich Albion and it was as if a light switch had been flicked. Instead of the 6–0 win followed by the 0–4 defeat, the second half of the season contained some of the most captivating winning football I had ever seen a City team play. The 2–1 defeats away at Wimbledon and Stockport were the only blots on an otherwise immaculate 2002.

Over Easter we faced an awkward tie away at Wolves and fortunately David was home from the States for the holidays to see it. He had made a successful transition to life in America, as his mother and I always suspected he would. It was probably that suspicion that confirmed for me the realisation the previous April that he was emigrating and not just going out to Dallas for a short trip to see Susie. They had both secured jobs with Bridgespan, the not-for-profit arm of Bain & Company, which was based in Boston. It was with a certain amount of relief that we heard the news because Boston was a city that appealed to all of us immediately, probably through the glimpse of it afforded by the successful 1980s TV sitcom *Cheers*. When Lynn and I flew out to see them during half-term in October 2001, we saw instantly why they were both so happy in the city. We had, of course, chosen the right time of the year to go. There are few sights in the world quite as spectacular as a New England autumn and our journey from Boston through New Hampshire and Vermont almost up to the Canadian border was deeply satisfying on so many levels.

It was a strange time to be in America. It was six weeks after 9/11 and you couldn't pass a residential house never mind a public building without seeing an American flag on display. There have been times when such a sight would induce in me nothing more than Samuel Johnson's definition of patriotism as 'the last refuge of a scoundrel' but 9/11 changed everything. The world was a different and scarier place, partly because of the violence that was now an ever-present threat and partly because politicians did a very good job of playing on everyone's natural anxieties. In the past, politicians had seized power on the back of the dreams of affluence they promised. Now they did it on the threat of the monster that lurked behind the door that only they could keep closed.

Still, the world kept on turning and David and Susie moved into a small flat in Charlestown near the Bunker Hill Memorial which is where I phoned him one Sunday lunchtime to learn that City had lost 2–1 to Preston North End. There isn't a foreign trip that I have made since the invention of the internet that hasn't involved some sort of memory of discovering City results in allegedly exotic places. A few days later it was the 4–0 home win against Grimsby which was found on a public computer in a tiny library in a place not much larger than a village in rural Vermont. Whatever was happening in the world, the thread of continuity provided by Manchester City remained unbroken.

That was why I was so pleased that David had decided to fly home the following Easter in time to see City's triumphant run-in to the title. The trip to Wolves was another of those father-son bonding times that I had missed so badly since he had left the country twelve months before. The game was exciting; a packed house, tickets found in desperation just before we were about to give up hope, an expectant atmosphere created by both sets of supporters. It threatened momentarily to be a game in which the passion of the crowd and the fierce determination of the opposition could have had dire consequences but the City defence weathered the storm and two excellently taken goals from Shaun Wright-Phillips, who had emerged during the season like a butterfly from a chrysalis, deflated the home crowd's certainty and secured the three points. The championship was won the next week with a crushing 5–1 demolition of Barnsley. I no longer went to watch City hoping they would win. I went to watch City knowing they would win and that hadn't been the case for at least twenty-five years. For sheer enjoyment I rate the second half of that 2002 season as the most satisfying time I ever knew as a Manchester City supporter. Of course the prize on offer was the lower one of promotion not the supreme one that comes with winning a major trophy. It was, however, comforting to see that on the last day of the season when the cup was handed over it was the same piece of silverware we had won with honour in similar barnstorming fashion at Newcastle back in 1968.

I drove up for that last match with Amy. It meant so much to me that I had successfully passed on my love of Manchester City to my children and that they appreciated the nature of the support I had committed them to. Amy and her brother had been born during the years immediately following the Mercer–Allison era so although they had heard all their lives about the great days of Manchester City they had never really experienced any of them for themselves (with the possible exception of the Gillingham match and that was memorable for its drama and its emotion rather than for its significance in the wider context of football competition). The match was against Portsmouth and in front of a full house there were further goals from Howey, Goater and Jon Macken to take the season's total to 108. It was to be Stuart Pearce's last match as a player and it seemed inevitable that the final act would be to offer Psycho the chance to seal a perfect season with a goal of his own that would be the hundredth of his distinguished and soon-to-end career.

The penalty that was awarded just before the end was, to say the least, a little dubious, but nobody much cared, not even the Portsmouth players. They had lost this end-of-season match and they were finishing in lower-mid table so whether they lost it 3–1 or 4–1 didn't matter so very much. Everyone was smiling because it was almost as if it were Stuart Pearce's ninth birthday party and his dad had arranged it so that he would score the winning goal from a penalty with the last kick of the match. (Excuse me, I thought every boy's father did that.) Pearce himself, also smiling, approached the penalty spot with none of the nerves that must have almost paralysed him during those infamous shoot-outs in the semi-final of the World Cup in 1990 and the redemptive success in the European Championships in 1996. He put the ball on the spot, took a few steps back, ran up and belted it high over the bar and into the back of the Platt Lane stand. If anything, it only increased the good humour. Even the referee was smiling and at peace with the fans and the world. Why couldn't football always be like this, I wondered?

Thanks to David Bernstein, I was a grateful guest of the club that memorable day. Some time after the end of the match in the company of my biographical subject, Mike Summerbee, I wandered across the pitch and spoke to Monsieur Benarbia in my carefully rehearsed O-level French circa 1964. 'Je suis très content de faire votre connaissance,' I burbled, hand outstretched, anticipating a torrent of French coming back at me. 'Hmm,' said my new hero, 'nice accent!' And he wandered away in search of someone less ludicrous. Summerbee, who had introduced us, then spotted Keegan and Mighty Mouse raised the considerably heavier former outside-right on to his shoulders and staggered a few steps in celebration. Everyone wore smiles. Everyone was kind and considerate to each other. This wasn't a football club caught up in the wild throes of ecstasy. This was a Manchester City comfortable in its own skin; well managed, deftly handled at boardroom level with excellent, improving players and a connection to its supporters. At that moment it was difficult to believe that this feeling of *gemütlichkeit* could not be sustained indefinitely.

And so I came to one of life's staging posts. It had been coming a long time and we had been in agreement about it for a long time but it was still a wrench when it happened. One of Lynn's attractions for me had always been her American antecedents. This blue-eyed, blonde woman from the beaches of Southern California had remained determinedly wedded to everything about California throughout her thirty-year stay in England. She liked certain things about England but it was very much an *Antiques Roadshow*/English Heritage/National Trust version of England that attracted her. Her body had sojourned in Cambridge, St Albans and Muswell Hill but her soul was comforted only by the sight of the rolling surf of the Pacific Ocean, furnish'd and burnish'd by Los Angeles sun. We had agreed some years before that we would spend our declining years together in California. It always sounded better to me than the English alternative, which was to end up like Mam and Dad, the parents in Alan Bennett's *Play for Today* 'Sunset Across the Bay', dying in a seaside lavatory in Morecambe.

Now that both children had left the parental home and were

living with their partners, Lynn wanted to make her break for freedom. I was hardly in a position to object. She had given me thirty years of her life. She was twenty-six years old in August 1972 when she arrived on a charter flight at Gatwick Airport at the height of an English summer and stepped off the plane into the Arrivals Hall wearing a thick, floor-length white overcoat. The coat could only be prised off her body when the room temperature passed 75 degrees Fahrenheit, which meant she wore it a lot. On the last day of July 2002 I drove her to Heathrow to take an American Airlines flight back to Los Angeles. I went through much the same conversation I had had the previous year with David and she easily maintained the fiction. She wasn't emigrating because she would be back for Christmas and if she got a job as a teacher, which was her intention, she would have those long summer vacations of two or three months to come back home to London. The enforced absences would re-inject some vitality back into a marriage that had inevitably started to pale for both of us over the course of thirty years, for we had married within a month of her arrival at Gatwick. I joked that what she was going through was the twenty-first-century version of the mass immigration of the turn of the previous century and I expected her to send money home to me from the country where the streets were paved with gold. In the end, inevitably, I ended up sending money out to her, a reverse Marshall Plan.

We might have both felt that the parting was slightly more significant than we were each making out. Neither of us could have had the faintest idea of just how significant it would be.

Chapter Four

IT WAS AN ODD SENSATION RETURNING TO THE EMPTY house after the trip to Heathrow. It was hardly the first time I had been alone in the house, but as the days passed and it became apparent to me that Lynn's exit wasn't a holiday but an emigration, I became increasingly depressed. The emotion that had overcome me when I realised that David had emigrated was intensified and I slipped into a profound depression such as I am not sure I had experienced up to that time. When I lost my mother in 1962, once I'd gone back to school on the Monday after the previous Wednesday's funeral, I wasn't allowed any self-indulgent wallowing. I remember apologising to the Physics master after the lesson that first day back for not having done any homework over the weekend. He stammered a reply, clearly as embarrassed by the spectre of genuine emotion as most people in England were at that time.

In 2002 I was under no such constraint and I slumped into what I supposed was just another attack of of Empty Nest Syndrome but certainly felt at the time to be considerably more serious than that. All my energy, which had always seemed to be boundless, now dissolved and I lay slumped on the bed for hours at a time. My friend, the playwright Jack Rosenthal, who had himself suffered a very similar reaction which he described so poignantly in his BBC play *Cold Enough for Snow*, knew instinctively that something was up but I kept the answering machine permanently on.

One night I was sitting in the dark as his voice left a message inviting me over to his house a mile or so away. Not only did I not have the energy to get there, I didn't even have the energy to pick up the telephone. When Jack had been describing to me his own anxieties, we had finished our discussion with my saying cheerfully that he should go home and make himself a cup of tea. Jack had sighed heavily, smiled gently at me and said quietly as he rose to his feet, 'But that would mean I would have to fill the kettle and switch it on, wouldn't it?' I now knew what he meant when he found that he no longer had the energy for the slightest physical exertion.

After seven weeks of being on my own and not doing it very well I flew out to see Lynn in time to celebrate our thirtieth wedding anniversary. At least that was the laudable intention but the trip was a disastrous mistake. She had already started work teaching Special Needs pupils at a junior high school in Santa Barbara and was fully engaged pouring her energies into the job. She suffered from insomnia, which made the short amount of sleep she was getting extremely important to her; so important, indeed, that she said she would prefer it if I slept in a separate room. It felt like rejection piled upon rejection even if, logically, I could see the sense in it. When she left the house at 6.30am she went into the integral garage that was accessed from the hallway next to the bedroom where I was sleeping. As the key turned in the ignition and the car engine roared into life I felt as though it was a knife being plunged into my heart.

I drove north to San Francisco to stay with Michael Chadwick, my friend from our primary school days, but not even talking about City with a sympathetic friend could soothe the raging beast. After a few days of this agony I flew to Boston to be with David and Susie, although just being in that city inevitably reminded me of the much happier visit Lynn and I had made together to New England the previous year.

I returned to England still depressed, unable to breathe easily, as if my head were trapped in the top of a jumper I couldn't manage to pull over my head. My hypochondria was lovingly fed by the discovery of the need for a colonoscopy. I dragged myself to the hospital by public transport feeling utterly miserable and deserted by the world, although I had asked Jack to pick me up after the operation on the remote assumption that I was still alive. The procedure from which I emerged entirely unscathed revealed not cancer of the bowel as I had fondly imagined but, somewhat to my embarrassment, piles.

I refrained from mentioning this episode in polite society, although I couldn't help passing on the story of the VHS cassette which the hospital gave me to go home with like a party favour. The operation is performed while the patient is under sedation with a small camera which is inserted into the rectum so everyone can have a good look round (and a big laugh, I always suspected). While they are watching on the monitor some nurse presumably says, 'This bloke's *tochas* is really weird. Let's record it and have a big laugh at the Christmas party.' Next morning I decided to see what it was that was so hilarious about my colon so I put the cassette in and waited for enlightenment – and waited and waited. After watching and then fast forwarding through fifteen minutes of snow I concluded that either I was dead or someone had failed to press the record button.

I checked the label. It said quite clearly 'Colin Shindler'. Somewhat disenchanted – this had cost PPP a large fee, after all, and my insurance would no doubt rise as a result – I rang the hospital and told them of the disappointing performance on screen and that, stretching the imagination, I'd seen better performances from Keira Knightley. They apologised, queried the reference to Keira Knightley and said they'd send another VHS cassette. Then I thought, if they do send another one how could I possibly tell that it's my *tochas* I'm looking at? It could be anyone's *tochas* and I would be none the wiser. 'Oh, just send him old Mrs Goldstein's *tochas*,' they might say, 'he'll never know.' And I wouldn't. So I said, 'Thank you but please don't bother', hung up and replaced the cassette on the shelf between *Lawrence of Arabia* and *Dr Zhivago*. It really needed decent sound effects, haunting music and possibly some kind of a picture to turn it into a David Lean film.

One other reason why life looked so bleak in October 2002 was that City had started their latest Premier League season with more than the traditional early optimism but had won only two of their first ten matches and scored only six goals altogether. Keegan had signed Peter Schmeichel, who had been a truly wonderful goalkeeper late in the previous millennium, along with Sylvain Distin, Nicolas Anelka and Marc-Vivien Foé, which gave the thrilling team that had won promotion a solid Premiership spine. They were shrewd signings which, allied we supposed to Keegan's instinctive desire to attack, would result in City finishing well up the table. None of the pre-season predictions from the pundits marked City down as potential relegation candidates. Maybe after six changes of division in the past seven seasons we were due a year of unspectacular consolidation. I saw an early season match at Highbury in which a final score of 2–1 to the home side flattered the visitors. More disappointing was the certainty that the Algerian magician Ali Benarbia was too slow to survive in the Premier League.

I was out in Corfu on a week's holiday with Howard and Archie his younger son when we received with grateful thanks the news of a vital 2–0 win away at Birmingham. I was back the following week for a trip to The Hawthorns on one of the foulest November days I can ever remember, but it resulted in a second consecutive away win with Anelka notching his sixth goal of the new campaign. It was the perfect time to start a run of victories with United due at Maine Road for the last-ever home derby there the following Saturday. In midweek, we were due to face Wigan Athletic whom we had last seen in that League Two play-off semi-final. They were still down there while we were examining our aristocratic robes which meant, inevitably, that they turned us over for a humiliating 1–0 defeat; just what we didn't need before the arrival of the Other Lot.

Conventional trepidation before a derby was intensified by the realisation that not only did we not have a locally born Mancunian in the starting line-up who understood the unique importance of the derby match but we only had two Englishmen, Howey and Horlock. Contributing nationalities included Denmark, Holland, China, Cameroon, Ireland, Israel, France and Bermuda. There was no Corrigan or Doyle or Lee, nobody from Collyhurst or Fallowfield; and yet we won and not only did we win but we won convincingly. United were thoroughly and totally outplayed. In the crowded Directors' Lounge afterwards I experienced two further thrills. One was meeting Bert Trautmann for the first time and becoming almost tongue-tied at the age of fifty-three in the presence of my first great hero. The other was meeting Bobby Charlton and saying with mock solicitude, 'I'm so sorry for the pain we've caused you today.' Sir Bobby is clearly something of a literalist because he looked straight back at me and said, 'I don't think you are.' This conversation, though lacking some of the wit to be found at the Algonquin Round Table in the 1920s, was nevertheless too perfect to be continued any longer.

That match was probably the highlight of the year, possibly of the next five years, because the clouds closed in almost immediately afterwards and the sunshine disappeared altogether to be replaced by a chill of demonic proportions. The week after the derby victory, I was on my daily constitutional trudge over Hampstead Heath and still ruminating pleasurably on the idiotic dawdling on his own goal line of Gary Neville, who was robbed by Goater who shot and scored from the acutest of angles for City's second goal. As I rounded Kenwood House, I found Jack Rosenthal and Maureen his wife standing in front of the beautiful house looking rather worried. I knew Jack had been having back pains but he was so stoical about it that it was hard to be too agitated on his behalf. This was the first day I saw the haunted look on his face that I was to get to know only too well over the next eighteen months. They had been to see the consultant haematologist at University College Hospital and the conversation had obviously not gone well.

Describing my relationship with Jack is like describing my relationship with my family. To all intents and purposes Jack and his family *were* family, so close were our daughters and particularly our sons. Most years the four Shindlers and the four Rosenthals gathered on high days and holy days to celebrate the fact that by combining two ovens and two sets of dishes we could put on a wonderful meal. Usually, while the two women were in the kitchen, the two girls were helping and talking, the two boys disappeared, and Jack and I sat round the dinner table discussing why Alex Ferguson reminded Jack of angry drunken Scottish dockers he used to meet in the pubs of Salford in the 1950s and 1960s and why Kevin Keegan reminded us of self-centred teenagers. Football was a constant topic of conversation between us and I felt so comfortable discussing the game with Jack because we shared a common heritage.

One winter's day we were looking at David and Jack's son Adam, who must have been about eight years old at the time, playing football in their garden. The lawn was covered in snow and the light was starting to fade so that the two little boys seemed like a rather ghostly presence in the back garden. 'Come and look at this,' called Jack. 'It's like old football, isn't it?' I knew exactly what he meant. It was a reference to the photographs in the sports pages of the newspapers in the 1950s. Twenty years later I still remembered that brief interchange with absolute clarity and the way it bound me so closely to Jack. If he went, I thought to myself, who could I possibly have these conversations with; conversations that needed the merest hint of a trigger word to summon up a shared world?

We also shared a common aversion to the very idea of shopping. 'You need a pair of shoes,' Maureen would say to him. 'I've got a pair of shoes,' he would reply. 'What do I need another one for?' It was a philosophy of conspicuous consumption with which I empathised entirely and which, if copied by others, would have plunged the British economy into recession many years before the bankers did it on their own. It was yet another reason why I felt so at home in his company. Many of my contemporaries had long shaken off the warnings handed out to us so freely in our Northern childhoods. Jack's childhood, as anyone who has ever seen *The Evacuees* knows, took place in the 1930s and 1940s and his background was humbler than mine. My parents were fortunate enough to bring me up during the expanding economy of the Macmillan boom years. It was odd, therefore, that I felt more sympathetic to the Depression era and wartime deprivation than I did to my own time. It was, perhaps, because those years formed the basis of my academic studies but it certainly helped to strengthen the bonds that tied me to Jack.

I had known him for thirty years but we only became close friends when we found we were living a few streets away from each other in the early 1980s. We had first met in Granada Television at the start of the 1971–2 season when we were both watching a live transmission of the Manchester United v Sheffield United match in a room in Granada Television in Manchester – it was later re-shown all the time as a tribute to George Best who graced it with one of his famous goals in which he dribbled through an entire defence before rounding the goalkeeper and rolling the ball into the far corner of the net from a difficult acute angle. Jack had no idea who I was that day, though I knew all about him and admired his writing more than I could then say.

A few years later, by now married with a recently arrived baby, I was so moved by his BBC play *The Evacuees* directed by Alan Parker that I wrote a fan letter to him. He still scarcely knew me at all but he replied with a handwritten letter on three sides of notepaper recalling in some detail his ecstasy at watching United beat Anderlecht 10–0 at Maine Road in 1956 and his sadness that he didn't think, as far as he was concerned, that any United side would ever match the glory of the Busby Babes. I suppose football had somehow crept into my letter to him and football became the tie that bound us for ever more.

When we moved to north London in 1981, I was a producer in the BBC Drama department and I was very keen to establish a relationship with Jack that would be either personal or professional but preferably both. I sent him a book to adapt that was the story of a cantankerous old Jew (it reminded me of my father), but after a number of hugely enjoyable conversations he decided to go off and write *Yentl* with Barbra Streisand instead. 'You'd have had a better time with me,' I used to tease him and he would nod happily and smile. It was the start of one of the most rewarding friendships of my life.

At one point in their early lives, David and Adam announced that they were going to buy a house in Manchester together and David was going to play for City and Adam would play for United. It was a slightly grander version of their games in the garden but, while it amused their mothers, it made Jack and me almost burst with suppressed emotion. When the boys were old enough to join a football team we would religiously drive them down to Regents Park where they played in a league operated by the American School in London. Jack and I revelled in this chance to pretend we were coaches of a First Division team, although I had to maintain some disinterest as I was also the referee. In their last year Jack and I coached the boys and their seventeen team-mates (numbers were unrestricted) to a league and cup double to our great delight, although there were doubts from the parents of the children from the other teams who weren't sure I should be refereeing the games and coaching one of the teams in it at the same time. In fact, Jack was the one going berserk on the touchline and I did volunteer to surrender the whistle to any American who actually knew the rules of what we called football, but they backed off at this point.

You couldn't find a more sanguine, jovial, kindly man than Jack, but his chance to bombard not only David and Adam but also eight-year-old American girls with the knowledge he had acquired standing on the terraces at Old Trafford watching Duncan Edwards and Bobby Charlton, was too great to resist. 'Man on!' he would shout at the little girl in pigtails. His team talk to a collection of cold children more interested in how many slices of orange they could cram in their mouths at the same time culminated in the cry with which we all used to tease him mercilessly in later years. 'Hard shots!' he would shout from the touchline to the mystified youngsters; of course, he was more than capable of sending himself up even more perfectly. On the Thursday before the Saturday game he would ring me up, the concern dripping from his voice, 'Colin, I've just heard Emily's got a cold. Do you think she'll be fit for Saturday? If not, who's going to be our midfield Colossus?' Whatever my state of mind, Jack could always make me smile.

On Christmas Day 2002, Jack could barely sit still, the pain in his back was so intense. He asked me if I knew how to get to the Royal Marsden Hospital in Sutton. I had to smile if a little ruefully. That was the journey we had to do with Amy when she was undergoing her chemotherapy for a childhood cancer that struck her when she was only twelve years old. It was fifteen years before but the memory of that horrible time was so strong it seemed like yesterday. Of course I offered to take him; he was due to go on New Year's Eve. He was just having an interview with the consultant, it wouldn't take long. I said that was fine as Lynn, who was back from Santa Barbara, and I had tickets for the Cole Porter musical *Anything Goes* that evening, and Christmas Day progressed as best it could with everyone conscious of Jack's situation.

Ironically, the room where the consultant saw patients at the Royal Marsden was in the refurbished wing on the second floor that had previously served as the children's wing when Amy was so sick. Now the children had their own purpose-built wing with a special entrance on the ground floor which seemed like a positive improvement. I thought the Marsden was a terrific hospital. I'd been a Friend of its charity since they had saved Amy's life. When we walked in through the front door that morning, the first thing we saw was a photograph of Maureen on the front page of the house magazine. She was standing by a new piece of hospital equipment which she had just 'opened'. It seemed like a good omen. Jack was such a positive person and people who learned he was over seventy were astonished. This was a man who was full of the joys of life and whose own life and work conveyed as much.

Hospitals always dampen an atmosphere and Lynn and I were a little subdued as we drove to the National Theatre to see *Anything Goes* that night. I was less subdued when I picked up the tickets at the box office to discover that they were for that afternoon's matinee. So when we had been staring out of the waiting room window at the Marsden, we should have been sitting in the Olivier Theatre revelling in the glorious words and music of Cole Porter. At the time, *Anything Goes* was the hottest ticket in town and I was furious with myself for believing that I'd booked evening not matinee seats. The sweet girls at the desk took pity on me. One of them disappeared for a minute and returned with the news that we could sit in Trevor Nunn's box for that performance. What a kindness. They didn't have to do it but I was touched by their solicitude. Why can't life, why can't all our lives be filled with such acts of kindness and mutual support?

Next day we were back at the Marsden to see Jack as an in-patient but whatever was going on medically, it was football that provided the basis of the conversation. City were in the middle of one of their periodic good spells and Jack and I watched Final Score on *Grandstand* insecure in the knowledge that City were winning 2–1 at Goodison Park. As ever, Jack was fulsome in his praise of City because, though he had been a United supporter all his life, as a Mancunian, he retained a soft spot for them. I tried to demur because the game wasn't over, though we were well into stoppage time which seemed to be lasting for ever. 'So what are you now?' asked Jack jovially, happy enough to think about anything other than what lay ahead of him. 'Eighth? Ninth?' 'Tenth,' I said miserably, having just spotted on the right-hand side of the screen that the Everton 1–2 Man City scoreline had now updated to Everton 2–2 Man City.

Although Lynn had done a lot of the driving between Muswell Hill and Sutton when Amy was being treated, I had done enough of it to remember the road very well – and to be aware that the traffic had got considerably worse in the intervening fifteen years. I wondered how often I would be bringing Jack round the North Circular Road and over Kew Bridge. I suspected quite a lot as he had a long course of treatment mapped out for him until the middle of May but we all fervently hoped that, like it had with Amy, the disease had been caught in time and there would be a happy ending. But Amy had been twelve and Jack was now seventy-one and somehow I was fearful. I was fearful about much in my life at this time.

Lynn's departure at the start of January 2003 hurt me even more than it had on 31 July the previous year. When she had left originally I wasn't sure if she would find a job and I had no idea that I would decline so precipitously. It wasn't that I was incapable of looking after myself or the house. Indeed, over the course of our marriage I was the Felix Unger and she the Oscar Madison of this particular odd couple. After my mother died I had been effectively on my own so I had never been unduly bothered by the prospect of running a household. I was organised and with a borderline OCD personality that made me well qualified to cook and clean and wash and sew. I would have made some lucky chap an extremely bad wife. I took over the maintenance of Lynn's brilliantly planned garden and, the more I dealt with it, the greater grew my admiration for her. So that's what she was doing out there all those hours – and how clever of her to have arranged matters so that something was in bloom almost twelve months of the year.

Perhaps, inevitably, our daily conversations now became tinged with a faint sense of mutual disappointment. I was disappointed that not only had she left me to redecorate the house on my own but that she showed only the most rudimentary interest when I complained about builders and floor-layers, the weather and the congestion charge. It all meant so little to her out there. Conversely, of course, she was disappointed that I clearly found what I felt was her endless belly-aching about the school and the kids and the teachers and the Federal Administration's education policy far less interesting than what was happening in *The Archers*, to which I had been listening a few moments before.

In those months I learned something that every divorced, separated or bereaved person learns soon enough – the emptiness of the house is matched only by the emptiness of the soul. The minutiae of everyday living, the endless complaints about the weather and the traffic and, in my case Manchester United, the sound of someone else upstairs, or on the phone or running a bath, those endlessly repetitive, seemingly inconsequential moments are the glue that keeps family lives together. I'm quite sure there are many people who enjoy the freedoms offered by living alone but I wasn't one of them. In the winter the house was always dark and cold when I came home and I hated it. The undrawn curtains seemed to reproach me for my neglect. 'Why weren't you here to draw us when daylight faded and the street lamps were turned on?' they seemed to pout. In the summer it was hot and stuffy and the stale fetid air performed the same accusing function.

One of the few pleasures I took from Lynn's departure was that I no longer felt personally responsible for the weather. I used to dread the weather forecast at the end of the television news if it showed clouds and rain hovering over the south-east corner of the country. Now that she was in California I felt like Gene Kelly with his umbrella holding out both arms and I could walk down the lane with a happy refrain singing, just singing in the rain. It was no longer my fault if it turned out to be the wettest February since records began or the coldest or the greyest or the most miserable. Weather returned to its original incarnation of being that grey stuff that hangs outside the window. Was it my fault that I felt guilty about something over which I clearly had no control? Or did she ratchet up the guilt because it was an easy way for her to punish me in revenge for having inflicted the rotten weather on her by bringing her to England in the first place? I know I apologised for the weather and I know she forgave me in the sense that, of course, she knew it wasn't *really* my fault. But I remained guilty so I couldn't have believed she meant the words of forgiveness she uttered. Or is the truth simply that human beings have an infinite capacity for self-deception?

Worrying about other people close to you is probably the best cure for self-obsessed worrying. Over the next few weeks I watched a lot of World Cup cricket in South Africa as Australia played their way to their inevitable retention of the trophy. I saw much of it in a waiting room at the Royal Marsden hospital in Sutton as Jack's treatment followed its prescribed course. Sometimes the journeys to and from the hospital were a delight for me if not for him. Easily prompted by me, Jack would reminisce about his days at Granada which always intrigued me. There was an age gap of eighteen years between us so that I was a teenager when he was starting his career as a writer and producer at Granada. The letters spelling out GRANADA TV atop the building at the bottom of Quay Street were illuminated in red at night and soon became a well-known landmark on Manchester's cityscape. I had often wondered as that teenager what magic was being wrought within its doors.

Granada in the 1960s was a hotbed of creativity, nurturing the talents not only of Jack but also of Michael Apted and Colin Welland, Arthur Hopcraft and Mike Newell. Jack learned his trade on *Coronation Street*, for which he wrote about 150 episodes, and that journey to the Royal Marsden was enlivened by stories about Albert Tatlock, who always seemed a miserable old bugger, and Pat Phoenix, who frequently failed to distinguish between her real self and Elsie Tanner, the larger than life fictional character she played. Jack was writing his autobiography in screenplay format at the time so I suspect he was testing out his material on me and I was delighted to be the fortunate audience, especially when he went back to the beginning of his script-writing career and talked about those early days on *Coronation Street*. I had always admired Jack but the more we talked, the more I loved him and the more I was self-conscious about the idea that I was driving him to meet his nemesis. I tried hard to think positively, like the United supporter he was, but I was a City supporter to my fingertips and it didn't take long for negative thoughts to intrude.

Even if the worst of the winter weather no longer tormented me as it had done when I saw Lynn staring at it mournfully from the bedroom window, it was still a relief to greet the arrival of spring in 2003. In April, when the magnolia bush which formed the focal point of Lynn's garden burst into the purest white blossom I had ever seen in my life, I became oddly aware that I must have seen this happen every year since she had planted it God knows how many years before. Of course I had seen it, but I had never absorbed its beauty. When the blossom started to fall, scarcely two weeks after it first revealed itself to my astonished gaze, I felt betrayed, a helpless spectator at this new Fall of Man.

*

Jack was supposed to go in for a high dose of chemo that it was hoped would complete his treatment but the date suggested was also Seder Night and, possibly more important for all the Jews I knew, it was the night of the Arsenal v Manchester United match which looked like being the decisive game on the run-in to the 2003 Premiership title. Arsenal had stumbled badly in recent weeks, losing a two-goal lead at Bolton and United had looked by far the stronger team. The Jews started their exodus from Egypt as Arsenal went ahead but as the Jews debated the importance of the Passover service, United fought back and scored twice, only for Arsenal to rescue a point. The draw was a much better result for United than it was for Arsenal, who had Sol Campbell sent off by referee Mark Halsey (whom I still couldn't bring myself to excoriate after those five minutes of stoppage time at Wembley four years earlier). United's eventual triumph, unfortunately, was a foregone conclusion from that moment.

At least Jack had the comfort of another Premier League title as he returned to the Marsden. This time it was stickier than it had been before and one morning in the hospital canteen with Maureen and Amy Rosenthal I tried to relieve the tension by relating a perfectly true story. Since Lynn had left I found myself constantly waking up in the middle of the night and in the middle of an otherwise empty queen-sized bed. I was also starving. My great vice, assuming you think it is a vice, is a fanatical devotion to the consumption of plain chocolate M&M's, and instead of cuddling my wife in the middle of the night, I was reduced to the less attractive alternative of stumbling into the next room, opening the cupboard where I keep the M&M's and taking them back into bed with me for company.

Now I was also trying to keep the growth of middle-age spread at bay and I was very aware that it was not a good idea to eat an entire packet of M&M's (a 'fun size' packet, I should add, in case you think I was devouring large 2lb bags) in bed every night if I wished to maintain any pretensions to a svelte middle-aged body. Unfortunately, every morning I would wake up next to an empty packet of M&M's but, mystifyingly, I had absolutely no memory of ever going and getting the packet. I was obviously sleepwalking into the confectionery cupboard. I just woke up with a packet of M&M's, as if the offending chocolates had emitted a seductive siren call that some instinct inside me could not resist. This was despite the fact that every night I went to bed determined to resist the allure and, indeed, invariably drifted off to sleep almost immediately I turned the light out.

What really upset me were the days when I genuinely thought I had triumphed over this mental weakness; when I woke up to find no evidence of an empty M&M's packet anywhere on the bed. I felt whole again, restored to my former condition of abstinence, despite the pangs of night starvation. You can imagine my surprise and frustration, therefore, when I went back upstairs after breakfast to make the bed and found an empty M&M's packet under the pillow on Lynn's side of the bed. 'No!' I cried involuntarily as I was confronted by the vision of that empty little yellow packet. It looked as if it were smirking at me. I not only had no memory of fetching the bastard, I didn't even have the remembered pleasure of eating it.

It was by now early May 2003 and time for me to go to Manchester to start filming a BBC4 *Timeshift* documentary programme about the changing lives of footballers since the abolition of the maximum wage in 1961. I didn't get back to London until the day Jack had to be picked up and taken home but it was a day we were all anticipating with enormous relish. It was mid-May and the sun was shining and the birds were singing and the grass was green and the sky was blue. Deliberately, I turned off the A3 at the Robin Hood roundabout and drove Jack through Richmond Park which was looking at its greenest and most enticing. 'Isn't this great, Jack?' I asked, knowing he had seen nothing but four hospital walls for weeks. 'It's bloody marvellous,' he replied with great feeling. He was going to have a good summer and we all clung happily to the information that he was 'in remission'.

I wanted to start the *Timeshift* documentary on location at Maine Road because the match against Southampton on Sunday 11 May was going to be the last game ever to be played there. From the start of the following season Manchester City would be playing their home games in East Manchester, at the stadium that had been built for the Commonwealth Games of the previous year. The two stadia seemed suitably contrasting locations in which to examine the changing public persona of the professional footballer, though ultimately, the programme was hacked about in the editing suite, so that none of the Manchester locations were even seen.

City were ending the season in comfort if not style. Fifteen wins contrasted with seventeen defeats and only six draws, leaving the team in ninth place and with the possibility of entry into the UEFA Cup through the back door of the Fair Play Award. On the face of it, ninth place was a satisfactory position in which to end this first season in the Premiership for ten years when mere survival hadn't been the primary instinct. The team had allegedly been strengthened by the January purchase of the French defender David Sommeil and much more controversially Robbie Fowler from Leeds, but the latter purchase was followed six weeks later by the departure of David Bernstein from his position as chairman of Manchester City. This was a calamity for the club, the full import of which was not to become evident for some time.

It seemed from the outside that the chairman had lost a power struggle with the manager but the manager didn't wear the look of a victor. Like Moses who had been the organisational genius behind the journey of the Children of Israel from bondage in Egypt to the very border of the land of Milk and Honey, David Bernstein was not to be permitted to lead his flock into the City of Manchester Stadium for which he had worked so hard and so long. Moses had yet again fallen foul of the Wrath of the Lord. It seemed that City's best chairman was to be deprived of his moment of triumph for far more trivial reasons. He had seen Fowler's medical file and quite rightly wondered whether the former hero of the Kop would ever regain full fitness. The player had pulled up no trees at Leeds and the damning medical reports suggested strongly that he would never be the potent goal-scoring machine he had been in his Liverpool days.

As a former Liverpool striker himself, Keegan had presumably felt an instinctive empathy with Fowler and had wanted him at City almost from the start of his managerial reign, despite City's then lowly status and fragile financial circumstances. Bernstein did his best to give his manager exactly what he wanted but, in view of Fowler's fitness record as well as Leeds's own financial crisis, he thought it sensible to negotiate the lowest fee possible to protect City against a possibly wasted investment. Keegan was appalled when he explained his proposed course of action. 'You can't do that, Mr Chairman,' he said in a positively poetic epigram. 'It's like bayoneting the wounded.' It's odd, isn't it, how ethics in football manifest themselves? For Keegan, the big cheque and the big player such as the world saw when he signed Alan Shearer for Newcastle United in 1997, was the right way to behave. A cut-price negotiation demeaned the seller and the player. It was not a viewpoint with which the chairman had much sympathy and the relationship which had worked so well in that first triumphant championship-winning year, was fatally flawed.

For all their great regard for Kevin Keegan, his aura, his belief in attacking football, the fans made it clear that they were sad to see Bernstein leave, crediting him, quite rightly, along with Joe Royle, with saving the club from the depths of despair into which it had fallen in May 1998. However, there is not much sentiment in football fans and for them the prospect of Keegan and more money (so it was wrongly assumed) plus a new stadium was enough to compensate for the exit of a chairman they had liked. On the one hand it was certainly exciting to move to a new stadium for the first time since 1923 and the Southampton game would mark the farewells of Schmeichel, Benarbia, Jensen, Goater and Horlock, so there would be the excitement of new faces to greet the new stadium. Huckerby, Howey, Nash and Wiekens had already played their last games so the clear-out had started. On the other hand, some of the dissatisfaction that I know I felt was precisely because we were moving to a new stadium and leaving behind the ramshackle but friendly place that had effectively been my second home for nearly fifty years.

I was a little six-year-old boy when I had been taken to Maine Road for the first time. Now I was leaving it at the age of fifty-four, seemingly none the wiser; certainly no less besotted with the boys in blue. I spent a lot of time that weekend in different parts of the stadium, writing and rehearsing a variety of pieces to camera, none of which made it on to the *Timeshift* programme that was eventually transmitted. It did, however, mean that I got to visit each of the four stands and sit in contemplative silence while I dredged up the memories of the matches I'd seen from that vantage. The old Platt Lane stand had been demolished and ineptly rebuilt during the Peter Swales regime but the view from behind the goal was still the same. It had been such a thrill to hand over the three shillings (Children 14 and Under), click through the turnstile, buy the sixpenny programme and run up one of the two less-than-completely secure fire escape staircases that carried spectators to the top of the back of the Platt Lane stand. That was where I'd gone in the early to mid-1960s to watch Bill Leivers and Cliff Sear and the young hopefuls David Wagstaffe and Neil Young.

Francis Lee had knocked down the old Kippax and built a towering three-tier monstrosity, from the top of which it was possible to see over the Main Stand directly opposite and all the way across town to Old Trafford. It was standing on the Kippax in my late teens that I watched the spectacular emergence of the team of 1968 and 1969, the Lee, Bell, Summerbee team – 'my' team, the team that belonged to me in my very heart and soul and which no other collection of individuals in a blue shirt has ever been able to match. When the crowds were packed in for a derby match and the excitement got too much for all of us, somebody would push you in the back and you'd be carried with the heaving mass down the terrace steps, swaying and running, unavoidably kicking people in front of you on the back of the calf and, as the crowd swayed back up the steps getting your own shins hacked by those same people as we all tried unavailingly to regain our balance.

The 'new' North Stand had been built in 1970 out of the funds that had swollen the City bank account because of the success of the Mercer and Allison triumphs. Before that it was the open Scoreboard End, so-called because at the top of the terrace stood a scoreboard with letters from A to S which corresponded to the half-time scores in the programme. So slow in those days were the communications from other grounds that it was well after the players in front of us had kicked off the second half before the last of the appropriate numbers would slowly be lifted into place. A loud cheer was always elicited if United were losing. Frequently, that was the highlight of the day. It was standing on the Scoreboard End terrace that I had seen Glyn Pardoe's debut against Birmingham City when the fifteen-year-old schoolboy prodigy became the youngest player ever to appear in the City first team.

The four stands of Maine Road were the structural equivalents of Jacques's Seven Ages of Man speech, for I seemed to age as I went into the different stands, finishing in the celebrated comfort of the Directors' Box thanks to the welcoming kindness of David Bernstein. David had worked tirelessly to get us into a new ground because it was clear that the future of the club depended on it but he knew very well that many of us would leave Maine Road with regret. Indeed, to this day, I still refer to any City home match as taking place at Maine Road. The City of Manchester Stadium was too much of a mouthful to catch on but I responded favourably to the name Eastlands, the part of East Manchester where the stadium is sited. I am not and never will be party to calling it after a Middle Eastern airline.

The game against Southampton was, perhaps predictably, a crushing anti-climax. Michael Svensson scored midway through the first half and that was it. City seemed entirely devoid of enterprise or energy. It was as if the ground itself was the star for the day and what the players did, kicking a football about for ninety minutes, was a complete irrelevance. With this defeat City gained entry to the UEFA Cup through the Fair Play Award, granted on the basis that they had kicked fewer players than other clubs. This tells you everything you need to know about the late unlamented competition.

The referee blew the final whistle for the final time and 35,000 people said goodbye to a stadium that deserved a better eulogy than the one it had received. I was due back the following morning to film an interview with Tony Wilson, fanatical Red and founder of Factory Records and The Haçienda. We had been friends since our days at university, when he had been the Editor of the student newspaper and commissioned my first newspaper column. I was glad that I managed to take a very quiet and personal farewell of the ground at the conclusion of the interview. I never wanted to see my home destroyed by the developer's wrecker ball.

The story has a painful coda. About seven months later I came up to Manchester for a dispiriting 1–1 draw against Leeds United. Driving back in the direction of the M56 I found myself irresistibly drawn towards Maine Road as the car headed down Lloyd Street North, scene of those number 75 bus journeys of long ago schooldays. I had both children in the car with me because it was close to Christmas. I told them what I wanted to do and they made no objection so I turned sharp left and came across the place where the Maine Road stadium had risen into the grey Manchester skies. To my horror, there was nothing there but a series of temporary walls erected by the builders – no Main Stand, no North Stand, no Kippax, no Platt Lane. I felt physically sick. It was like stumbling unexpectedly on the grave of someone you'd loved. Hot salt tears started to prick at my eyes. It must only have been a matter of seconds but I wrenched at the steering wheel and put my foot down on the accelerator, burning rubber in my desperation to get away from the scene of the crime. How I wished I had never gone back in the first place. I loved Maine Road with all my heart and I feel its loss to this day.

Chapter Five

THE SUMMER OF 2003 PASSED ALL TOO QUICKLY, AS summers do, as I suppose everyone finds as they get older. I remember when I was eight or nine, we broke up from school for the summer holidays around 20 July. We didn't have to be back at school until the first week in September. Six long glorious weeks of sunshine and holidays lay ahead with their endless games of cricket, visits to Old Trafford cricket ground and a plentiful supply of what we then thought was ice cream, though apparently, according to later EU regulations, it was actually some random collection of animal fats. Chocolate, strawberry and vanilla were the usual flavours with the occasional dalliance of exotic Neapolitan. At some point there would be a week or two of holiday by the beach, invariably in Cornwall which was so far from home my parents had to order the *Manchester Guardian* in the local newsagent. It would arrive as if from a foreign country the day after it was published in Manchester. It was worth the wait for me because there was a guaranteed report on the previous day's Lancashire cricket match. At some point in August the weather would be miserable, my friends away on holiday with their families or otherwise occupied and my mother bad-tempered, and then the cherished freedom from the jail of school seemed like another form of punishment and the days were endless.

There were no such feelings of ennui this summer. I had arranged a tour of Tuscany and Umbria for us to take together shortly after Lynn arrived back home after nearly eleven months in California. As we drove out of Bologna airport and on to the autostrada towards Florence it was as if we had left all our domestic troubles at home in a box in the loft. For eight magical days and nights we were transported not just to Tuscany and Umbria but somehow, magically, to the land of our former selves. We took off the cloaks of hurt we had each worn like a hair shirt for twelve months and rediscovered what it was that had drawn us to each other in the first place. Released from the cares of her job, Lynn relaxed in the sunshine of Tuscany and the years seemed to drop away from her.

So often in a marriage it is the family holidays which become battlegrounds. Christmas and New Year is traditionally the time that the Samaritans regard as their busiest. Long-anticipated holidays fall short of expectations and the disappointment leads to arguments and worse. This last summer holiday lingers in the mind like nostalgia for the elegiac summers of Edwardian England which haunted the memories of people in the interwar years who remembered them, not as a time of social unrest and possible civil war in Ireland, but as distant worlds of lost enchantment.

It seemed as if Lynn were packing to return almost as soon as our plane landed back in Stansted from Bologna. Term started for her before the end of August and she had lessons to prepare. We went to a friend's house for dinner the night before she was due to fly out and we held hands on the couch like teenagers, I'm not embarrassed to report. I suppose watching her as she disappeared again through Passport Control at Heathrow and into the ever-lengthening queue for Security Clearance, possibly with a sigh of relief, served me right. Possessiveness, jealousy, call it what you will, it's an ugly and ultimately dispiriting emotion.

It might have still been August and the cricket season still had a month to run but summer was over and life was starting to darken. From where I sit and type in an upstairs room I look out over a small but delightfully secluded garden with a profusion of trees and bushes on all sides. The tree directly in my sight starts to turn red before any of the others begin to show their autumnal colours and it always induces in me a small sensation of panic, as does the ubiquitous Back to School notices and the erection of goalposts on sports grounds where previously nets and the slip-catching cradle had held sway. The evenings no longer stay light until after 9pm and there is a nip in the air by 8pm. Like Matthew Arnold outside Rugby Chapel in 1857, I've always had a problem with autumn. Despite the fact that it tends to appear on a regular and utterly predictable basis, it always rather takes my emotions by surprise. Arnold described it rather better:

> Coldly, sadly descends
> The autumn evening.
> The field
> Strewn with its dank yellow drifts
> Of withered leaves, and the elms,
> Fade into dimness apace,
> Silent; hardly a shout
> From a few boys late at their play

Not even the prospect of buttered crumpets and the signature tune of *Sports Report* on the radio can snap me out of this melancholy once I am immersed in it. I know we are supposed to admire the wonderful autumnal colours and to rejoice in the prospect of rubbing one's hands and/or backside before roaring fires. However, I am a dissenter. I find the whole business of raking those withered leaves which have fallen off next-door's tree and clearing the buggers out of the drains to be tedious in the extreme. To me the end of the summer is the end of the year.

The new academic year begins in September/October. The new Jewish year begins at much the same time. Even television schedulers begin their year in what they call Week 36, when the family returns from holiday and starts to congregate for worship round the flat screen. The 31 December seems to me to be an entirely arbitrary and unsatisfactory date on which to end the year, an end which really arrives three or four months earlier. More significantly I have always felt autumn to be a harbinger of death. I fully expect to disappear for good sometime in October/November, having decided there is no longer much of a reason for living, the next Lancashire county cricket match being too far distant to offer any comfort.

I always greet the end of the football season with pleasure, assuming City have not been relegated and then, even if they have, sometimes it's a relief to have it over with. The end of the cricket season, on the other hand, induces nothing but regret and melancholia. As the pads and bat are zipped up in the cricket bag and the bag itself is kicked further towards the back of the bedroom closet, I always feel that there goes another season chalked off on the stately progress towards death – and that applies if I've just made a gritty 17 not out or been wrongly given out lbw for 3 by a deaf and blind team-mate who is umpiring only to redress a grievance he has been harbouring from the previous season when I gave him out caught behind off his thigh pad.

Enough of this merry frolicking. We're back in the autumn of 2003 and there was the usual careless optimism about the season that was to unfold in front of us. The new signings did not fill me with any sense of great expectation. Michael Tarnat the German international left-back came from Bayern Munich to replace Jensen, Paul Bosvelt provided some necessary midfield steel, Claudio Reyna came from Sunderland, and the ancient David Seaman arrived from Arsenal. It was as if, at least in those days, only Keegan in the whole world didn't know that Arsene Wenger never let anyone leave his club unless he was crocked, hugely overpriced or considerably over the hill. They joined Antoine Sibierski, Steve McManaman and Trevor Sinclair, signings which carried with them a tangible lack of excitement. It was a deeply dispiriting collection of Has-beens, Never Weres and Never Will Bes; it was like playing fantasy football with no money, which I suppose is what it was.

At first it seemed I was entirely mistaken and that the changes in playing personnel and the opening of the new ground had combined to create an irresistible forward momentum. The Eastlands ground was impressively well constructed and the 47,000 crowds (compared to the 35,000 which was the final capacity of Maine Road) revelled in its newness as if the modern clean lines of its design were part of the club's own regeneration. Unlike August 2000, this time the first match of the season against Charlton resulted in an impressive 3–0 victory, and after three games City had scored seven goals and gained seven points. Even the compulsory defeat to Arsenal, who were now setting off on their famously unbeaten season, seemed to be only a blip, as by the start of November with just over a quarter of the season already completed we had accumulated eighteen points scoring twenty-two goals on the way. At that rate we would have nearly eighty points at the end of the season and have scored nearly ninety goals, so that would make us almost certain candidates for a top four finish and a first Champions League place. Want to know where we did actually finish? The answer is sixteenth, with just Everton between us and the relegation zone.

It was to be a season when the football was unappealing, the manager seemed disenchanted, though with what we never knew because he appeared to get his own way on everything, and the team went backwards instead of forwards. The most symbolic match of the season was going out of the UEFA Cup in November against Groclin Dyskobolia, though I suppose it could have been Groclin Dyslexia for all we knew. In any case, they were an unknown bunch of Polish no-hopers who scored a goal at Eastlands in a one-all draw, which took them through after a miserable 0–0 in Poland. 'We came in through the back door and we went out through the back door,' observed Keegan quite accurately. He seemed as depressed about being the manager of Manchester City as we were watching him disappear into his anorak, bringing to mind the image of his head slumped in the wake of the heart-breaking 4–3 defeat at Anfield that polished off his attempt to win the championship in 1996 for Newcastle United. That season he wore his head as well as his heart on his sleeve.

The run of nine points from fourteen games that lasted from the start of November 2003 till the end of February 2004 just about mirrored the rest of my life. In addition to the usual feelings of frustration with attempts to raise money to make a feature film and with the feelings of loneliness that overwhelmed me at home on a regular basis, there was also more bad news about Jack. The monthly check-ups he'd had since he'd come home at the end of May had all gone well. The blood count numbers were healthy and the Jacob's Cream Crackers box, which had been full of his out-patient medicines, had been placed in storage. I delivered him back to Maureen after one such successful sortie with the words, 'I think he's just malingering. I'd cut off his state benefits if I were you.' We had to be confident if we were treating it all so lightly.

We celebrated with utter certainty the seeming triumph of the Righteous over the Malign.

Then in October it all changed.

From my own family's experience I knew that the really dreaded words were not just 'It's malignant' but, even more so, 'It's come back.' Jack's cancer had come back and on the way home round the North Circular Road after we'd absorbed this latest unwelcome information we were silent almost for the first time on that mind- and buttock-numbing journey. I tried to think of cheery things to say but they all seemed trivial and stupid and pointless. We both knew what he was facing.

A week before Christmas, Lynn arrived home for her brief Yuletide sojourn from her latest four-month spell in California. I was distressed when I saw her. She looked exhausted. She had maintained her beauty for so long, it was shocking to see her face appearing so lined. I really thought that age would never catch up with her and, though she discounted the merits of her beauty as being superficial, I knew she was always pleased when I told her, with complete sincerity, how beautiful she was.

The following day I left her to adjust to Greenwich Mean Time and drove the children up to Manchester to see my father who was recovering from a stroke, after which we would watch City play Leeds United. I couldn't help wondering which would be the greater ordeal. My father lay on a bed near the entrance to a large ward. He looked very old, small and frail but he had lost none of his ability to complain about almost everyone he came into contact with; in this case the nurses who made their point by ignoring him completely. In the end, I had to go and find the nurse and apologise on his behalf and, though it solved the problem temporarily, I'm quite sure the *status quo* was restored the moment we left. David and Amy did their best with him but they had never had a real relationship with him, which was hardly surprising considering neither had I. He lived two hundred miles away from them as they grew up but he never saw it as part of his role as a grandfather to show much of an interest in their lives, unlike Lynn's parents who lived six thousand miles away but became extremely close to their grandchildren.

We drove with some relief to the gleaming new City of Manchester Stadium. I had kindly been given tickets in the Directors' Box and, as ever with City, everything behind the scenes was wonderful. But after Sommeil fell over the ball in the middle of the first half and gifted struggling Leeds a goal, the football on view was diabolical. Ten minutes from the end, Sibierski equalised with a header but, as with too many games in recent years, watching City failed to lift my heart in the way it had done in the past. This growing sense of disillusion had less to do with the club's success or failure – I knew from experience how best to ride the crashing waves of triumph and despair – than with the unpleasant and dispiriting atmosphere in which football as a whole now lived.

There was one bright spot in this otherwise unremitting gloom – I had been invited to give three lectures on board the Cunard liner the *Caronia*, on a New Year's cruise to Madeira and the Canary Isles. The deal is you and your partner get free passage in return for writing and delivering the lectures. Nice work if you can get it but you can only get it if you try very hard. It was such a pleasure to drive to the Southampton dockyard where someone took the cases out of the car and up to the cabin while the car itself was driven away to await our return in twelve days. Feeling rather like Noel Coward sailing to exotic parts in order to write about England, this pampered luxury had the effect of making me never want to travel by air again.

Lynn, who, I had anticipated, would be such a doughty sailor, struggled as the liner ploughed its way through the stormy Bay of Biscay. The weather wasn't particularly good throughout the trip but we greatly enjoyed the cosseted life on board and even the ever-present sound of the clash of Zimmer frames failed to dampen the enjoyment. The *Caronia* was an elegant ship, built in 1949, and it brought to mind the golden days of ocean-going travel, which must have been the interwar years and into the late 1950s before the widespread growth of air traffic. It was only as we slid out of the harbour in Lisbon, our last port of call, with the floodlights of what I immediately assumed must be either Sporting Lisbon or Benfica shining brightly in the middle distance that a conversation with Lynn brought home the awkwardness of our situation.

I was so enjoying our time on board that I was keen to experience it again the following year if they wanted me to return as a guest lecturer. Lynn, however, firmly rejected the idea because American schools only get ten days or so off for Christmas (and even less for Easter) and the only way she had been allowed to go on the voyage, which didn't return to England until 10 January, had been to beg a week's additional holiday from her Principal. It was clearly not going to be possible to repeat it on an annual basis. I was, probably unjustly, really annoyed – another example, I felt, of how that wretched job of hers was destroying our marriage. It was an easy accusation to make. Whatever assailed our marriage it was more than the irritations caused by her job.

She wandered away from me into the darkness of the prow knowing perfectly well how I felt about her bloody job and, as ever, after thirty years of marriage, it all went into the unmarked jar where we deposit our raging emotions so we can continue with the orderly life of a long relationship. Except, I asked myself not for the first time, was this a marriage at all? Was I just being, as she implied quite forcefully, unreasonably selfish?

I didn't think I was being selfish. A great part of the pleasure I derived from the comfort of that voyage was the knowledge that Lynn was luxuriating in it. Like the holiday in Italy six months before, I had worked hard to ensure that she had nothing to do but turn up and enjoy herself. When I worried about the future of our relationship and asked myself if I still loved her I had only to remind myself of the number of occasions when I tried so desperately to please her to convince myself that I certainly did. Sometimes, though, as on that night in Lisbon, it was hard.

We docked in Southampton on a miserable Saturday morning and drove home under the most funereal of dark grey skies. She was thinking that the next day she would be back in the sunshine of California and, though the job was hard and she'd enjoyed much of the cruise, she was exhibiting few signs of regretting her imminent return to the west coast of America. I was thinking that City were losing 4–2 at Portsmouth and that I wouldn't now see Lynn until 20 June and the next five months promised a struggle on all fronts – with Jack, with my work, with my father. And in times of struggle you really want the person closest to you to be close to you and not six thousand miles and eight time zones away.

I was now constantly worrying if, after thirty-one years, our marriage was sustainable in its present guise. I suspected Lynn didn't want to address the subject for fear of breaking the tenuous thread that held us together and, of course, I didn't either. Life, even a life like that, seemed to both of us better than a divorce. I'd been married since I was twenty-three and I couldn't imagine what it would be like to be single again. And besides, for all these frustrations, I loved Lynn, I really did; which I suppose was why I got so cross with her when she upset me. When she disappeared once more through Passport Control the next morning, I felt a moment's uplift that there would be no more disagreements and no more angry silences in the house, but by the time I got out of the Terminal 3 car park at Heathrow I knew that didn't matter. What mattered was love, actually or otherwise.

So Lynn returned to California and I tried to immerse myself in work, looking up constantly to hope that Keegan's City could somehow recapture that spirit of derring-do that had permeated their football during the promotion season, two years earlier. When the uplift came it did so from a highly unpredictable source. In the fourth round of the Cup, City drew 1–1 at home to Spurs, prompting a replay at White Hart Lane ten days later. Even though I can see the floodlights in Tottenham from my bedroom window, proximity was no help because I am invariably in Cambridge on Tuesdays and Wednesdays in the Lent term, getting back usually about 9pm, so I had made no plans to acquire a ticket.

At 5pm that Wednesday, Howard rang me to say that his evening appointment with Charles Clarke had been cancelled by the Education Minister's office and he was now free to go. Fine for him, now in residence in the Aldwych as the Director of the London School of Economics, but I was in Cambridge at rush hour. Obviously if I'd known what was going to happen I'd have chartered a helicopter but I only arrived back in the driveway as they kicked off. I collected my things from the car and phoned Howard, who had left a message saying he had one of the stands to himself, to discover that we were a goal down in the first minute. Any possible desire to race to White Hart Lane for the second half was eliminated by what happened in the remaining forty-four minutes of the first half; we conceded two further goals without reply. I settled down to watch on television the second half and the last rites of City's 2004 FA Cup campaign go the way of so many others and was sharply reminded of why I continued to support this uniquely infuriating club.

As if being three goals down at half-time were not a sufficient handicap, Anelka came off injured and Joey Barton managed to get himself sent off between leaving the pitch after forty-five minutes and arriving at the dressing room. This has set the bar for ludicrous red cards quite high for Mario Balotelli but I have no doubt that one day soon he will clear it with ease. After the game, Keegan revealed that he had spent most of the interval not talking to his team at all but trying to elicit from the referee the reasons why he had sent off Barton. Total silence is certainly a stark contrast to the Ferguson hairdryer but, on this occasion, it turned out, probably to the astonishment of the manager himself, to be just as effective.

We all expected some sort of pointless show of resistance in the second half, along the lines of the defeat at the same venue in the League Cup two months earlier when they had also been 3–0 down at half-time and eventually lost tamely 3–1. However, Distin pulled the inevitable goal back only a couple of minutes after half-time and the luck that had deserted us since November suddenly returned. A wicked deflection from a hopeful shot by Bosvelt brought the second goal and a fractionally offside Shaun Wright-Phillips scored the equaliser with a delicate chip over the sprawling Spurs goalkeeper. At the other end the debutant Iceland international goalkeeper, Arni Arason, made three brilliant saves to prevent Spurs from closing it out.

Despite the gripping 3–3 scoreline, after eighty minutes I still feared for the lads if it went into extra time. Those ten men had run their hearts out and were clearly going to find another thirty minutes with the demands placed on them by being a man short simply too much. In the last minute of stoppage time, Shaunie went on another mazy run, Sibierski tumbled over but got it out wide to Tarnat, advancing for the umpteenth time down the left wing, and his beautifully flighted cross was met by Jon Macken's head to send the ball back across the frantic goalkeeper and into the far corner of the net. It was unbelievable. I was on the phone to my daughter after every goal. She had texted me at half-time that she was suicidal. Now, like the rest of us, it appeared that she had made a miraculous recovery.

For all my attempts to find in football an explanation for life, rather in the way previous generations would scour the Bible for the answers, I am constantly disappointed in my efforts to emerge triumphantly holding aloft the equation like the FA Cup on a trot round Wembley. The amazing comeback at Tottenham was not the start of a period when everything I touched turned to gold but the exact reverse. Indeed, troubles in my personal and professional lives started to increase to the extent that when an invitation arrived from Salford University to present an award to Bert Trautmann, the brilliant and brave Manchester City goalkeeper from 1949–64, I fell on it with a cry of relief. Bert joined City six months before I was born and only left just before I was about to take my O-levels. In neither case were the two events causally connected. Bert was my first great hero and, despite what I subsequently learned about his life in Germany before he was captured by the Allies in Normandy, he has remained one. I had met him at the derby match in 2002 but it was a brief, hurried meeting and I was looking forward to spending some time with him.

Unfortunately, Bert cancelled his trip from Valencia because of his now frail health after I had already bought the train ticket which took me to Manchester from St Pancras along the Midland line passing through Kettering and Market Harborough. This route takes half an hour longer than the regular Virgin West Coast line which runs from Euston but it was much quieter and seemingly more reliable. It's a toss-up which is worse – being stuck in a traffic jam on the M6 or on Piccadilly station platform as successive trains are delayed and cancelled.

In the event, I presented Bert's award to Ken Barnes, father of Peter and a clever wing-half in the successful City team of the mid-1950s, who accepted it on behalf of the great man. I said to Ken and the other players from that vintage who attended the lunch that the nearest goalkeeper I ever met to the great Bert was the great Peter Schmeichel – a truly magnificent goalkeeper and more responsible, I believe, than any other individual for United's run of success in the 1990s. 'Oh no,' they all said, 'Schmeichel did a lot of punching; Bert caught the ball.'

I took a taxi from the university to the Jewish nursing home off Leicester Road where my father was currently living. He was glad to see me to the extent that he thought I would instantly take his side against the manifold injustices that were being perpetrated on him, but of course the staff were actually extremely pleasant and I had no reason to suppose it all turned into *One Flew Over the Cuckoo's Nest* the moment I walked out of the front door. I suppose the staff could have been humouring me but I didn't get that impression. Dad certainly wanted to go home but he was palpably too much trouble for my stepmother Lena who was simply not up to the task of being a full-time carer since she was herself eighty-seven years old and fairly frail. Dad fell over too often and she had no chance of hauling him upright. He also burst into tears which I hadn't seen him do since my mother died.

I couldn't help but admire how my father clung so tenaciously to life. I'm not sure that in a similar situation I would have wanted life to continue. I wondered if Dad believed in an afterlife but I never found the opportunity to ask. Was it perhaps a childlike presumption that in death he would rejoin my mother or get his sight and mobility and general health back? Surely he couldn't have been frightened of dying. The life he was living was not worth clinging to so why was he doing it with such grim determination? Thinking back to those times now I sometimes wonder why we never had a conversation about these philosophical musings, but since we'd never really had a conversation in fifty years about anything other than the price of petrol or the traffic on the M6, perhaps it was optimistic of me to suppose we could have started at that point.

I left him without the slightest twinge of guilt after I'd wheeled him down to the living room at 5pm which is when the nursing home serves its evening dinner. Like my brother, I felt I had spent too much of my life apologising to staff for my father's behaviour, but if you got my wife on a bad day she would no doubt have said much the same thing about me. Indeed when she wanted to twist the knife all she had to do was intimate that I would one day end up exactly like my father. I denied it vehemently, of course, but as I looked in the mirror every day when I was shaving I couldn't help but be aware that the shape of my face was changing slowly but inexorably into something that looked much more like my father's even as my father's face and body was turning into a cadaver.

How could I have behaved in such an unfeeling, unfilial manner? The fact was that Jack's plight moved and engaged me on an emotional level which my father's fate never did. Maybe at the age of eighty-eight it felt simply as though Nature was taking its course but even at the time I was aware that I loved Jack and I had honestly never felt that way about my father. It was a consequence of a childhood in which he rarely featured in my life. My mother, on the other hand, was a constant nurturing presence and since she died before I could turn into a rebellious teenager I never discovered if I might have found in my father some kind of refuge from an overbearing mother who wouldn't let me grow up.

I returned to London that Friday night full of these thoughts only to have them driven straight out of my head by a remarkable derby match on the Sunday afternoon in which Manchester City beat Manchester United 4–1 in a game they could easily have lost by an equally convincing margin. The luck which had so painfully deserted us all season suddenly returned. United hit the bar and the post, had all the play until half-time after City's second goal went in and could have buried us. For no accountable reason it never happened. After half-time Shaun Wright-Phillips kept Ronaldo quiet, van Nistelrooy kept falling over and the United defence caved in spinelessly. Their heads dropped and they had no stomach for the fight, much like the last derby match at Maine Road in which United finished third out of the two teams.

Unfortunately, instead of raging on the touchline with a stream of foul-mouthed abuse which we would have enjoyed watching, Ferguson sat silently on the bench, numbed by the disaster unfolding in front of him, helpless in the face of his team's feeble capitulation. There wasn't a lot of sympathy heading his way in a stadium that resounded to the triumphalism of City supporters temporarily released from the misery of a deeply depressing season.

We assumed that this spiritually uplifting victory would herald the start of the final quarter of the season in which we would rediscover the careless rapture of the first quarter and finish in a blaze of glory and a torrent of goals. It didn't quite work out that way. We lost the next match at Leeds and then embarked on a series of draws which kept us in the maelstrom of the relegation dogfight. I was at Upton Park as one particularly ghastly defeat unfolded because I was the guest of a delightful American academic called Chuck Korr who is a fiercely partisan West Ham supporter. I have absolutely no memory of the match I watched with him but I had brought my transistor and, although my corporeal presence was in East London, my heart and soul was in East Manchester as City contrived to lose spinelessly 3–1 to the mighty forces of Southampton.

It was one of those numbing, utterly pathetic home capitulations that are the hallmark of relegation sides. We should have lost at home to Wolves the previous Saturday, Shaun Wright-Phillips grabbing an undeserved last-minute equaliser, and on Easter Monday I had been to a sun-drenched White Hart Lane to see us throw away a 1–0 half-time lead to a desperately poor Spurs side. Keegan at this point was on sick leave with a bad back, leaving the shop to be run by Arthur Cox, the man with a long black coat and a charisma bypass. It seemed like a long tube journey back home. Another relegation was clearly on the cards and I couldn't help wondering why the triviality that is football retained the power to upset me so much, particularly in view of what else was going on elsewhere in my life.

Then, suddenly, it got better. The crunch match at Leicester ended in a hard-fought, desperate, slightly fortunate 1–1 draw which was followed by an equally desperate 1–0 home win over Newcastle. This was relegation football at its most stomach-churning and buttock-clenching. Wanchope's goal at Eastlands was all the more precious because, the following day, Bolton walloped Leeds 4–1, condemning the Yorkshire side to the drop along with Leicester and Wolves. After weeks of anxiety those particular storm clouds suddenly lifted. Well, God be Praised as the seventeenth-century Puritans would undoubtedly have said, had they been able to afford a ticket to Premiership football. The

Puritans probably wouldn't have approved of football on the Lord's Day but they would surely have given thanks for Wanchope's goal fifteen minutes into the second half at a very nervous City of Manchester Stadium. In the end we were saved not really by our own efforts – the Newcastle win was only the fourth victory out of eighteen attempts at home – but the greater ineptitude of others.

As if to underline the point, City, relieved of the deep-rooted anxiety induced by such a close acquaintance with the despair of relegation, went up to play Middlesbrough in the penultimate game of the season and lost. The inescapable conclusion was that this was a poor team, devoid of inspiration, heading nowhere, so it must have been a sense of filial duty as much as any expectation that City might achieve a mighty victory that took Amy and me back to Manchester for the last game of this depressing season. My father was now back home after his enforced stay in the nursing home, which was what he wanted, but the strain this imposed on my stepmother Lena did not improve her humour. What Dad wanted was some sort of Jane Eyre, a companion who could do everything for him, from reading the paper to making his meals and talking about the Middle East. I don't remember Jane Eyre talking to Mr Rochester much about the Middle East but it's a long time since I read it. Actually, I didn't think he wanted Jane Eyre from Haworth but Jane Eyrbromovich from Whitefield. What added to my father's sense of isolation was that he and Lena were at that point pretty much the sole survivors of a group of forty or fifty families who brought Jewish civilisation to the suburbs of north Manchester after 1945. The rest were dead and I thought it must be the curse of old age to be left so alone with all those memories.

It was with some relief that we made our excuses and set off for the City of Manchester Stadium. Free from the paralysing fear of relegation but still mired in a run of poor form, City played an Everton side just one point above us and boasting the prodigious talents of the Boy Wonder, Wayne Rooney. City won 5–1 and could have scored ten. Rooney was anonymous and we drove home full of joy and optimism about the future. The new season couldn't come too soon. When would the fixture list be out? Sometimes I despair of the idiocy football induces in otherwise perfectly sane and rational people, particularly when it's my own idiocy.

Chapter Six

IS LIFE INHERENTLY ABSURD OR IS IT JUST THAT SOME PEOPLE respond more easily to manifestations of the absurd than others? Or is that an entirely absurd observation?

One Friday night towards the end of April 2004 I went round for dinner with Jack and Maureen, as I did most Friday nights because Jack was back from hospital and the Friday night ritual gave us all a sense of comfort and normality. When I got to the house, however, it was apparent that Jack was in considerable distress again. His face was otherworldly with pain and poor Amy and Maureen didn't look a whole lot better. It was obvious that he had to get back to hospital quickly. Again, I said I'd drive but he needed to lie down and he couldn't do that in my car so they called an ambulance. There was a private nurse at the house but she looked even more terrified than the rest of us. She was South African, looked about twelve years old and appeared to be quite overwhelmed by everything. I thought she belonged in a hospital in Cape Town taking temperatures and emptying bedpans. The awfulness of final-stage cancer was understandably beyond her limited experience.

After Maureen and Amy set off with Jack in the ambulance, I went back inside the house with the young nurse and we made a pathetic attempt to eat the roast chicken Maureen had cooked but neither of us felt much like eating for different reasons. I was depressed and she was, as she put it in that charming accent of hers, 'a bit sceered'. Since the patient she had been hired to look after for the night had left the building there wasn't much for her to do but I was still a bit surprised when she asked if I thought it all right if she went to stay with a friend of hers in Leytonstone because she was 'a bit sceered' to be left in the house overnight. I said I thought it probably was, although frankly she might be a lot more sceered walking the streets of Leytonstone on a Friday night at chucking-out time, but suggested she ask Maureen first; so she rang Maureen on her mobile and ascertained that it was, in fact, all right.

She reminded me of the teenage babysitter we once hired to look after our small children when Lynn and I went to the cinema. On our return, I walked the girl, who was the daughter of a neighbour, back to her house in the quiet streets of middle-class St Albans. On arriving at the front door, she asked me if I wouldn't mind waiting with her until her parents got back in half an hour because they didn't like her to be in the house on her own. Presumably our toddler children had spent the night looking after her.

After the latest emergency passed, Jack was moved to the Royal Free Hospital in Belsize Park where I next saw him in rather a nice single room on the twelfth floor with a stunning view out, looking south to Camden and Euston. I usually go for a walk every afternoon when I am writing at home – rain or shine. It's a circular walk of about five miles lasting about ninety minutes, or eighty-seven minutes if I am strictly accurate since I go the same route at pretty much the same pace at the same time every day. Just as President Kennedy claimed to get very irritable if he didn't have sex every day or every couple of days, so I tend to get irritable if I go more than a day or two without my walk across Hampstead

Heath. Jack being where he was, I easily managed to adapt the walk over the Heath to Parliament Hill and then down to the hospital.

I had been toying with something I wanted to say to him for weeks but it never seemed like the right time. Either there was someone in the room or he was too ill to listen to me being emotional or he was in too much pain. I talked about it to my friend Lee who worked for a branch of local government in Cambridge specialising in the NHS, and for whose sound common sense I had developed enormous respect. She had recently lost her stepfather to cancer and she was adamant that I had to say something to Jack about how I felt. I have to confess that I did so with some trepidation and it still took a few days before I found the right moment.

I was finally alone with him as we talked about football and I searched the room looking for the weirdly shaped egg carton thing that you have to pee into if you can't get out of bed. Once more I was thinking that, if Jack went, there would be very few people left who had the same range of historical associations about Manchester football. Jack had been going to Maine Road and Old Trafford since the late 1930s; I had been going since the late 1950s. Who was I going to moan to on a daily basis about the awfulness of modern football and particularly modern footballers when he was gone?

I said, very self-consciously, almost as a new train of thought about the Premiership or the FA Cup, 'Jack, I just want to tell you that I love you.'

'Do you, love?' He looked up. A bit surprised but not a lot.

'Yes, Jack,' I ploughed on like Magnus Magnusson after the buzzer has sounded, 'I absolutely adore you.'

'Well I love you, too, love,' he replied possibly a bit dutifully. 'In fact,' he went on encouragingly, 'I think I admire you more than anybody I know. But we're going to beat this thing, aren't we?'

'Course we are,' I confirmed. But it was too late. The tears were already spurting from my eyes as if someone had turned the hot water tap on or Richard Attenborough had suddenly announced his arrival.

I raced to the sink and tried to splash cold water on my face to hide the salt tears that were flowing down it as this story flashed through my mind. We had such a history together. I couldn't stand the thought that it was ending. There was a perfunctory knock on the door which was flung open as I made my way back to the single chair. It had to be Richard Attenborough to complete the story but of course it wasn't. It was the assistant Rabbi from the West London Synagogue. I left, relieved. It was time for a philosophical discussion that I was in no mood to share but I was glad Jack had someone else in the room to take his mind off my hysterical outburst.

One of the reasons I had been so reluctant to make that declaration of love was not that I feared rejection or ridicule. Jack would have known instantly that it was sincere and he was constitutionally incapable of exploiting that kind of vulnerability. However, he would also have known that I wouldn't have said it unless I had thought he was going to die. I did not want him to think I was writing him off but I knew that the end wasn't far away and I couldn't let him go without saying what I said. Looking back on it now I suspect it was very selfish of me to do that because Jack must certainly have known that I had given up on his struggle for life. I walked home with all these thoughts spinning round in my head like in a spin dryer without any feeling that the thermostat would ever intervene to end it.

Maureen told me later that Jack had related to her and Amy what had passed between us during the afternoon conversation.

They were both pleased and touched that I'd said what I said especially as it brought from Jack a classic Jackism.

'Oh,' said Amy, temporarily overcome with the emotion of the moment. 'That's wonderful. And what happened after he told you he loved you?'

Jack thought for a moment and then replied in that deadpan Northern voice, 'Oh, then we had sex and he went home.'

By this time, the middle of May 2004, I had almost given up the idea of working on anything new. Ian Marshall, my editor at Headline who had successfully managed my three football books, had moved to Orion and commissioned my proposal to write a non-fiction novel about the love affair between Greta Garbo and John Gilbert, an idea which I'd also sold to Radio 4 as a Saturday afternoon play. This new project gave me the chance to write about an area of history I knew pretty well in a new and original way. I was looking forward to writing about the origins of twentieth-century celebrity and this constantly engaging enigmatic Swedish actress but somehow I just couldn't get started.

It was with some relief that I got away from the house to give what was then an annual lecture on Film and History to the Cambridge undergraduates who were shortly to take their examinations, one of the papers being a more general paper on historical theory and practice for which this lecture was specifically designed. I invited as my guest for the day David Bernstein who had been a friend since we first met in 1997 and became an even better one after he stepped down as the chairman of Manchester City. David has a genuine passion for modern American history, not something I suspect has appeared very often on the CV of past chairmen of the Football Association. We were invited to lunch in Clare College by Tony Badger, Master of Clare, Mellon Professor of American

History, Newcastle United and Bristol Rovers supporter and all-round good egg. It is friends like Tony and David who make life a pleasure in good times and supportable in bad times.

The day was utterly beguiling. There is something about Cambridge in the early summer sunshine that is always very seductive. The stone of the buildings seems to be lifted by the increased light and the combination of river, bridges, college courtyards, trees, formal gardens and the limited noise, which has followed the banning of cars from the centre of town during the day, gives the place a timeless feel. Earth hath not anything to show more fair than the view along the backs of the colleges from Clare Bridge, which can certainly no longer be said of the view from Westminster Bridge, though it has its moments.

It was now the middle of May and I had finalised the arrangements for the next holiday Lynn and I were due to take in Italy, two weeks after she arrived back in England on 21 June. It was all carefully woven around the tickets I had bought for David and me to go to see the one-day international at Lord's between England and the West Indies. I was looking forward to the holiday with considerable anticipation, as was Lynn who was always complaining about being overworked and now sounded ill as well as tired and depressed. I tended to attribute that to the fact that the only time we seemed able to speak to each other because of the time difference was at 2pm our time which is 6am in California. She always sounded as if she had just woken up – which, on most occasions, she had.

I knew she would appreciate the itinerary I had arranged through Florence and Chianti-shire, down to Orvieto and up Umbria through Spoleto. Wonderful countryside, food and guaranteed sunshine. I was becoming fixated on the holiday and I was starting to fantasise about Tuscan bean soup and the Uffizi Gallery and walking over the Ponte Vecchio, staying at those delightful out-of-the-way hotels I had painstakingly discovered on the internet. There is only so much misery your mind can take at any one time.

I desperately wanted Lynn to be with me for the ending. She knew how close I was to Jack and she remembered perfectly well those silly times we spent together such as coaching the boys' Saturday morning football team twenty years before. Lynn, however, to my increasing frustration, was clearly more engaged with the dyslexic kids in Santa Barbara and she wasn't with me when I needed her. I started to become frustrated with Santa Barbara and everything it stood for.

It was 22 May in the new football calendar before we reached the FA Cup final, traditionally the climax of the football season but now just another televised match before the Champions League final and the start of the European Championships. That year the FA Cup competition had surprisingly resolved itself into a final contest between Manchester United and Millwall, leaving me with a difficult dilemma to resolve. Normally I would have no trouble in supporting the opposition but Millwall had such a deservedly unsavoury reputation, they were managed by Dennis Wise and I genuinely wanted Jack to experience some pleasure from the season because I knew he wouldn't be around for 2004–5.

United apparently won 3–0 comfortably but I avoided watching the highlights, as I always do when I know United have won. I find life is so much more bearable that way. I am delighted to say that I have never seen the goals that won them the European Cup in 1999 or the penalties against Chelsea in Moscow but, particularly in the days immediately after the finals, it took considerable ingenuity and a lot of dashing out of rooms or holding my fingers in my ears while diving for the remote control and the safety of the on/off switch.

I was genuinely pleased that Jack's last footballing experience was of United winning the FA Cup – greater love than that I do not know exists. Ironically, it was a victory that probably meant more to Jack who loved the FA Cup than it did to the Manchester United manager whose refusal to defend the trophy in 2000 offended every traditional supporter of the competition. Yes, I know United claim that they were ordered to do so by the FA, but their manager has never previously exhibited a reluctance to let his feelings of opposition to the FA be known if forced to comply with an FA decision of which he disapproved.

Adam brought Jack back to the house to watch the match. He had collected a row of photographs of United's great players of the past so that his father's heroes were carefully lined up on the mantelpiece. Starting at the end was Duncan Edwards, Jack's favourite player, and next to him were the other members of the pantheon – Bobby Charlton, Denis Law, George Best. Jack's head nodded in happy acknowledgement as he ticked them all off – Bryan Robson, Eric Cantona, Ryan Giggs and then right at the end was Diego Forlán – one of Ferguson's horribly overpriced misfits from South America who could possibly have managed to hit a cow's arse with a banjo but couldn't put a football in the back of the net from any distance. Jack thought his position among the greats appropriately comic, which at the time it was, but at the start of the next season, after signing Rooney, United sold Forlán to Villarreal where he couldn't stop scoring, which is probably an even better joke.

Jack was now in the peaceful, serene atmosphere of the North London Hospice. The day after the Cup final we collected him and took him out for the afternoon but we couldn't travel too far and we ended up in the nearest park in Friern Barnet – a nasty patch of scrubland with one of those depressing kiosks selling Wall's ice cream that looks unchanged from the 1950s. I looked at Jack, asleep in the wheelchair, like a parent looks at a sleeping child in a pushchair. For years Jack had always looked younger than his real age. His hair still had more pepper than salt and having a wife and two kids the same ages as mine made me think we were almost contemporaries, despite the eighteen years of chronological difference separating our births. Jack always seemed to me to epitomise youthful vigour but looking at him that afternoon, it was obvious that was no longer the case. We only stayed out about half an hour because he was uncomfortable in the chair and breathing rather heavily.

The end was so near that everything else just came to a halt. I went to see him again on the Wednesday night to watch the Champions League final with him – the unlikely meeting of F.C. Porto of Portugal and the French club Monaco. It's hard to imagine now that he's the most famous and successful manager in the world but back in May 2004 José Mourinho was best known in Britain for running up and down the touchline at Old Trafford, after his Porto side had knocked United out of the last sixteen of the Champions League with a goal in the last minute. Porto's victory over Monaco confirmed Mourinho's inauguration at Stamford Bridge, but a Champions League final with neither an English nor a Spanish club in sight seems to belong to the 1990s rather than the noughties. Football fashions can change with bewildering rapidity.

Jack lay in bed and watched the match but clearly comprehended little of it. I used to love bantering with him during matches but by then he was on very high doses of morphine to deal with the pain and as a result he simply vanished into a world of his own. He made the occasional reappearance over the next two days. On the Friday morning I rang my Amy and told her to go and see Jack that day because I wasn't sure he would last the weekend. She did so and apparently he smiled at her and said, 'Hello, kid'; to which she very properly responded, 'Hello . . . man.' It was shortly after this brief conversation that Jack lapsed into unconsciousness again. I rang David in America, who was taking the news hard, as I feared he might, because Jack had been like a second father to him for twenty years.

In the evening, those closest to Jack gathered for a last attempt at a Friday night supper, after which we took it in turns to remember some aspect of our relationship with him. To have been a friend of this man for twenty years was an honour I would treasure for the rest of my life. If there was any comfort to be gained from the sadness that overwhelmed us all it was in the wonderful way that Maureen, Amy and Adam had looked after him throughout his long illness. Their steadfastness, their dedication and above all their deep and abiding love for the man was an object lesson in how to behave well in the midst of such desperate circumstances. I admired them all as much as I loved them.

It was difficult for me to leave Jack that night. It was like being on a station platform as the train leaves and watching the face of someone you love and might never see again recede into the distance. Just turning round and walking out to the car park seemed wrong. I felt I had to be there until I could accept that nothing was visible but at midnight we broke up. I was asked to go home and wait for the phone. I recognised that although I'd come a long way with them, at that moment my presence was superfluous, if not intrusive, so I drove home with a heavy heart.

I couldn't ring Lynn to talk about it because she had flown to Maryland with her parents to attend the wedding of her niece; one of those coincidences which life frequently throws up of birth, marriage and death intersecting almost brutally. David was there, too, so I couldn't talk to him either and it was far too late to ring Amy. In any case, I was still feeling that I needed to protect my children from being upset, a fairly silly anxiety given that Amy was twenty-nine and David nearly twenty-seven. If he had been that age in 1943 or 1917 he'd have been a major in the army and seen many of his friends and the men under his command blown to bits in front of him. I suspect that, like most of my psychological positions, this pathological need to protect children who are quite capable of looking after themselves stems from what happened to my brain after my mother died when I was thirteen.

Jack died just after eleven o'clock the following morning. The phone rang twice between ten and eleven and, for reasons I cannot explain, I knew it wasn't him or, at least, in the circumstances, I knew it wasn't about him. Then it rang again at 11.20am and before I picked up the telephone I knew that this time it was. Maureen's voice sounded very tired but resigned. 'He's gone, love,' she said simply. My heart sank like a stone. It was hardly at the news itself but at the finality of it all, I suppose.

For all the fact that this death was long expected, I cried when he died. Great gushing fountains of tears spurted from my eyes in a manner that would have done credit to Richard Attenborough at his most tearful. When they eventually stopped I made myself useful by collecting the death certificate and was then weirdly surprised when I looked at it because it had my friend Jack's name on it. Cause of death multiple myeloma, it said. How bald that statement was. How could such a plain factual summary do justice to the fight that had obsessed him and us for nearly two years?

He was buried two days later on a bright spring Bank Holiday Monday. Afterwards we went back to the house and, within minutes, entirely appropriately, the television was on and those of us who wanted to spend the afternoon in the traditional manner were watching the First Division play-off final between West Ham United and Crystal Palace. One goal won the game for Palace – it had been a remarkable rise in the second half of the season for a club that was in turmoil until Iain Dowie appeared to sort them out. Until, of course, he didn't and he was sacked. Despite the fact that I have many friends who are West Ham supporters and none, as far as I know, who are Palace supporters, I was glad Palace were coming up as they were far less likely than West Ham to establish themselves in the Premier League so if Palace held on to that goal lead, there was one relegation place sorted out for 2005. They held out and Palace were indeed duly relegated a year later.

I came home and rang America, finally making contact with David and with Lynn who were both, naturally, devastated. I had left messages on their answering machines at home but I knew they wouldn't get them until they returned from the wedding in Washington. Both were crying when they talked to me, just as I had been when I had left the messages for them. David had gone back to Susie's parents' house in Metuchen, New Jersey, and Lynn was with her parents in California. Though I didn't feel particularly lucky, I appreciated that there had been an advantage to being in London as the tragedy unfolded and Amy and I could join in the communal grieving. In Metuchen and Santa Barbara, Jack's passing made no rustling sound in the palm trees. I don't know if they have palm trees in New Jersey – probably not, though they do have the Sopranos – but they certainly do in Santa Barbara.

Lynn sounded more than normally distressed. I knew that she had been feeling ill for a few days but, unlike me, she usually bore all her aches and pains stoically so I was surprised when she complained so vehemently. Also I was six thousand miles away and it was the era before Skype so it was impossible for me to judge quite how serious her illness was. I believe it is traditional for women to see the doctor as a matter of routine and men to resist such visits but with us it was the other way round. It took consistent pressure from me and her mother for Lynn to agree to visit her family practitioner as they call GPs out there. We agonised over Jack on the phone, looked forward to her return in three weeks time and eagerly anticipated the holiday in Umbria. I always felt that whatever emotional distance had grown between us it could be solved by our simply being together again in the same time zone and in the same house. We'd had a good summer in 2003 and there seemed no reason why we shouldn't experience the pleasure of another one in 2004. Its limited time frame somehow ensured it.

Although I continued to mourn the loss of Jack, I was looking forward to all the things I was planning for Lynn and me to do together in the limited time we had available. I had booked seats for a Cole Porter musical at the Chichester Festival Theatre, along with an overnight stay in a very romantic inn just a few miles up the road. Amy and her long-term boyfriend Matt had stayed there and she recommended it enthusiastically. I had told Gill and David Bernstein about it and we were going down there as a party of four. In addition, I had booked tickets for all of us at the National Theatre to see *A Funny Thing Happened on the Way to the Forum* and for the great hit of the year Alan Bennett's *The History Boys* – a play I was sure we would both like enormously as everybody else who had seen it had raved about it without exception. David and his girlfriend Susie were coming over to spend a few weeks with us and the tickets for the England v West Indies one-day international at Lord's were already sitting on the mantelpiece. The healing process had started and I felt sure my life was going to begin its upward curve once more. Which just shows you how wrong you can be, I suppose.

Chapter Seven

TWO WEEKS AFTER PORTO WON THE CHAMPIONS LEAGUE, on Wednesday 9 June, I went to see a dreadful Hollywood blockbuster called *The Day After Tomorrow* – a horrible mess of special effects and paper-thin characters starring Dennis Quaid which I squirmed through for what seemed like hours.

It was a warm, pleasant night when I gratefully emerged on to Piccadilly. That lunchtime I had spoken to Lynn who was still complaining of feeling ill but, sympathetic as I must have been to a point, I had no real measure of what was ailing her, although she mentioned that she hadn't been in as much pain since her last experience of childbirth twenty-seven years before. She said she was expecting to receive the results of her blood tests from the doctor later that day and that might tell her if it was anything worse than a bad virus. I told Graham my next-door neighbour when I saw him on my return from the cinema as we performed our neighbourly task of setting out the recycling boxes and wheelie bins for the next day's collection.

Although it was around 11.30pm, the air was still warm and it was a delightful night in high summer so Graham and I talked for quite a long time before I went up the steps and inside the house. I closed the curtains in the sitting room because it had still been light when I'd left to drive into town, saw the light was flashing on the telephone answering machine and pressed the 'play' button. To my surprise I heard my mother-in-law's voice. In that matter of a second when my brain registered the identity of the voice I knew something terrible had happened. There was no reason for news not to be conveyed by Lynn unless Lynn herself were the subject of the news, which must necessarily be bad. It was. Lynn had collapsed on the floor of the garage at her parents' home in Santa Barbara. Paramedics had arrived and taken her to the Emergency Room at the Cottage Hospital where it was soon discovered that she had total renal failure – in other words her kidneys had packed up.

The message wasn't long but I had remained standing stock still as it unfurled its horrific news. At its end I sat down heavily on the couch and immediately pressed the 'delete' button, as if by doing so I could delete the message's content as easily as its existence but of course I knew, even as I did it, that the forty-second message had just changed my whole life and not for the better.

I rang my parents-in-law in California but their phone line was engaged. I rang my son in Boston and so was his. I assumed they were talking to each other. They were. I went upstairs to get the piece of paper on which Amy had left the details of her trip. She was on a cruise ship somewhere in the Baltic with other members of *The Archers* cast and many *Archers* fans, known as Archers Addicts. There was a contact number in Norway which I assumed was the cruise ship's port of origin. It was past midnight in London but later in the Baltic. I would have to take the risk and ring her. By the time I woke up in the morning they might have left for the day and I knew that the three of us had to get to Santa Barbara to be with Lynn as soon as possible.

Eventually I got through to David and after that to his grandparents. He was very shaken, as was I of course, but he was hanging on to the reality that she was alive. It now appeared that Lynn had suffered some sort of brain haemorrhage — a word I was to get used to spelling so, reluctant as I was even to think about it, it meant that Lynn had had a stroke and nobody knew what kind of physical and/or mental damage that would leave in its wake.

It was now well after midnight but I rang Graham because I had only left him twenty minutes and a whole lifetime ago, and then I rang Maureen who immediately volunteered to come round but I said no, the morning was soon enough. I left a message on Lee's mobile phone because I knew it would be turned off and she'd pick it up in the morning. She had counselled me through my father's decline and Jack's death. I was hoping she wouldn't think this was going to be one journey too many for her.

I dragged myself upstairs and ran a bath but my mind was racing. I was mentally composed enough to run through in my head the list of things that had to be done. I had to get on a plane as soon as possible but I had all sorts of things to do first, including making sure Amy could get back from the middle of Eastern Europe. To make these sorts of snap arrangements is difficult enough; to make them when staggering under the heavy load of knowledge that had just dropped on top of my head was significantly worse. Somehow I got to bed and slept fitfully. All the time I heard in my brain the sound of someone saying to me, 'Your life has changed, your life has changed, your life has changed.'

Around 2.30am the phone rang. There was a surgeon at the other end of the line who sounded slightly irritated that he had had to ring England to talk to his patient's next of kin. He told me that blood vessels had burst in Lynn's brain and that there had been extensive bleeding. He was going to open up the brain and staunch the bleeding and then clean out the blood but I should know that there was likely to be significant brain damage. I asked in a voice thick with fear and sleep if she was likely to die on the operating table. He thought about it for rather longer than I had hoped he would and then replied in something of a monotone that she should make it through the operation all right but it rather depended what he found when he went in there.

I kept the phone cradled next to me in the bed; it was resting on her pillow where her head usually lay, her head that was actually being sliced open at that moment. Some time later the phone shrilled again and I was informed that the operation had gone well, the surgeon had done what he had wanted to do and she was back in recovery prior to being returned to the Intensive Care Unit. When I woke up for good at 6am there was a brief split second of hope that, like the conclusion of so many school essays, it had all been a dream. But it was only for that solitary split second and the weight of sorrow lying on my chest soon told me that it was all for real.

Inevitably my thoughts strayed to my mother who had died after she had banged her head on the skirtingboard while doing her keep-fit exercises on the floor. The story of her banging her head I was later informed was true enough but it wasn't the whole story. She had had an aneurysm, an abnormal enlargement of an artery. The similarity between these two events happening to the two most important women in my life was unbelievable enough. That this should happen ten days after Jack's funeral made it, if it were possible to imagine, that much worse. I had to think as clearly as possible what had to be done in the few hours remaining before I would have to fly to California and remain at her bedside for an indeterminate length of time.

Somehow it all got done. The plane tickets to Santa Barbara were booked and the Italian hotel reservations, the car rental and the theatre tickets were un-booked. Easyjet would be flying to Bologna with at least two empty seats since there was no chance of a refund there. The man in the box office of the National Theatre, however, sounded positively thrilled that I was giving back the tickets to *The History Boys*, such was the demand for them. Amy and Matt flew back to London from Gdańsk, David was going out to California on the Friday and we would be there on the Saturday. It was the day of a garden party in Cambridge to which Maureen and I had been invited to replace the invitation the previous year when we had failed to show up for another medical reason. Somehow we must have been fated never to go there.

There was a local election going on that Thursday and at lunchtime, having been on the phone for three hours, I took the polling card off the mantelpiece and walked down to the booth to vote. I ran into Michael and Ruth my neighbours on the other side and instead of making fun of the Conservative party candidate, which is what I usually do on polling day, I had to tell them what had just happened. They were shocked, of course – how could they fail to be shocked – but all the time I was thinking, 'How can I tell them how frightened I am?' Or perhaps, 'Can't they tell how frightened I am?' I knew their shock was genuine but while they would be shocked and upset for a while, I had to live with this thing for ever and I didn't know how I was going to do that.

By now the news had travelled in the way bad news gets instantly transmitted and the telephone was ringing constantly. The doorbell sounded as neighbours came round to see if they could do something (if only they could). Maureen arrived with her Amy and we sat there staring at each other and thinking, or at least I was, of the time two weeks before as Jack neared his end of how we had sat in the same seats round the same table while I made them

111

chicken soup and pasta with mushroom sauce. Now the situation was reversed and we none of us knew quite what we should do or say. The sister of one of Maureen's former housekeepers had had a stroke and had recovered to lead a full and active life but, though she came and pressed a booklet about stroke victims into my hand, my mind simply refused to accept that Lynn, my Lynn, was a stroke victim. That was the sort of thing that happened to people in their eighties. Wasn't it? I'm somewhat embarrassed to look back at my ignorance of those matters. I wasn't to remain ignorant for much longer.

The news from California was that she had stabilised. She was in the Intensive Care Unit in the delightfully named Cottage Hospital (how can you put a whole hospital into a cottage?) but she was still unconscious and the extent of the damage was therefore unknown. Was this a good thing or a bad thing I wondered? She was stable so she wasn't going to die shortly but until they knew for sure what caused the renal failure there must be a chance that it could happen again. More frightening for me was the impact of the brain haemorrhage and those words that would have condemned her to a living hell. Was this to be Lynn's fate? How could life be turned on its head like this?

What state would Lynn be in when she came out of her coma, assuming she did? The news from the hospital was that they couldn't tell but, given my previous experience, I assumed they did know and it was too horrifying to tell us immediately and that they had decided to wait to let us adjust to her current condition before giving us the soul-destroying news that she would be permanently crippled. The brain surgeon with the poor bedside manner had effectively already told me that the damage was extensive, which might have been code for permanent, but I couldn't be sure. The ray of hope to which I was clinging was that, in my limited experience, doctors are frequently clueless and are as surprised by their patients' recoveries as anyone else. It was important, especially in my dealings with my grown-up but now understandably worried children, that I remain as calm and strong and positive as I could. I tried, I really did, but I suspect I failed abysmally.

I met Amy and Matt at Heathrow as Maureen kindly dropped me off at the United Airlines check-in counter. It was a bright and beautiful Saturday in mid-June, a day for driving out to the country and playing or watching cricket. It had been just two weeks to the day since Jack had died. I said goodbye to Maureen, wondering what malignant fate was at work here, sensing that somehow she in her widowed grief was going to have to find some kind of emotional reserve to be able to offer support to me as I had done for her these many weeks past. I couldn't go through this on my own and she knew better than anyone in the world what I was going to have to face. For weeks I had been feeling a fraud because it wasn't my life partner who was dying and, though I meant every word of the love I tried to show, I could still go home to my bedroom and talk to my wife and discuss it with her. That was no longer the case and Maureen, who had always shown us that it was possible to be successful in show business and still have a strong and loving family life, was now my corridor to sanity from a very different sort of madness that was going to close over my head.

I was relieved that Matt was showing such support for Amy by coming out to California with her, particularly as I knew Susie was accompanying David. It was going to be important that they had someone else to turn to apart from their father who was clearly going to be under different pressures. How long ago was it that all I had to worry about was whether City would avoid relegation? It was in fact five weeks but it could have been five years.

There was one crumb of comfort; we would miss the European Championships. I had grown so tired of Sven and his 'Yes, I think we should always try to play football' shock revelations and the mess that revolved around the ghastly Gary Neville leading a walk-out of England players before the vital qualifying match in Turkey the previous autumn, that I was hoping desperately that England would be knocked out swiftly and return to Luton airport in disgrace with Fortune and men's eyes. With a bit of luck the tabloids would then be calling for the whole bunch of overpaid, self-indulgent prima donnas who make up the bulk of Premiership teams these days to be boiled in oil – something lingering anyway. Presumably, too, all those flags of St George, flying from every white van in London with a pair of ladders strapped to the roof, would be taken down and tossed sorrowfully into the wheelie bins of Olde England.

Then I realised what a delight and a release for the tortured soul football can be. To fix my contempt on the man who should never have been made captain, the over-rated and under-performing David Beckham and his partner in luckless tabloid notoriety, Sven-Göran Eriksson, allowed me a brief respite from the cares of the real world. Who wouldn't prefer to bemoan the fact that Beckham was no longer worth his place in the national team than to confront the reality of what lay waiting for us in a hospital in Santa Barbara?

David was waiting for us at the airport. Santa Barbara had two principal attractions for me, one of which had always been its tiny airport which suggests to me what flying must have been like in the 1930s when small planes flew into aerodromes. The other is the fact that there is no such thing as a traffic jam in Santa Barbara unless it rains, in which case the city slithers to a halt. Since it rarely rains, driving around Santa Barbara always brings to mind what the roads must have been like in the 1950s when the first freeways opened up the prospect of endless driving at top speed without the restrictions caused by too many cars on the roads. As we drove to the Cottage Hospital for the first sight of my poor wife I thought how I would happily take the misery of being stuck in the predictable traffic jams of the North Circular Road or on the M6 between Stoke and Knutsford if it meant I could have a healthy Lynn back.

Outside the Intensive Care Unit was a telephone. You had to announce who you were through the phone before the doors were opened and you could be admitted. God knows what tragedy had occasioned this sort of security but I was in no mood to inquire. In the following days whenever I picked up the phone, the person at the other end could never make out what I was saying and I could never understand why they could never understand me. Confusion reigned and confirmed me in my belief that the United States and I were meant to become lovers not spouses.

When we finally saw her it was something of a relief. That seems like an odd thing to write since she was in a coma and hooked up to half a dozen machines all bleeping away impressively. I think the relief stemmed from the fact that she was stable and ostensibly in such good hands. There was one nurse for every two beds so her condition was being constantly monitored. She seemed peaceful, not contorted, and since she could have been asleep in bed there was no way yet we could know how bad the damage had been to her brain and her body.

I was glad there were no mirrors around in which she might have caught a glimpse of herself. It wasn't that she was vain because she wasn't, but she had been pretty all her life and, though in her younger days she had been increasingly irritated by the unwanted attention she unwittingly attracted from men, she took a pride in her appearance and she would not have liked what she would have seen. That is assuming she could comprehend what had happened to her. At this point and for some time afterwards we just had no idea how she might respond to any kind of stimulus.

After a troubled jetlagged sleep that Saturday night we returned to the hospital on the Sunday morning to meet the internist, the doctor who had officially admitted her and who was the point of contact for all the other doctors – the kidney specialist and the neurologist in particular. His name was Kyle Lemon, which had caused a short palpitation. A lemon was a car that came off the production line at British Leyland on a Friday afternoon in the 1970s. I didn't fancy one of those treating my wife but, in fact, he proved to be sympathetic and charming, if never on time, although, in my experience, hospital time is always told by sundial rather than electronic clock.

Dr Lemon told us that it was likely the brain bleed had damaged some of her memory and there would be large blanks in her remembered history. This was by no means a frightening prospect. Her memory had never been her strongest asset. As far as her recovery in other areas was concerned, it was impossible to tell until she woke up. He was ready for her to wake up at any moment but she had been out since she had collapsed on the floor of her parents' garage on Wednesday morning.

I found it difficult to process a lot of the terrifying information he gave us when my own mind was in such turmoil but the one statement that Lemon made which haunted me for the next few days was that they needed to find out what had caused this kidney failure in the first place and then hope that it could somehow be reversed. I comforted myself with the thought that it was probably his job to tell families the worst-case scenario so that any improvement on that felt like a triumph.

Gradually, over the next few days, Lynn began to recover consciousness. It wasn't, as we have come to expect from the movies, a case of one of her eyes opening and five seconds later there is a halting line of dialogue. Lynn was clearly paralysed down the whole of her left side, the consequence of the blood vessels bursting in the right side of her brain. Her eyes could be open and she would be uncomprehending but slowly it transpired that she was able to make a fist with her right hand to indicate 'no' and hold up a finger to indicate 'yes'.

I kept telling her how much I loved her until David pointed out in his very logical way that we still didn't know if she knew who she was or indeed who we were. It could be that the sight of three or four people she had never seen before standing at the foot of the bed telling her how much they loved her was simply freaking her out. We just didn't know what was going on inside that poor damaged brain of hers and the biggest irony of all was that she would have been the one who could have told us. Her work as a teacher of dyslexic children made her very conscious of the workings of the right side and the left side of the brain. She would tell me over dinner after a difficult lesson with a severely handicapped pupil, and frequently at inordinate length, how fascinating were the workings of the brain. I just hoped that her neurologist knew at least as much as she did.

They decided that they had to take a biopsy of the damaged kidneys to determine what had started this chain of medical catastrophes. It was going to be a painful experience and I saw Amy holding her hand and explaining to her in great detail how she could help the process and counselling her against the discomfort. She was utterly magnificent and I was so proud of her, but as she had said continuously since we had arrived in Santa Barbara, her mother had looked after her with such love and devotion when she had cancer as a child that this was 'payback time'.

The emails I wrote at the time, which I have rescued from the hard drive with extreme reluctance, remind me forcefully of the following weeks in which hope alternated cruelly with despair. Writing about what was going on at the time was a practical way of communicating with our friends and in its own way was a cliff top I could stand on and howl at the unfairness of life. Reading them now, from a position of relative emotional stability, what I wrote then remains, however, extremely upsetting. On the other hand, I am now better able to make sense of a time when my life seemed to have no meaning, no stability and no end to the misery.

Ten days after she had collapsed, Lynn started to form words but we had no means of knowing whether the words had any thought behind them or were just like the imitations of a small child struggling for the same command of language. If I said 'I love you', she would parrot it back but at the same time I wasn't at all sure she knew who I was so to have someone tell you that she loves you while being entirely oblivious as to your identity is a mixed blessing. 'Boiled beef and cabbage' would generate the same effect. The swelling on the brain was gradually reducing which gave her more functions but we still had no idea what had caused the renal failure and what state the brain would be in when it finally settled down.

In retrospect and at the time I thought the Santa Barbara Cottage Hospital was wonderful. The nurses and the facilities were first rate. When Lynn came out of intensive care she went into a single room that was better than a good many three star hotels I've stayed in. I looked out of the window one day towards the mountains that form the dramatic backdrop to the cosseted wealthy sprawl of Santa Barbara and I thought that people in the hotel down the street paid a fortune for this view, probably nearly as much as Lynn's healthcare provider was paying. It was quite a contrast to my experience of life at the Whittington Hospital in Archway and the Royal Free with the hassle of parking and the constant sense of the hospital being dirty and the anxiety that the nurses might administer the wrong dosage or the wrong medicine. This naïve belief in the innate superiority of the American healthcare system lasted about a week.

The longer I remained in California that summer the more I missed England. When the children were at school we had spent every summer at the home of Lynn's parents and had revelled in the easy lifestyle of the Golden State and tried to ignore the brown cloud of noxious pollution that sat permanently over the town of Riverside where they then lived. Apart from the struggle in the days before the internet and cheap overseas phone lines to discover the latest Test scores or the progress of Lancashire's unavailing attempts to win the County Championship, California offered our family a measured portion of delicious hedonism. Just reading the word California on the page induced in me a sense of delight and desire in the way that the name of Manchester City on the page always gave me a sense of comfort and belonging. No doubt some of my romantic notions about California had been stirred by my long-time academic study of Hollywood in the first half of the twentieth century, a place which, in its simple ostentation and worship of sensual pleasure, must have seemed to the economic and political refugees that flocked there the closest they could ever come to paradise on earth.

There was something incongruous about Lynn falling ill in California. It just seemed wrong that the land of sunshine and angel-hair pasta should now become the setting for tragedy. Quite how deep the tragedy would run became apparent nine days after I arrived at her bedside.

It was a Monday night and Amy and Matt had disappeared to the cinema with David and Susie to see *Dodgeball*. I was sitting by the bed looking at Lynn as she lay in what was fast becoming her constant state of torpor when the door opened and the latest doctor walked in. I never caught his name but I was very aware that he was blond and extremely handsome. For a moment I felt I was in an episode of *ER* but, having introduced himself, he left and Lynn and I reverted to our traditional one-way conversation.

An hour or so later I was returning from the water fountain in the corridor outside the room when I saw the actor/doctor looking at something as he sat at the desk behind the nurse's station. I smiled and waved at him as I felt it was not possible to be too nice to the people who seemed to hold your wife's very existence in their hands. The handsome doctor called me over. I speculated as I walked towards him if he had been an actor and had discovered his true calling while playing the part of Handsome Doctor in a soap opera or whether he was perhaps thinking of jacking in the med biz and acquiring an agent.

'I've had the results of the biopsy back from UCLA.'

'Oh,' I said, my heart beating more rapidly than Tony Blair's, whose heart palpitations had recently been the source of popular concern.

'It looks like myeloma,' he said.

I heard the words as they were spoken but they didn't really register. I knew myeloma like an unwelcome relative who arrived unannounced, took over the house, showed no inclination to leave and was always in your bathroom when you wanted to go. I didn't know anything about kidney failure but the idea that it had been caused by cancer simply had never occurred to me.

The kids came bouncing back from the stupid movie. I shep-herded them out of the room and into the waiting area before telling them the news. It broke my heart to do so, knowing the inescapable nature of the journey on which we would all now have to embark; then we kissed Lynn goodnight and went back to tell Lynn's stoical parents. I rang my brother in Manchester and started to cry.

Further desperate inquiries elicited the information that the biopsy had been sent elsewhere for a second opinion. Hope sprang eternal. On Friday, four days after the original diagnosis, we were told to be in the waiting area at 3pm as a family and Dr Lemon would come and talk to us. I had barely slept since the Monday night. We had all spent our time researching the disease and ringing everyone we knew who might have the slightest acquaint-ance with myeloma. We pretty much convinced ourselves out loud that it wasn't cancer. I did not think the horrendous sequence of events that had enveloped me could possibly confirm the cancer diagnosis. It had to be something else.

We were there ten minutes early. The doctor arrived nearly an hour late. I kept thinking that his tardiness, though no different from any other time he had been late for a meeting, was in fact a sign that Lynn was going to be all right. He couldn't possibly behave like that knowing our whole family was twitching in our seats waiting for him. I couldn't remember a more agonising wait in the whole of my life. He showed up just before 4pm and sat down, and then proceeded to tell us in a very calm voice that, 'The diagnosis has been confirmed. It *is* myeloma.' I don't think I have ever felt as wretched in my whole life as I did at that moment.

Chapter Eight

WHEN DID I START TO FALL OUT OF LOVE WITH THE England football team? I know I was still emotionally involved during the European Championships in England in 1996 because I can remember racing between television sets in the house during the successful penalty shoot-out against Spain in the quarter-final, trying to make the Spaniards miss and the English, particularly Stuart Pearce, score – small thanks I ever received for my efforts from either Mr Venables or the Football Association. I also know that by the time the same competition was held in Belgium and Holland four years later I found defeats against Portugal and Romania to be both predictable and not worth getting upset about. The 1–0 victory against Germany, which had naturally sent the tabloids and the country into a ferment, turned out to be entirely meaningless and four days later both the tabloids and the country were spitting with venom after the hapless Phil Neville gave away an eighty-ninth-minute penalty which effectively presented victory to the Romanians.

I detect, therefore, that the disillusion must have begun around the time of the World Cup in 1998. I know that the 3–2 defeat by Argentina in the round of the last sixteen produced a number of conflicting emotions. One was a sense of burning injustice that a late goal by Sol Campbell had been cruelly disallowed because of a foul by Shearer, another was a sense of fascination that the vengeance of the mob was to be wreaked on David Beckham for the sly kick that got England reduced to ten men. I remember the delight I felt in Michael Owen's wonderful goal which suggested the emergence of an eighteen-year-old prospect who would carry the world before him and the aching disappointment when a slow motion replay clearly showed that he had cynically dived for the penalty that had brought England level at 1–1. Somehow cranking up the patriotic fervour for the 2000 European Championships was going to be a tough task and going out to Brazil in the 2002 World Cup was just confirmation of the inevitable.

I was seventeen when we won the World Cup and the revenge defeat at the hands of West Germany in Leon in 1970 had hurt as badly as any City disappointment. The 3–1 loss to the Germans when Günter Netzer ran the game at Wembley in 1972 told those of us who were prepared to face the hard truth that the defeat in Mexico had been no fluke and when Brian Clough's 'clown' Jan Tomaszewski heroically sent Poland to the 1974 World Cup instead of England, that was it for eight miserable years. Even when we returned to the world stage in Spain in 1982, it ended in a series of deflating 0–0 draws. Maybe the flame had all but died at Wembley in October 1973 after the trauma of the 1–1 draw with Poland and the 1996 Euros simply fanned the embers. What I do know is that when England began their 2004 European Championship Finals campaign the day after Amy and I arrived in Santa Barbara I wasn't expecting very much from the England football team. If anything, I thought it would be entirely appropriate if the country had to suffer as we all had to suffer that month.

The arcane nature of the rights to screen football matches on television meant that we had no idea where or indeed if the Euros would be on American television. It was hardly a matter of high priority in the circumstances but we managed to find a bar in downtown Santa Barbara where they were showing the England v France match. We got there minutes after the game had finished and we could tell from the stunned expression on the faces of the emerging England supporters that things had not gone well. As it transpired it had gone particularly badly, despite an outstanding competition debut by the Everton teenager Wayne Rooney. Lampard had headed England in front but when Beckham had the chance to seal victory from the penalty spot he missed and, with a predictable groan rising from England supporters all over the world, they gave away two goals in the last three minutes, both scored by the imperious Zinedine Zidane. My poor children. As if they didn't have enough to worry about.

As it transpired, two solid victories over Switzerland and Croatia, which we saw at the house having coughed up the required subscription, took England into the knock-out stages where they met the hosts Portugal and their nemesis, Cristiano Ronaldo. The quarter-final, England's traditional farewell performance at major tournaments, took place three days after the news about the myeloma and the day before the final crushing blow of the con-firmation. At that stage I don't think I cared one jot about the result. It was enough that football would come to our rescue and for ninety minutes we would have nothing to think about but beating Portugal in front of their own supporters. As it turned out, it gave us respite for over two tumultuous hours. It seemed that Michael Owen's third-minute goal was going to be enough to secure another appearance in a semi-final but seven minutes from the end of normal time Portugal equalised. They went ahead in the second period of extra time but five minutes from the end of that torture Lampard brought the scores level again and when, in a bizarre recreation of the 1998 Argentina game another late headed 'goal' by Sol Campbell was disallowed, this time because John Terry was busy fouling elsewhere on the pitch, once again it was back to the scourge of penalties. Beckham, that brave captain of his country, heroically displayed his patriotism as he blazed the first penalty over the bar. Portugal helpfully missed one of theirs but England's determination to behave as perfect guests on the host's big night could not be faulted as Darius Vassell handed Portugal the chance to claim victory.

If I'm being honest I was actually pleased we'd gone out. When terrible personal tragedy strikes it is somehow exacerbated by the fact that the rest of the world carries on unmoved and unaware – eating in restaurants, laughing in the cinema, kissing in the park – uncaring and oblivious to your suffering. There is a moment in King Vidor's 1928 classic film *The Crowd* when the hero's little child has been accidentally killed and a well-meaning cop says to him on an intertitle: 'The whole world can't come to a halt just because something's happened to you.' It's perfectly true, of course, but it's a very understandable human emotion to want to scream to the rest of the world, 'Look at me. I'm in terrible pain.' To know that after another penalty fiasco, the country was to be plunged into its traditional biennial frenzy of self-analysis and self-loathing on the back pages was somehow comforting.

My problems were not, however, going to be solved by dropping Vassell or kicking Ronaldo, although both courses of action had their attractions. The moment the myeloma diagnosis was confirmed, even as the tabloids were calling for heads to roll at the FA, I knew we were heading in one direction only and that was down. How long it would take I did not know but I was sure that all my future held was more dying and death. It seemed unfair and insupportable. Why me? It's the question everyone asks and nobody can answer.

And then, quite unexpectedly, things started to get better. The prognosis was still negative and we still had the implications of the brain haemorrhage and the stroke and the paralysis, but slowly and perceptibly every day started to bring some small sign of a physical recovery. Everyone was thrilled with the speed of it and the doctors were suggesting she might regain more of her memory skills than they had anticipated, although there were still bound to be large gaps. Words started to emerge, although they were sometimes devoid of meaning and frequently extraordinary in their combinations: 'marvellously acceptable' meant 'yes'; something that sounded like 'stella mallen expression!' meant 'turn the television off before I go mad!' The frustrations were both heartbreaking and comic by turns.

At the same time we had also been told by the oncologist that her life expectancy was between three and five years. Despite what I had seen happen to Jack only a month before, I really believed by that stage that doctors spent a fair amount of time guessing. It wasn't that they were entirely ignorant; it was more a case of the famous Hollywood aphorism best expressed by the screenwriter William Goldman as 'Nobody knows anything.' That wasn't quite true in the hospital, of course. They all knew something based on what had happened before but every cancer is different, every body is different and every body's reaction to the treatment is different. When the oncologist told us that the average life span for a myeloma patient is three to five years I saw no reason why Lynn should be an average patient. The batting average of a county pro might be 36 but he is still capable of getting a century every time he goes out to bat and I became increasingly, stupidly optimistic.

A few days later Lynn was moved from the big hospital, whose charms had by now worn thin for me, to the Rehabilitation Institute a few hundred yards up the road. I had no idea what would be the equivalent facility in the London Borough of Haringey but I doubt very much whether it could have been any better. Although she was initially placed in a two-bed room, a single became available shortly afterwards and she was moved there. The staff were uniformly helpful and her physical recovery grew apace but still the anxiety about the impact of the cancer tore at me constantly.

We took it in turns to be with Lynn, who spent more time asleep than a newborn baby. In my off moments I watched as much Wimbledon as I could and I started to write the non-fiction novel about the affair between Greta Garbo and John Gilbert. The writing was a helpful way of blotting out the reality of the con-temporary world and instead I immersed myself in the cinematic *demi-monde* of Hollywood in the twenties and thirties. However, these refuges from reality were of brief duration and, like the sequence in *The Crowd* I quoted before, I was constantly aware of the fact that life for everyone else continued normally. On the Fourth of July America celebrated its Independence Day by towing boats to the Pacific Ocean and barbecuing hamburgers. To my surprise all the doctors went off to jet-ski and play golf, which is no doubt what Washington would have done at Valley Forge in 1776 if he'd had the money.

I was aware that the two masks of tragedy and comedy were constantly present. Lynn was being treated with a very strong steroid called Decadron and, ironically, thalidomide – which is where the comedy started. The doctors were very keen on using thalidomide but the manufacturers wouldn't release it (it cost $5,000 for a bottle of thirty pills) unless we went through a whole series of cross-checks. First, Lynn was supposed to sign her under-standing that she would not have unprotected sex which might cause her to give birth to a deformed foetus. Now my wife, God bless her, was nearly fifty-nine years old and the last time she had had unprotected sex when in real danger of getting pregnant was probably around the time of the poll tax riots, though the two events were not linked. She was instructed to make both a written and verbal declaration. It was explained to the manufacturers of thalidomide that, in the circumstances in which we were currently mired, it was going to be rather difficult but they insisted.

The brain haemorrhage had left Lynn paralysed down her left side and since she was very left-handed I signed my name in place of hers and faxed it off. The form was then rejected because the signature did not match the name of the patient. The following day I persuaded a willing female friend to forge her signature – only partial success because it had to be accompanied by a verbal declaration. Lynn, of course, couldn't talk but again the thalidomide people appeared to be uninterested in what the rest of the world might consider to be a salient fact. This kind woman who had known Lynn for many years then agreed to pretend to be Lynn on the phone so that my wife could be treated for cancer but, being a law-abiding citizen and never having run for public office, she was not well versed in the art of public lying.

They started with what they obviously considered the hundred pound question on *Who Wants to be a Millionaire?* 'What is your name?' asked the woman on the end of the telephone. My co-conspirator, however, was giving all her concentration to sounding like a patient with a stroke and terminal cancer so the question rather caught her by surprise. 'Nancy Lynn White,' she murmured with pretend difficulty. I was horrified and made frantic signals at a clearly mystified actress. The woman at the thalidomide head-quarters in San Diego was obviously now looking at the forged document that read *Nancy Lynn Shindler*. The last time Lynn was Nancy Lynn White was on 23 September 1972 before she said 'I do'. Surprisingly, in the face of this ludicrous mistake and the palpable lying that was going on, the conversation continued.

'Will you be having unprotected sex?' yodelled the earnest young woman down the coastline. They seemed obsessed in San Diego by other people's sex lives to the point of paranoia. By now I was screeching with disbelief. The idea of my wife, who basically had no quality of life at all, having unprotected sex with anyone while hooked up to a dialysis machine was worthy of Joe Orton. 'No,' came the grim reply. Eventually, farcically, the application for Lynn to be administered thalidomide tablets was formally approved and the manufacturers kindly agreed to take the insurance company's five grand and cough up a month's supply of the drug. It probably seems more comic now than it did at the time. If you think the NHS is in a bad way, this was the performance put on by the world's greatest healthcare professionals (allegedly).

Lynn remained in the Rehab Institute, re-learning how to walk and talk. Everything was a major effort for everyone, leaving us all wrung out like a wet dishcloth. 'My communication is up the creek without a paddle,' she would suddenly say, which initially suggested exactly the reverse but immediately afterwards she would say 'yes' when she actually meant 'no', leaving us to try to make sense of her increasingly frustrated demands while her blood pressure rose like the red anger in a cartoon figure.

Still, it helped that this was the time when Lynn was making steady if not spectacular progress in other areas – getting to her feet from her chair unaided was a spectacular victory and she was justifiably proud of herself. Watching her learning to walk again was tinged with a bitter sadness because it took me back to the time when our children were learning to walk, when we could take pleasure together from every day of dogged progress. I didn't dare to share these feelings with Lynn. She might have been experiencing the same emotion but I could see very little value in reminding her of those happy times.

Our conversations were one-sided and therefore rather stilted because I was learning to censor everything that was racing along my brain before it emerged from my mouth in case it upset her. I wanted to indicate that I was having only positive thoughts because I felt instinctively that this was the best way to help her but at the same time I didn't know how much she resented hearing of what became trivialities and what might have seemed to her a refusal to acknowledge the seriousness of her condition. Also the truth was that I myself was beset by the most negative of thoughts.

More significantly, I was never sure of the effect of the brain damage. How much did she know of how badly she was impaired? And who did know exactly how badly she was impaired? The neurologist who was supposed to be dealing with her case was conspicuous by his absence and ostensible lack of interest. One day in the middle of July, just over a month after the calamity had started, Lynn took a basic general knowledge test and the next day the doctor came back into the room waving the score – Lynn had achieved 98%. That was wonderful and she was genuinely thrilled. Was it possible that she was going to make a full recovery after all? I scarcely dared to hope. Like a side facing almost certain relegation who suddenly wins two consecutive games, they stimulate hope in their supporters but have no ability to sustain it.

Our children eventually reconnected with the rest of their lives and I stayed on with Lynn's family as we waited to see what happened in the next match. One Saturday I drove the hundred miles from Santa Barbara to Los Angeles, intending on the way to call in to see Maureen who was staying with friends in Malibu and then mooch around the second-hand bookshops of Westwood which were fast disappearing beneath the onslaught from the internet. It was a day to myself, the prospect of which I had been relishing. At 2pm I was entering the second hour of sitting in six blocked lanes of traffic on the Ventura Freeway when Maureen called to inform me that she had heard, though I can't now remember how, that my father had been taken back to hospital. Maureen, understandably, asked me if I was going to fly straight back to England. My response was to laugh more than a little hysterically since at the time I had no immediate prospect of getting to the next exit on the freeway, let alone the airport. Again I ask the question, 'Do we all laugh at those weird junctions between comedy and tragedy?' Or perhaps more pertinently, 'How many tragic events piled on top of each other do we need before our only reaction is to laugh?'

I thought frequently about the solemn passage in the Yom Kippur service, 'On the first day of the year it is written and on the tenth day it is sealed, who shall live and who shall die.' I've always liked the majesty of that phrase and with this latest news I was starting to feel that anything accomplished by a human hand is pretty much insignificant because the writing in that Great Ledger has already decreed the dates of our time on this earth. I had made my peace with my father last December when my brother and I thought it was all over. If I ever got on to a plane it would probably be too late. I had no doubts that I should stay on in California and let events in Manchester unfold as they might.

As soon as I was 'cleared for transfers' by the Rehab Institute, which meant I knew the best way to lift Lynn from the wheelchair to the car and from the bed to wheelchair, I took her out for non-medical reasons. Before I had been trained and 'approved' to do so, I'd sneaked her out in the wheelchair for a walk round the block one balmy summer evening and was fiercely castigated by the

Authorities for having done so without permission. Frankly, I didn't give a toss. It felt like being assigned to the spare bedroom before we were married but sneaking into her bedroom after her parents were in bed. It made me smile to realise that the highlight of our marriage was now an illicit twenty-minute push of her wheelchair.

I also learned how to give her showers, which wasn't quite the erotic experience it might have been thirty years before. Yet there were times I can recall quite distinctly, when she was in bed at the end of the day with her hair washed and dried and clearly benefiting from the clean body in the clean nightdress on the clean sheets, I felt as I did all those years ago when we used to do the same for our very young children. Such tenderness, so much hoping.

Then the children showed me yet again that they were children no longer. The following weekend David and Susie went off to Half Moon Bay just south of San Francisco. When they returned they were engaged. No matter what the immediate problems, life moves on and even in the midst of death we are in life. David's engagement to Susie was the only unalloyed piece of good news to come our way for a long time and everyone was thrilled. I know Lynn understood the nature of the news and was delighted. If she thought her time was now finite, at least she had known and entirely approved of her son's choice of wife.

There were many days around this time in mid- to late July when I wheeled her into a private corner and sat opposite her holding her hand while I tried to talk but then became overwhelmed by the situation and burst into tears. I cried a lot. I cried in bed waiting for the bliss of unconsciousness, I cried on the phone to friends and relatives, and I cried, despite my best endeavours, when I was talking to Lynn. She would look at me with a weird expression on her face – it seemed to be a mixture of contempt for my weakness and scorn because what the hell did I have to cry about? It was she who was going through the torments of the damned and, with every justification you could argue, she could become very awkward and wilful. I think we all understood that it was because she had no control over her life so if she made life hard for me she was at least getting a bit of revenge on the fate that had maligned her so cruelly.

That was when I found it increasingly difficult to stay in Santa Barbara, a place I had grown to hate with a passion. People would say to me that 'at least you're in the most beautiful town in America' and it was impossible to convey to them how much I loathed the place – false, superficial, obsessed with wealth and ostentation, it was very much not my kind of town. The people were allegedly very laid-back but since I was trapped in a situation where I was very far from being laid-back their laid-backness was irritating rather than helpful. It wasn't so much that I longed for the deprivation of the inner-city ghettoes of Olde England but I was left hoping that their ubiquitous shopping malls, seemingly the justification for the town's very existence, would shortly host a bunch of tanked-up England football supporters on a rampage, as they used to be back in the good old days of the late twentieth century. I suppose it was just my way of expressing the considerable rage I was feeling. I couldn't do it in front of friends and family and I was still impressed with the level of skill and care among the support staff of the Rehab Institute so I just allowed the hatred I felt for Santa Barbara and the people who lived there to fester. Lynn had loved the place and look where it got us all. Just as Lynn's rage and frustration found its outlet in my availability so I turned my own anger on the town where I was trapped.

Santa Barbara, unfortunately, proved an insufficient outlet for my rage and when I asked to have my own blood pressure checked the doctors at the Rehab Institute looked a little askance at a reading of 161/100. Since I had never previously been troubled by high blood pressure, which was remarkable given all those years of supporting Manchester City, it was apparent to all of us that this new development was entirely a consequence of 'the situation' in which I found myself. The doctors ('That'll be $350, please') didn't want to medicate the blood pressure down because we all thought that when 'the situation' resolved itself it would return to normal. They did, however, recommend a full check-up ('That'll be $800, please').

Even at the time, the ludicrous elements of what was happening to me continued to make me smile. One morning I sat downstairs in the hospital having blood and urine extracted before going up to the second floor of the same building to fix an appointment with Lynn's oncologist. I was idly wondering how much a family season ticket for a hospital might cost when the oncologist's receptionist suddenly started quoting facts at me about my wife's illness which I knew were wrong. Aggravation levels and blood pressure rose accordingly until the receptionist asked anxiously, 'This is Betty Schindler we're talking about, isn't it?' Marvellous. Now I knew there were two cancer patients with almost identical surnames being treated by the same oncologist whose medical skills were not necessarily in question, although I do recall that his name had been introduced to me by the equivalent of the hospital registrar with the words, 'He's a bit weird but don't worry.' Worry? Moi?

By this time I was fairly adept at transferring Lynn's body from the bed to the wheelchair and from the wheelchair into the car, packing up the chair and then reassembling it at the other end. One bright gorgeous Saturday at the end of July I suggested we went to the beach. I hoped that the proximity of the Pacific Ocean

135

and people enjoying themselves on the beach might have some kind of positive effect on the two of us, but when I wheeled her into the Goleta Beach Restaurant all we could do was look at each other with eyes of sadness.

I don't know whether we both felt the same sort of sadness but I had the strong sensation as I talked and she made the occasional response that for all the physical improvements she had made since 9 June this was going to be as good as it got. We were a hundred yards or so away from the campus of the University of California at Santa Barbara. Lynn had been an undergraduate there and in the summer of 1966, at the age of twenty, she had won the Miss Santa Barbara beauty pageant. She had always been some-what dismissive of her triumph, genuinely relieved that she hadn't won the Miss California contest and gone on to compete for the title of Miss America. She had hidden her trophy in the loft but her family had always regarded it as something to be proud of and I'm afraid the children and I teased her about it mercilessly.

It was the end of the day as we sat in the restaurant and, though it was still midsummer, it felt as it had when the children were small and we were getting ready to go home from the beach – it had been a wonderful day but it was over and all that was left was the mechanical business of packing up, driving home, supper, bath time and then bed. That was how I felt about our lives. Somehow we had come to an end. I had no idea if she was thinking anything along those lines.

She ate little of her dinner and soon complained of feeling tired. She wanted to go back to the Rehab Institute. It was a clear sign that she was getting used to the routine of the institution. It was the last clear sign I had for a while for, as we emerged from the restaurant, she decided she wanted to turn right, away from the car park. I was happy to push the wheelchair wherever she wanted it to go but unfortunately the path ran out quite quickly as we reached the edge of the sand. I turned the other way and went past the car and headed in the direction of the campus but after a few minutes she wanted to go back where we had come from, even though I tried to explain that I couldn't push the wheelchair through sand. Nevertheless that's where we went until she decided she had had enough of the view in this direction as well and wanted to go back towards the campus. As we approached the car I persuaded her that it was time to return to the institute. Somewhat mutinously she agreed.

Getting her to bed that night was difficult and I did not distinguish myself. Next morning all hell broke loose and, as the situation became clearer, I wished with all my heart I had been more patient and loving with her the previous night. At some point on the Sunday night she was rushed back to the hospital. The scan showed no tumour but her condition continued to deteriorate and she was re-admitted to the neurology department of the Cottage Hospital a month to the day since she had been released from there. All the indications were that she had suffered another bleed of some sort in the brain. Just to make sure the comedy element wasn't ignored entirely, my own blood pressure now reached 206/117 so I was checked into the Emergency Room of the same hospital while my wife was lying in a coma upstairs. The ER doctor looked at the blood pressure figures and asked, 'Do you know you're in danger of having a stroke if your blood pressure remains this high?' Thank you. Yes. 'Who is your next of kin?' asked the bored woman at reception. 'Your wife?' 'Well, yes, but she's not really available right now.' 'Where is she?' 'She's upstairs on the fifth floor in a coma,' I replied truthfully. You really couldn't make this up.

I was sent off, back to England. I was no use to anyone and a danger to myself. I went to see Lynn before I left for the airport, though I wished, as soon as I saw her new condition, that I hadn't. On the journey to the airport I wondered if I'd ever see her again. All the way back to London, through interminable stopovers in Los Angeles and Washington, I thought about what life would be like if she died before I got back and if I did see her how much worse could she possibly get. I landed at Heathrow and made a sorrowful journey back to the house I had left in such high anxiety two months earlier. Well, I thought, back to some form of normality. England are playing the West Indies at Old Trafford, Lancashire are struggling against relegation from Division One of the County Championship and City kick off a new season at home to Fulham the following Saturday. The phone rang. It was my brother. Our father had just died.

Chapter Nine

I HAVE ALWAYS HAD A GOOD MEMORY. FRANKLY, I'VE always attributed much of whatever success I've ever achieved in life to the luck of having been blessed with one. If you can remember some obscure fact and reproduce it in the right manner and at the right time it will get you through quite a few exams. The good memory also extends to football. I can remember matches, City matches in particular, back to the early 1960s, so that when I look at a season's fixtures and results I know exactly where I was and what state my life was in during the course of that season. At university, my time as an undergraduate coincided with City's three most successful seasons to date – 1967–8, '68–9 and '69–70. I used to have a party trick in which I could tell a year or two after the event which day of the week any particular named date had been simply by referencing the City fixture list in my head. Clearly this trick only worked if I were asked to identify a particular date during the course of the football season.

As I write this chapter, I have open on the desk in front of me a copy of the City fixtures and results for the 2004–5 season kindly provided by my friend Geoff Watts. I have just stared at it in bewilderment. I think I went to just two games – Spurs away with Geoff and Middlesbrough at home. There were good reasons for that, of course, but what astonishes me is that I am looking at the two derby matches – a 0–0 draw away and a 0–2 defeat at home – and I can't remember a thing about them either, even if, from the scorelines, they don't sound particularly memorable. I have vague memories of a 4–3 defeat at St James' Park, a spectacular equalising goal by Shaun Wright-Phillips at Highbury and Delia Smith at Carrow Road on a Monday night shouting 'Letsby Avenue' at half-time in a match won by a Robbie Fowler flick five minutes from the end. And that is it. Other than that, the season is a complete blank in a way that no other season has been since 1954–5, the year when I first knew for sure I was a City supporter. Other events have simply driven the football clean out of my head.

I had talked to my brother in Manchester quite frequently during my two months in California so I was aware of my father's slowly deteriorating condition. His death came as no surprise and in its way was something of a blessing all round. He was in his eighty-ninth year but the way he had fought so tenaciously for a life that didn't seem to be worth living was a surprise to me. If that was courage or bravery then I saluted him for it but ours hadn't really been a classically troubled father-son relationship; it had been perfectly cordial and I was always solicitous for his welfare although, as a relationship of any kind beyond the biological, it had never really existed. In the early days he left all matters of child-rearing to my mother. After her death we were rather locked into our own worlds of pain so, instead of growing closer and discovering a world of mutual support, we drifted even farther apart emotionally.

I travelled to Manchester not sure if I was mourning my father's death or my wife's current tragic condition. After the funeral, some semblance of normality appeared as I played football in the garden with my five-year-old great-nephew, Nathan. He was very keen to win, a trait that reminded me of myself at the same age. His London-born father has ensured that he has become an Arsenal supporter which, of course, I think is wonderful considering the fact that he lives in north Manchester in the heart of a United-dominated family.

I was intrigued to see that at the age of fifty-five I was pretty much an irrelevance as my brother, the elder son, held sway during the service. I was perfectly happy for Geoff to read Kaddish, the mourner's prayer and he did it with impressive *élan*, but I knew that though I came from this community I wasn't part of it any longer. The black-hatted social misfit who led the evening prayers confirmed this impression. Did my father's death mean that the ties to Manchester were loosening or did my wife's possibly fatal illness mean that they were being renewed? At the time I was so bewildered by life that I had no idea.

A week or so later I was lying in a blissfully lukewarm bath in a guest room in Gonville & Caius College after delivering a lecture on Civil Rights in a temperature that matched the humidity of the American South when the mobile phone rang. It was Amy. David had just rung from California to say that their mother had woken up again. They were all thrilled and delighted but my heart lurched. What state was she in now?

As it turned out, she was even more physically impaired than she had been before the second stroke and, at the same time, she was aware of the fact that all the gains she had previously made had been wiped out. It was like coming back from 0–2 down to equalise and then conceding a dubious penalty to lose the game in the last minute. No wonder she was so depressed. If she were losing the will to fight I could hardly blame her. The various doctors for the kidney, the brain and the cancer rarely talked to each other, let alone us or her, so none of us knew what was happening and my naïve belief in the wonderful American healthcare system was being exposed for its childlike stupidity. I wanted to confront each of these men and scream at them but the words that wanted to come out of my brain were those of the leering Terry-Thomas, the comedy actor with the cigarette holder and the gap between his teeth: 'You're an absolute shower!' I don't suppose that would have helped anyone.

As has been my constant habit I turned to football and cricket in a desperate attempt to return my life to some semblance of normality, just to keep hold of my own sanity. England continued to reel off Test match victories against New Zealand and now the West Indies, which brought hope for the Ashes series due to be played the following summer. Lancashire, who had briefly been top of the County Championship in May, had not won a match since then and, despite fielding a batting side that boasted the prolific talents of Carl Hooper, Stuart Law and Mal Loye with the bowling in the more than capable hands of Dominic Cork, Glen Chapple, Gary Keedy and Saj Mahmood, they lost heavily twice to Surrey and were now facing relegation from Division One. I had always thought it odd that the England Cricket Board in its infinite wisdom had decided that three of the nine teams in Division One would be relegated to be replaced by the three top teams in Division Two. Relegating and promoting a third of the division every year meant only the Championship winners were likely to be safe from the prospect of relegation. It added interest to the season no doubt but it induced a sense of impermanence. There was no reason why Lancashire, who clearly couldn't win the Championship, or at least hadn't done so outright for the past seventy years, should be immune from relegation. In 2004 they would be a perfectly respectable side who played uninspiring cricket and would finish eighth in the table, nearly twenty points short of safety. It seemed a particularly low blow sustained at a time when I was ill-equipped to withstand it and it depressed me further. Still, it felt good to get angry with Mike Watkinson for coaching a competent side into Division Two rather than with the doctors in Santa Barbara. I couldn't do much about either but at least, in his defence, Watkinson had in former years made runs for Lancashire, which is more than any of those doctors in Santa Barbara had managed.

Certainly I revelled in Chelsea's 1–0 win over United on the first day of the new season, a scrappy victory but an indication that Mourinho, in his first match in charge, was going to make life difficult for Ferguson. As for City and the lethargic 1–1 draw at home to Fulham, if Keegan stayed and behaved like the sullen teenager he had been the previous season I thought we had a good chance of going down. It would be appropriate in the year that Lancashire, too, had gone down. It would be the dawn of Armageddon and frankly I didn't have the strength to complain any longer. Fortunately, from City's point of view, the three teams coming up, Crystal Palace, West Bromwich Albion and Norwich City, all looked weak, but it is desperation time, quite frankly, if your hopes of a successful year are pinned on the poor quality of the teams promoted from what I still think of as the Second Division.

My GP counselled me to take things easy at home for a few weeks while my blood pressure slowly returned to a managable high from its stratospheric past. For obvious reasons, though, it stayed worryingly high as I remained in constant touch with events in California. As best I could I immersed myself in my old routines, emerging at Lee's suggestion at the end of August to visit Norfolk for a couple of days. It was a county whose attractions had previously escaped me entirely. Now, the very Englishness of it all enchanted me. The tea shop in Holt was such a contrast to the fast-food places I had relied on in Santa Barbara and the bookshops in the town were a blessed relief after the endless Borders of California shopping malls. Even the admittedly tacky charms of Wells-next-the-Sea proved a pleasing contrast to the rolling surf of the Pacific Ocean, whose appeal felt overstated but that was only because I had been staring for so long at its timeless splendour while feeling so profoundly depressed.

I was reclaiming my English heritage which I had in a sense cast off when I fell in love with all things American as a teenager. America had the best of everything, it seemed to me then, except of course football and cricket teams, and so persuasive was the combination of that culture and my new wife that I found myself in the early years of our marriage and, much to my own surprise, somehow defending American foreign policy in South East Asia. That admittedly was a blip, and my instinct that Richard Nixon was a crook and was heavily involved in Watergate as soon as the news leaked of the break-in, only confirmed my admiration for the American political system that rid itself, tortuously but in full view of the world, of a corrupt President. The combination of George W. Bush and the fall-out from Lynn's illness had caused me to re-evaluate how I felt about America. I couldn't perform a complete *volte-face*. My children were half-American and my interest in American history had not diminished one jot but it was a pleasure to be out of the country and back in England during a glorious summer. Even the rare days of rain and cloud were incapable of depressing me.

Still, those stolen forty-eight hours in Norfolk were filled with memories of Lynn. The drive from London took me past the perimeter of the American air force bases at Mildenhall and

Lakenheath in Suffolk. When we were first married and I was completing my Ph.D. thesis Lynn used the teaching credential she had gained in California before she met me to acquire a wonderful job teaching what I always referred to as 'parsing' to American pilots who felt they did not need to know that an adverb was a word that modified the verb in order to drop bombs on someone.

Feeling something of a stranger in England in general, and the rather arcane world of Cambridge postgraduate work in particular, Lynn was thrilled to be working with Americans and able to buy American products at the BX, the huge supermarket on American overseas bases where goods from home are on offer at subsidised prices. As a student on an annual grant of five hundred pounds we ate better than most of the dons of my acquaintance. For five bob we could buy huge steaks hewn from the flesh of cows that had only a day or two previously been basking in the sunshine of Texas. It was also the ability to buy infinite amounts of plain chocolate M&M's that began my susceptibility to their charms, which still rears its head at night. Thanks to the air force base, we also had a petrol allowance enabling us to buy petrol at 1972 wholesale prices – i.e. before British government tax and the quadrupling of the price of crude oil the following year. A gallon of petrol cost Lynn two shillings and sixpence (all right, twelve and a half pence), which meant that we could drive in our Mini on a Saturday morning to watch City play in Manchester for the grand total of seventy pence. Petrol at the pump for less fortunate Britons cost about fifty pence a gallon at the time.

After two years, Lynn gave up the job with some reluctance when we left Cambridge to live in St Albans. The Americans were rather more relaxed about security in those days and nobody asked for her ID back which meant, we were both thrilled to realise, that if we were prepared to drive to Suffolk we could theoretically carry on buying steaks from the BX on a regular basis. Unfortunately, shortly after the move, her handbag was stolen in Regents Park Zoo and her precious American ID went with it. I hope the thief was caught eating pancake and waffle mix from the packet and was sent to serve time on Death Row in Florida or Texas. I suspect, however, that the precious card was tossed casually into a rubbish bin in Camden Town.

My head was filled with these thoughts of our former life and how much we had both taken it for granted. As soon as I got back home, however, it was immediately apparent that nostalgia was a luxury I could no longer afford as Lynn's condition continued to deteriorate. Her legs had become increasingly useless so she could no longer stand and the new brain damage affected her ability to understand what was being said to her and even more so her ability to respond. I wondered when the Elizabethan wheel of fortune, in which I have always professed a strong belief, would start to climb again. At the time it appeared to be lying uselessly at the roadside waiting for the RAC to arrive. I knew that in all probability, while still hoping for a miracle, my own recovery would only begin after Lynn had died.

In early September she made sufficient gains for the medical authorities to permit her to be transferred back to her parents' home. This was a beautiful house overlooking the ocean and, when Lynn was capable of communicating, it was clear that what she wanted above all was to be out of range of a nurse with a needle or a basket of medications and at home on the sun deck gazing at the Pacific Ocean. However, although the house was adapted to fit her needs, it soon became obvious to everyone that she simply had to be in hospital. Trained staff were needed twenty-four hours a day and after only a few days at home her blood pressure dropped to a very low level (if we could have added hers to mine and divided by two we'd have each had normal blood pressure) and she was rushed back to the Cottage Hospital. It took a while for her system to stabilise before she was booted out of hospital and back to the Rehab Institute again.

I flew back to California in the middle of September with a heavy heart. When I had flown out in June I was terrified because I did not know what I would find but now I knew exactly what I would find and I was just as terrified. The day I arrived she was back late from the dialysis clinic she went to every Monday, Wednesday and Friday afternoon. I had been travelling for nearly twenty-four hours but I stood in the corridor outside her room in the Rehab Institute and waited for the first sight of her wheelchair. I knew it wasn't going to be a long conversation and it could even be just a bad-tempered response on her part because that had been the trend after dialysis sessions, which kept her alive but exhausted her. As soon as her wheelchair hove into sight at the far end of the corridor I walked swiftly towards her with a smile on my face and my arms outstretched saying, 'Hello, remember me?' 'Oh,' sighed Lynn in immediate response, 'I love you!' in that lovely soft tone of voice. I was so overcome it was me who brought the conversation to a premature end.

And that was pretty much as good as it got. The following day on a routine check of her vital signs it was discovered that her blood sugar had dropped alarmingly low again. They gave her a piece of chocolate to get it back up but it failed to respond and back she went to hospital. It was in that room in the Cottage Hospital that I started to say goodbye. I remember only too well that though she was dying and paralysed she retained enough of the Lynn-ness that I had always loved to make me want to hold her and kiss her. At one point, when the IV had been taken away I actually wanted to crawl into bed with her and cuddle her. I told her how I felt but unlike a similar moment in Jack's final days this time there was no response, certainly not a joke.

She now spoke rarely and when she did it was without much expression but it was still recognisably Lynn's voice – a very beautiful voice that contained a great deal of music and poetry in it. In thirty years of living in England she had not lost her American accent and I always found the tone of her voice to be extremely attractive. When I picked up the phone to hear her say the words 'Hi there!' it was always a pleasurable sensation, whatever comments then followed.

Dr Lemon told me it was time to start thinking about the quality of the life that remained to her. I asked how long he thought she had left and he was non-committal. I asked how he thought she would die and he said there might be another 'event' – apparently a favourite medical euphemism but, of course, I immediately called to mind three-day eventing and the Burghley Horse Trials – odd how stupid irrelevant things like that pop into your mind at moments of great significance. What Lemon did know for certain, was that if she were not sent to dialysis she would die within two weeks – a painless sort of death, he emphasised. Lynn would gradually fall into a deep sleep and pass away quietly as her systems shut down. It wasn't much of a comfort as comforts go but it was all that I had to cling to.

The only passably good thing that could be said about Lynn's situation as we celebrated, as best we could, her fifty-ninth birthday at the end of September, was that we all now had the chance to say a long, slow, sweet farewell. If she had died on the floor of the garage when she collapsed on 9 June we wouldn't have had that chance. While she was in the relatively pleasant surroundings of a modern single room in the hospital, I spent ten to twelve hours a day alone with her, watching her sleep but frequently falling asleep myself. Occasionally, for the big treat of the day, I was allowed to wheel her out of the room and into the lift taking us up to the terrace where she could feel the sun on her skin. There she could face the beautiful view of the mountains she loved. If I turned the chair in another direction she could just about see the Pacific Ocean and absorb the comfort (I hoped) of that feeling of serenity that accompanies the contemplation of the infinite. Those days were bright with soft autumn sunlight and the flora and fauna which were evident everywhere in Santa Barbara were startling in their luxurious growth. They seemed unable to accept the fact that they should have been reacting to the onset of chilly nights and dank days. 2004 was turning out to be a year when my usual fear of the approach of winter had been made to look a pathetic self-indulgence. There were matters to consider now far weightier than when I should turn the central heating back on again.

I was still getting my own mind round the inevitability of the final outcome of Lynn's illness when the doctors, to my surprise, decided to tell her that she was going to die. They and the hospital administrators asked to meet Lynn's family, ostensibly to discuss the way forward. Lynn was insistent that it all happened in front of her which at the time pleased me. It meant she was mentally strong enough to deal with things and it was very much the old Lynn, who would not have wanted to hide from anything. However, what I thought was going to be a discussion about nursing homes and insurance turned out to be a death sentence.

Lynn's myeloma might give her twelve to eighteen months of life, said one of the doctors, which would be the maximum but, unfortunately, such were the problems caused by the kidney failure and the brain damage that she wouldn't get that long. They wouldn't put a time on it too precisely because it would to an extent depend on what treatment was selected. It was clear that her estimated longevity was now directly in conflict with the quality of life she could expect, which meant that her family would now have to take an appalling decision. We never knew for sure, though we certainly supposed, that the hospital administrators and the insurance company were in collusion because it was abundantly clear now that the latter had decided that it would no longer pay for her to stay in hospital. In their opinion, presumably confirmed by the doctors, she was dying and not worth spending any money on. She would have to be shipped out to a nursing home – it was the only place that would take her.

This is where the flawed American healthcare system contrasts starkly with the equally but differently flawed National Health Service. One of the many panic attacks I suffered in those few days was over the cost of Lynn's treatment. I knew she had good health insurance because it was almost the only perk she got from working for the disgracefully under-funded California state education system. However, I also knew that if she was in for the length of treatment and, more to the point, the sort of treatment that Jack had undergone, then there was always the possibility that the insurance might somehow run out or that some things would not be covered and then what did we do? I had heard too many horror stories of the catastrophic financial consequences of being seriously ill in the United States. I was already nostalgic for the tender mercies of the NHS although I knew perfectly well that British patients are just as affected by money as Americans. It's just that in Britain the financial consequences affect the way that patients are cared for. Their families can suffer the disastrous effects of poor healthcare because it is badly funded but their families are rarely bankrupted by it.

I hated the cold, calculating decisions made by the bureaucrats at the hospital and the insurance company, yet at the same time I could see only too plainly that Lynn had no life, only an existence, and after the doctors told her to her face she knew, as we knew, that she would never recover. Always I think there had been the hope, no matter how overwhelming the apparent impossibility of her physical condition, that somehow something would work and she would start to climb the mountain. That hope was dashed when she was deported from the hospital and sent off to a nursing home.

It was as horrible a place as I had feared, the nearest that shiny, affluent town could manage in the way of a Dickensian nightmare and I knew as soon as we got there that Lynn had been sent there to die. It was, of course, the least expensive of the alternatives and therefore the only one the insurance company would pay for. There was no view of the mountains and the corridors were filled with the sounds of the elderly crying out for help in their pain or in their stupor. The nurses did their best in trying circumstances but this was not the way my fifty-nine-year-old wife should have to end her days.

As I succumbed to despair, Lynn slipped slowly but agonisingly behind a curtain of impenetrability. Whatever I did, I could no longer reach her. It was the start of the last act but there was no sign in the room, which she now shared with two other women, when the curtain would finally fall. I hoped there might be some kind of catharsis and, to that end, I engaged a therapist/counsellor to go in and try to discover what Lynn herself wanted. If we could have extracted from her a sense of what she desired for herself, it would have made some of those appalling decisions so much easier to make. Unfortunately, we never really knew.

*

The last few months of Lynn's life contained occasional moments of joy. The greatest of them all was when our son gave his mother one last present. David and Susie had decided to bring forward their wedding plans from the summer of 2005 to Boxing Day 2004. A wedding! After all the tragedies of the past year the idea that we could talk about wedding cakes and travel plans, about caterers and hotels and invitations and honeymoons was thrilling to all of us. All the petty details of wedding preparation which can lead the best of families into bitter disagreements became the stuff of life for us, because it brought out the best in all of us.

David and Susie were going to be married in the garden of Lynn's parents' house in Santa Barbara, overlooking the ocean. Ralph and Ava, Susie's delightful parents, took over most of the organisation with no fuss, great taste and wonderful efficiency. Jack's son Adam Rosenthal was going to perform the service and, as his best man, David chose the ultra-reliable Refik, his best friend when they were undergraduates. Refik achieved the top First Class degree in Medicine in the university when he graduated and he had been particularly helpful when I needed to clarify some of the medical information I was being given about Lynn. It was of necessity going to be a small wedding but it was going to be a joyous one. If I, as the father of the groom, were experiencing tears of happiness at the prospect, I had no doubt that Lynn would be feeling something similar. What a thrill to be clinging to something as life-affirming as a wedding.

There was something so pleasingly symmetrical about it that Lynn must surely have been thinking of our own wedding as she contemplated that of her son. As an American woman she had been married to a Manchester City supporter in Cambridge thirty-two years before. Now here was the fruit of that marriage committing himself in similar fashion to another beautiful American girl. It augured well, I felt, despite the knowledge that they would be afflicted by the same conundrum that Lynn and I had never really solved – at some point one of the parties is always in the wrong country.

It had dogged our marriage, certainly disfigured it and might eventually have destroyed it, so wretched and abandoned did I feel when Lynn left Muswell Hill and went back to California in 2002. If I honestly listed those things that united Lynn and me they were significantly outnumbered by the interests that appealed to only one of us. She liked antique fairs and tabloid television, undemanding Hollywood movies and Mexican food. I liked sport and broadsheet newspapers, theatre and Jewish food – no meeting of minds there. We frequently asked each other out loud, and not always in jest, how the hell did we ever get together? Yet what did unite us, apart from the obvious elements of children and home and education, was an intensely passionate love that owed nothing to rational behaviour. What a weird impenetrable sensation is love, how open to misinterpretation it is, how desirable do we all find it, and yet how many of us who believe we have experienced it acknowledge that it has actually made us permanently happy – briefly, yes, briefly ecstatic, yes, but permanent happiness through love – perhaps just for the fortunate minority?

I had met Lynn in 1972 – the year City were deprived of the league championship by a single point. The champions turned out to be Brian Clough's Derby County whom we had destroyed 2–0 in the last match of the season. Significant football memories is the way in which I remember years. I'm sure if I had been around in 1914, I would have been greatly irritated that Germany's invasion of Belgium and the consequent start of the Great War had deprived a blossoming Manchester City side of a certain League and/or FA Cup triumph. I make no pretence that our love was in any way greater than anyone else's. I just know that what I felt for Lynn was so overwhelming that it seemed in a way a thing apart from the actual state of our marriage down the years.

There were only twenty-three people who attended the wedding but since just five of them actually lived in Santa Barbara that meant a lot of trips to the airport and a lot of hotel rooms to be booked. The great thing about the constant arrivals was that with the appearance of each new face in Lynn's room the sense of occasion grew. Just as important, the prospect of the wedding distracted the children and me from confronting the inevitable fact that this was to be Lynn's last Christmas.

For the three of us Lynn was the very spirit of Christmas. Although hopelessly disorganised about most things outside of her teaching work, she took Christmas very seriously and prepared for it meticulously – a character trait much appreciated by the bridegroom-to-be who as a young boy had to be hauled out of his mother's closet by the collar of his shirt during the months of September and October as he rooted around in the back for the Christmas presents he was rightly convinced she was storing for him. In fact, Lynn frequently started Christmas shopping in January and it wasn't just the attraction of the sales that made her do so. She threw herself headlong into the purchase of cow bells, antlers and musical ties that played 'Santa Claus is Coming to Town'. Despite doing most of the present-buying and wrapping, and for many years after the children had starkly been confronted with the truth about Santa Claus, Lynn maintained a touching childlike delight in the somewhat secular version of the Yuletide.

As a child in Manchester my family had regarded Christmas as if it were a pogrom. As Jews we knew it was no concern of ours but if we kept our heads down maybe the Cossacks would just ride through Prestwich where we lived and not start looting and burning until they got to Whitefield, a more prosperous suburb two miles further north. Lynn changed all that and made me feel that the best thing about Christmas was not necessarily the large tin of Roses chocolates that mysteriously always came down the chimney and the season of Hollywood musicals on television.

The night before the wedding I hosted a dinner for the bride and her family along with my children and Adam and his fiancée Taina who had just arrived. Again I was left with the feeling that I was probably doing everything wrong and that if Lynn were there I wouldn't make the terrible social *faux pas* that I felt sure were bound to follow. I apologised in advance to David lest my worst fears came to pass and explained that I was still asking myself, 'What would Lynn do or say here?' He hugged me and told me I was doing fine – and I felt the remorseless tide of change sweep over me. It was the first time I had ever admitted openly to him that I couldn't cope and I knew it was the first of many such occasions to come. Slowly David was going to become the man of the family. As Lynn faded, so in a sense did the lustre of my star as the patriarch. It wasn't planned and neither child wanted it but not only had they both grown up so fast in the wake of Lynn's illness but the ceremony we were shortly going to experience was confirmation that our little dyslexic son was now a strong, self-confident and responsible adult. I hoped Lynn could see it. I was sure she must, even if she would be unable to confirm it by word or gesture.

The wedding was inevitably arranged around Lynn, when she would be picked up and delivered to the house, where she could be wheeled to, where she could sit at the table, what medications she would need, how we could be sure it was the right time for her to be collected and returned to the nursing home. It occurred to me that a wedding day traditionally revolves around the bride rather than the mother-in-law. I asked David rather anxiously how Susie had responded to the challenge, for she would have every justification for feeling that the biggest day of her life was being overshadowed. When David told me she had never mentioned it and showed no inclination to be resentful I was certain he had made the right choice of wife. What an unselfish supportive attitude Susie and her family brought to this meeting of north London and New Jersey in Southern California.

It had been sunny California from the day I had landed early in the month but as Boxing Day loomed the weather symbols on the television chart started to change from bright sunshine to drops of rain. It was like the day before filming a big outdoor scene with lots of extras when the production team could only stare at the sky and pray that the gamble to leave the shooting schedule un-changed came off. Walking through the nearby university campus, Lynn's alma mater, after a Christmas Day brunch of bagels and lox, it was warm in the strong sunshine and it was hard to believe that all the forecasts were unanimous in predicting a drastic change in the weather, starting at some point during the day of the wedding. The ceremony and the meal were all set to happen on the sun deck and in the garden. Would the rain hold off long enough for us to complete the occasion without disaster? I wasn't optimistic. Prayers had availed us little in the previous six months.

The rains of biblical proportion began just after the main course had been served. During the ceremony itself I had been casting constant nervous glances at the gathering clouds as if I were watching Lancashire at Old Trafford and trying to estimate how long they would have to knock off the runs before the umpires consulted and took the players off. I was also conscious that on my wedding day City had been hammered 5–1 at Stoke City but on this, my son's wedding day, they had managed to lose more respectably 2–1 at Everton. What import that would have for the health of the marriage I had no idea, though Adam was comforted by another United win.

Adam had written and delivered a beautiful wedding service but unfortunately he had arrived too late to be officially deputised to marry the happy couple and the service was completed by Amy who had signed the form permitting her to intone 'By the power invested in me . . .' etc. She was hoping that this power might last for twenty-four hours so she could race into the street and marry a lot of people possibly against their wishes but sadly it only lasts for the duration of one marriage. Even as she said the fateful sentence its potency started to diminish and, like Tinker Bell, no sooner had she pronounced David and Susie husband and wife than, as far as the state of California was concerned, she returned to a prosaic reality.

Lynn had been bought a new outfit and was transported from the nursing home just before the bridal car arrived. I had acquired a new surgical collar for her neck because when she sat in the wheelchair her head would slump forward and we all wanted her to see everything. Unfortunately the collar was only partially successful and she had her eyes firmly screwed shut during most of the show but she seemed to absorb everything that was going on, partly through hearing and partly through my attempt to imitate Richard Dimbleby in her ear. 'And now the Great Lox of State is being wheeled on to the buffet table . . .'

It was a memorable occasion but inevitably more than a little tinged with sadness. By this time Lynn was sleeping about twenty hours a day and though much of the day passed her by she must have been conscious for enough of it to be affected by it. However, just as she had seemed to perk up when the wedding guests had arrived, their departures and farewells had the reverse effect and I felt my mood slipping, too. I felt badly about it and I tried ever so hard to burst into her room every day with a smile, a song and a terrible joke, but I was having difficulty in sleeping because I did not know how much longer Lynn wanted to continue this existence and it was torturing me.

I had to return to the UK to teach but I had arranged to take a break after three lectures of the new university term at Cambridge. Lynn's family wanted me to come back more often but for shorter spells so I was doing my best to comply with their wishes. How long this commuting would go on for I didn't know but as it transpired, the agony lasted barely another month. Lynn had scarcely said a word the whole time I was there in December and January until right at the very end. On my last day there before heading back to the UK, I stayed at the head of the bed as the nurses went about their jobs in the room. She turned her face towards me and I held her hand tightly as I had done all those years ago when she had given birth to our children. I put my lips next to her face and whispered as gently and as comfortingly as I could, 'Oh darling, I love you so much!' to which she said, quite angrily and with perfect diction, 'Well, I don't love you at all!' I know she didn't mean it, though maybe she did at that exact moment, but it was like a dagger through my heart. They were the last words I ever heard her speak.

I came home in mid-January depressed and exhausted. I left the house only when I had to. My first attempt to engage with a normal social life had been in the previous October when I had gone to Greg Dyke's book launch at Stamford Bridge. It had ended in abject failure. The people there I knew but who did not know what had happened to me were brought up to speed against a background of party small talk so loud that I had to shout the circumstances of my current travails. It was horrible and I soon gave up and drifted out of the room. I regarded any further attempt as pointless so I remained closeted in the house apart from my weekly trips up the M11 to lecture.

On Wednesday 2 February I taught my Hollywood & Race class and drove back from Cambridge to follow the progress of City's match at home to Newcastle which ended in a dull 1–1 draw, the equaliser coming from a Robbie Fowler penalty. I remember nothing of it. Whether this was the result of what was happening to me elsewhere or what was happening to City I couldn't be sure. Keegan had turned City into a reflection of his own darkening mood. The euphoria of May 2002 or even that last derby match at Maine Road six months later was long gone. When I got into the house I found a long message on the answering machine. Every time I heard an American voice giving me medical details my mind flashed back to 9 June 2004, the night my life changed for ever. This time it now appeared that Lynn's pain was clearly worsening. The next day something had clearly happened.

Telephone calls to the west coast were now assuming the frequency and urgency of the very first days of her illness and we could all see that sending her to dialysis was increasingly pointless. No sooner had the family united around this decision than it was discovered that there was a tear in her stomach and that air was seeping in. This was likely to speed up the process of dying but I was still labouring under the illusion that it would take some days for her to die once the dialysis was withdrawn.

The doctors were going to have a meeting at 11am local time (7pm GMT) on Friday 4 February to decide the best course of action. At twenty past seven I was just sitting down to my home-made chicken soup with matzo balls when the phone rang. The hospice nurse told me that the doctors had decided it was inadvisable to operate. There was no guarantee of success, she might very well die on the operating table and it would be an extremely painful process for her. I could only concur with their decision. 'She'll pass away sometime tonight,' concluded the nurse. I was extremely disconcerted because I was still mentally preparing myself for that ten-day Victorian deathbed scene. I was desperate to be there for the end but this news made it quite clear I couldn't be and I was distraught.

I phoned the children and then rang the hospital, eventually getting through to the ward where my wife was lying and quietly expiring. Her mother and sister were there, sitting with her as she drew her last breaths. I had been told that the hearing is the last of the senses to go so I thought that, though she was unconscious, she might just be able to process my words as they held the phone to her ear.

I was struggling for control of my emotions and predictably failing. I didn't want my sobs to be the last sound she heard so I jabbered about how much I loved her and how I had loved her at first sight and how we had loved each other for thirty-two and a half years (with time off for bad behaviour). I said that wherever she was going I was going to follow her and she should put a coat on the seat next to her and I would join her as soon as I could get a ticket. 'I love you, darling,' I intoned over and over, until it was quite clear that if she was hearing me she had got the message and would by now be getting fed up of the repetition. When different words resolutely refused to come I put the phone down and cried until I thought the salt water might stain the new wooden floors.

At six in the morning the telephone shrilled by my ear. I picked it up. Lynn's father intoned quite simply, 'Lynn passed away a few minutes ago.' 'Thank you for telling me,' I replied politely. What do you say at moments like this? 'I'll see you tomorrow.' I replaced the phone and went back to bed. The house was cold. It was a freezing February morning and the central heating wasn't due to come on for another two hours. 'Lynn is dead,' I said to myself over and over again, as if by repeating them I could make sense of them but the words felt artificial, like saying a sentence in a foreign language to see if the grammar is right. What did I feel inside? Nothing. I felt a huge void.

I flew in to Santa Barbara for what I knew would be the last time. After that week I would never want to go back to a place that would for ever be associated in my mind with disaster and death. The children stayed with their grandparents and I went back to the lovely apartment down by the beach lent to me by my friend Jo Apted. Jo's kindness in lending me that apartment could never be repaid. It had been a godsend, a place of temporary tranquillity amid the tension and heartbreak of the hospital and the incessant bad news.

We did what we had to do – the gravestone and the funeral arrangements, sorting the clothes and the books, the estate and the obituary, the cremation and the interment. The children took over. My job felt like it was at an end. The weather was gorgeous throughout this final week, the constant sun, the splendour of the nearby mountains and the eternal captivating serenity of the Pacific Ocean mocking the solemn and tragic rituals being carried out in front of them.

My beautiful wife was laid to rest in the family vault next to her young brother who had predeceased her. She had returned to the California soil from where she had gathered her strength. Her soul had long been there even as her corporeal presence had nurtured her husband and children six thousand miles away in north London. I hoped simply that her spirit, wherever it was, was now at peace. I knew, without a shadow of a doubt, that whatever the travails of life and death, I had always loved her and I always would. Her premature death meant that she would remain in my mind, and in the minds of all those who had known her, as young and as beautiful as she had been the day the lights went up in that screening room in Beverly Hills. Hollywood had given and Hollywood had taken away. The lives of those who had loved her were diminished by her departure but there remained in all of us an image of her loveliness that would never die.

Chapter Ten

SO OFTEN IN THE PAST I HAD TAKEN REFUGE FROM THE storms of life in my devotion to Manchester City. In a sense the team didn't even need to be any good to offer that cloak of security for me to huddle inside. Idle transfer speculation, the idea that a good new player was going to sign for us, was a balm for the hurt; an unexpected away win could raise my spirits far beyond the lift three points gave to their position in the league table. Even the prospect of a win in the next game, an unexpected outpouring of goals in one match, the selection of a player for the England squad, these would invariably provide a sense of well-being and a feeling that all was not lost, prosperity was just around the corner and it wasn't just Liverpool supporters who could walk through a storm and not feel alone.

Maybe it was because the losses I'd suffered in 2004 were so enormous that I now found that I couldn't bounce back. I did not expect bereavement to be like a dose of influenza which a few days in bed or a course of antibiotics would cure but I did not think that I would find it so difficult to recover for so many years. Twenty years before I had written and produced *1914 All Out*, a film for ITV about life and cricket in a Yorkshire village during the Great War. Like most films it had taken many years and many script drafts before we had obtained the money to make the film and when it was finished it was transmitted by the scheduling geniuses at ITV on a Saturday night where it performed respectably but didn't make the impact that a Sunday night audience would have accorded it.

The reviews were similarly respectable rather than ecstatic, except about the cricket, but one in particular has stayed with me ever since, partly because it was written by Nancy Banks-Smith, *The Guardian*'s television critic whom I greatly respected, and partly because what she wrote was so blindingly obvious that I was castigating myself for years afterwards. The critical line referred to a scene in which the hero returns to the village on leave from the Western Front. His fiancée brings him up to date with the death toll in the village and mentions the doctor, an engaging character to whom we have been introduced earlier. The doctor's wife has also been seen sobbing decorously into a hand-kerchief. 'You can see she's not over it and the telegram arrived two weeks since,' says fiancée to fiancé.

At this distance I could pretend that it was a line written if not delivered in irony but that wouldn't be the truth. Nancy chided me gently that few people get over the death of a spouse inside two weeks and I kicked myself at the time I first read it for my stupidity but it was during the extended period of mourning I was now experiencing that the real idiocy of the line struck home.

As I had suspected, with Lynn's death, the long slow process of healing began. It was aided by the time I spent as an Affiliated Lecturer in the History Faculty at Cambridge University, lecturing mostly at the request of Tony Badger who, along with his wife Ruth, had been the staunchest and most loyal of friends. Tony's particular field of interest, as is mine, is twentieth-century American history, and for him it is especially the South and civil rights. I started to re-shape my lectures on Hollywood's portrayal of civil rights and the South until it became a more general and interesting series of lectures on Hollywood and race, depicting the change in the African American stereotype from the evil mulattoes, as mixed race people were called in *The Birth of a Nation*, up to the time of Spike Lee and Denzel Washington.

Cambridge has always nourished some part of my soul in a way that no other town has ever done. I first saw it when I went there with my father to see my brother who had taken up residence at Gonville & Caius College a couple of weeks earlier, two weeks after our mother's death. It was during my school's half-term holiday in October 1962, the week of the Cuban Missile Crisis when Kennedy and Khrushchev were threatening to make City's poor start to the season an irrelevance, although in the end the Russians backed down and City went down. As far as Cambridge was concerned, however, it was love at first sight.

The Cambridge I saw in 1962 seemed very traditional, almost clichéd, as if carefully arranged by a film production designer looking to convey in visual shorthand the traditions of the university – students on bikes racing down Trinity Street between lectures, gowns worn after dark, the streets patrolled by bulldogs (the university's own military police), fines of six shillings and eight pence levied for minor infractions of the arcane rules – but the seductive appeal of the university town was instant and overwhelming.

Five years later I arrived there in my own right, having doggedly believed in that destiny despite the deep and understandable scepticism unwittingly demonstrated by most of my teachers at Bury Grammar School. Staying overnight in Tree Court for my interview at Caius I was amused by the arrival in the morning of a jug of hot water borne by a porter who greeted me and the new day with that unique mixture of deference and contempt I was soon to know so well. Nevertheless, everything about the place lifted my spirits – the buildings, the libraries, the old courts, the river, the ubiquitous concerts, recitals and plays and, above all, the sport.

I had learned to play sport in the north of England where there wasn't a lot of grass around. The football and rugby pitches were heaps of mud in the winter and brown, arid, grassless wastelands in the spring and summer. The tennis courts were made of either hard concrete or red shale. The cricket pitches tended to nestle in the shade of looming factory chimneys or soot-blackened railway bridges, rather than Norman churches or rolling downs. No school-boy batsman dared unfurl a flashy off-drive or a delicate late-cut for fear of being punched in the face by the coach, a gnarled old pro from the Lancashire Leagues. Then I got to Cambridge and I was overwhelmed with the sight of so much green grass.

Wherever you looked there were beautifully kept sports grounds with their immaculate lawns and charming wooden pavilions with thatched roofs. In the summer term, and particularly after exams were over, college grounds were filled with cricketers and tennis players revelling in the grass courts and the lovingly rolled pitches. It fulfilled all my fantasies which had been stimulated by boarding school stories written by P. G. Wodehouse and Frank Richards about schoolboys who played sport every afternoon. Those deadly dull mornings in the old Mill Lane Lecture Rooms, the new History Faculty or the grandiloquent University Library were made bearable by the prospect of sport at a college ground after lunch.

The football we played still retained echoes of its Corinthian past, a spirit far removed from the hacking and cheating which had been integral to the Manchester Jewish Soccer League. The three cheers for the opposition at the end of each game surprised me every time I heard it. Caius had a pretty good team in the late sixties and I was glad to be part of it. The photograph of the team I eventually captained is on the wall as I write, symbolically fading into oblivion with each passing summer.

Returning to Cambridge to lecture was, and still is, something that I greatly enjoy doing but, however much it resonated with my need for romance in my existence, it took only a few days in the academic year and it certainly wasn't enough to fill the gaps that were increasingly appearing in my life like the holes in a piece of scrap metal used for target practice. I needed to be as busy or even busier than I had been before I had become so involved in the deaths of people close to me but now that I was heading into the second half of my sixth decade on earth I discovered that my traditional diligence was not resulting in paid employment the way it had in the past.

As I had done so often, I turned to Manchester City in that miserable winter and early spring of 2005 but what I found was a side and club and a ground that didn't nurture me as they had once done. Cambridge with its limitations couldn't do it and neither could City. Kevin Keegan had produced a side three years before that played some of the most entertaining, delightful and exhilarating football I had seen from a City team in thirty years. I wondered just how exactly he had managed to turn that team into the one I saw collect one of the most dispiriting away victories of all time at Carrow Road.

It was this match that saw Delia Smith's big moment at half-time when she cried 'Let's be 'avin' you!' into the Sky cameras as she bewailed the absence of a vocal home crowd in words that she had never employed during any of her cookery programmes. It was also one of only eight City wins in the twenty-eight games so far played during 2004–5 but, whereas a 3–2 win with a goal in the last five minutes sounds like it should have been exciting, the miserable nature of Keegan's demeanour depressed me still further and told all the supporters that he was not long for our world. It was the same at Newcastle, the scene of his great triumphs in the 1990s, when he had run out of steam and enthusiasm, his head slumping further behind the zipper of his anorak. It was now happening here and it was ironic that, after all the efforts that the board had made to placate their precious manager, including jettisoning a chairman who was prepared to say 'no' to him (see above for philosophical justification), he still decided that unemployment was a preferable alternative to managing this Manchester City club. The week after a mirthless 1–0 defeat by Bolton Wanderers at Eastlands, Keegan was off to Spain for an early tee-off time in the morning.

I was watching television when the BBC Radio sports desk rang to tell me of Keegan's departure for the airport. There was an initial confusion when, for a moment, I thought that as part of the BBC's stated desire to engage interactively with its licence fee payers, it was developing a new policy of ringing them up on an individual basis every time they felt they had news which might be of interest to them. It soon became apparent that what they actually wanted was for me to comment on the resignation for broadcast on the next sports bulletin. Again, I couldn't help feeling that, as with the call after relegation at Ipswich in 2001, I was only required to comment on negative aspects of the club and the positive ones would be dealt with others better psychologically qualified.

The arrival of Stuart Pearce as Keegan's replacement was as unsurprising as the time when Howard Kendall had scuttled back to Goodison Park amid jeers of 'Judas' and had been replaced by his trained successor, Peter Reid. David flew into London in the middle of March to attend the memorial service I had arranged for Lynn, so he and Amy and I went together to White Hart Lane to watch the start of the Pearce regime – a 2–1 defeat after a bright opening.

The new manager didn't seem to be the harbinger of much comfort. The season appeared to be tapering out in a disappointing whimper, which pretty much matched my nihilistic mood, when it suddenly sprang into life again. During April, City, under what now appeared to be the magical touch of Stuart Pearce, won three and drew three of their six matches leaving them, suddenly and quite unexpectedly, with an outside chance of a place in the following season's UEFA Cup. At the start of May they went to Villa Park and won 2–1 with goals by Shaun Wright-Phillips and Kiki Musampa (who went by the splendid appellation of Chris as in Christmas hamper), so all they had to do was to win the last match of the season at home to Middlesbrough and Keegan would have bequeathed to his and our astonishment a legacy that none of us could have predicted when a nightingale sang at Carrow Road.

By a remarkable coincidence the game was to take place on the same day as the unveiling of my father's headstone. Usually these things happen twelve months after the funeral but for reasons that I never quite understood the date was set for the same Sunday as this now crucial Middlesbrough match. Unfortunately, it was also set for almost the same *time* as the Middlesbrough match and my attempt to get the unveiling brought forward by an hour was in vain. It might have been easier to have persuaded the Premier League to have shifted all the last day matches back by an hour than to get the synagogue to allow the younger son of the deceased this one last favour.

The compromise reached after what appeared to be protracted negotiations with the Almighty was that the unveiling and the synagogue service would take place as arranged but that Amy and I (David being back at work on his MBA course at Tuck School of Business in Dartmouth, New Hampshire) would be in a position to get to Fastlands just after half time, which we did with the game still scoreless. Pretty much the moment we sat down Musampa scored and the result appeared to be a foregone conclusion. It seemed like those negotiations had produced a win-win result. It didn't, of course. It produced a draw-draw result because Middlesbrough equalised but not without the sort of finish that at least made the journey a memorable one.

As the fourth official was about to hold up the board for the time added on at the end of the ninety minutes Pearce did something entirely unexpected. He looked at Jon Macken, his reserve striker on the bench, and decided, instead of utilising the talents of this player for whom Keegan had shelled out £5 million of City's hard-earned gold and currency reserves making him for five minutes the club's record signing, he would prefer to utilise as a striker in this ultimate crisis of mankind the talents of David James, his goalkeeper. Apparently, we later learned, James had been jolly good as a striker in the five-a-side kickabouts that ended the training sessions.

Nicky Weaver was summoned from the bench to take his place in goal as James trotted up the field to bemused cheers from the crowd, while Macken presumably sat there seething. James's first contribution to the attack was to swing an enormous boot at a cross from the right, which, predictably, these things being a lot harder in a vital match than in training, he missed completely and fell over. In the ensuing kerfuffle the referee spotted an infringement elsewhere in the penalty area and pointed to the spot. We all rose to our feet and cheered lustily at this moment of supreme good fortune/tactical genius. The kick would be taken by Robbie Fowler, an ice-cool experienced penalty-taker who had scored eleven goals in twenty-eight games and could be relied upon to guide the ball safely into the net from a distance of twelve yards.

This, however, is Manchester City we're talking about. Are you watching, Joe Royle? Predictably, Mark Schwarzer in the Middlesbrough goal dived the right way and saved Fowler's feeble strike so the game ended 1–1 with the City players keeping their passports firmly in their pockets. It was a disappointing contrast with the mood that had surrounded Pearce's own missed penalty at the end of the 2002 season. Nevertheless, it was, in its own way, a memorable anti-climax and entirely in keeping with what we had all grown to expect over the years. Hope sprang eternal but results remained firmly rooted to the immaculate turf of Eastlands.

I couldn't help but spend much of the return journey comparing how I had felt after the last match of the previous season with what I was feeling now. The trauma that the children and I had emerged from was never far away. It took very little to stimulate the tear ducts even if I could look in the mirror and say to myself that I was on the road to recovery. Months after Lynn's death I would find myself unaccountably but helplessly crying in the most unlikely places. Going into the bank to change the name on the joint account, writing out a cheque to the Probate Office (it wasn't the size of the cheque) and once in a shop buying tile-cleaner liquid. All it took was some small trigger to set me off, anything that reminded me of happier times because times had been so unhappy for what seemed to be so long.

I had plenty of help and plenty of coping stratagems. I had friends like Lee and Maureen and David and Gill Bernstein and Ruth and Tony Badger in Cambridge who, whether by instinct or by thought, seemed to know exactly how much support to offer, the manner in which it should be offered, and the right time to offer it. As in previous unhappy times, I retreated into my routines of exercise and work. I got up and went straight to the exercise bike, listened to a book on tape while pedalling furiously but never leaving the basement, showered, had breakfast, started work, broke for lunch, worked some more, strode off on my daily yomp over the Heath and then back for more work before dinner. It was a boring way to live but it was the best way I knew to ameliorate the tortured moments that surrounded me.

At least during the summer of 2005 cricket rediscovered its place in the heart of supporters because the 2005 Ashes series was simply the best series of Test matches played in my lifetime. I can only dimly recall the 1956 series won by Jim Laker's astonishing haul of forty-six wickets in the five Test matches. There was a wonderful reversal of fortune in 1981 marked by the flamboyant performances of Ian Botham, but 2005 contained the greatest Test match I ever saw (Edgbaston) and a series whose result was in doubt until the post-tea session on the last day of the last Test. It was breathtaking in its capacity for a seemingly unending series of dramatic moments, not the least of which were the high-angle television cameras transmitting pictures of long snaking queues of cricket supporters desperate to get into Old Trafford to watch the last day's play of the third Test match which ended with Australia's last pair, McGrath and Lee, together at the crease and batting out the last four overs to scrape a draw.

No such crowds followed county cricket at Old Trafford but at least Lancashire redeemed themselves somewhat with an instant return to the top division of the County Championship. It was, however, with a side that didn't arouse much enthusiasm in me, partly I fear for arguably antediluvian reasons — there weren't enough Lancastrians in it. Of course we'd celebrated over the years a number of overseas players, particularly Farokh Engineer from India, Clive Lloyd from Guyana, and Wasim Akram from Pakistan. These men were not only indisputably great cricketers but they enhanced their reputations by embracing Lancashire and thus they were in turn embraced by Lancastrians.

By 2005 this sort of relationship was quaintly out of date. Overseas players now only fitted in a brief spell of lucrative county cricket between even more lucrative international engagements. In 2005 Lancashire entertained Brad Hodge for seven matches, Andrew Symonds for seven matches, Marcus North (like the other two a visitor from Down Under) for three matches and Muttiah Muralitharan for six matches, while the Indian Murali Kartik donated his services for two games. In addition, Dominic Cork, Mal Loye and Iain Sutcliffe had all been signed from other counties and the idea that Lancashire County Cricket Club somehow represented Lancashire now seemed to be as relevant to modern life as a Gilbert Scott telephone box or a typewriter. These symbols of a vanishing age were admirable in their way, no doubt, but they were deemed no longer relevant to life in the twenty-first century. It was a judgment which I occasionally applied to myself.

The very fact that I still cared passionately about county cricket started to make me feel old. County cricket, during my childhood, had been the cake and Test match cricket had been the icing. In the bright new dawn to which Giles Clarke has been leading English cricket (by way of a quick visit to the now-imprisoned Allen Stanford) we had been told that the basis of English cricket was now the England Test team. Nobody watched county cricket and nobody cared about it. Well, it might be true that first-class county cricket doesn't fill cricket grounds (has it ever since about 1948?) but it is a travesty to imply that nobody cares about it. I just wished that the caring I felt for Lancashire did not mark me out as a man on the verge of acquiring a bath chair for mobility.

*

In the summer of 2005 I turned fifty-six. It didn't strike me as a particularly advanced age. As a widower at fifty-five I felt very strongly that I had been prematurely bereaved and that eventually I would find someone else to join me on my journey through to the end of life, which still felt some way distant. As a creative person I felt no diminution in my powers. As a self-confessed sports fanatic I felt no less fascinated by sport than I had ever felt. I did not, however, feel that my interests were being reciprocated. I spent too many evenings in the theatre and the cinema from which I emerged, slightly surprised that the play or the film had ever found its way to an audience at all. It wasn't just that this stuff was being made and what I wanted to make could attract no interest at all but I knew perfectly well that my lack of interest in what the BBC was offering was the reason why they and other potential employers were much less interested in what I had to offer than they ever used to be.

I thought I should be in love with Manchester City to the extent I had always been in love with the club but I could see that already something was starting to shift, for many of the same reasons that my feelings for Lancashire cricket were beginning to change. Crowds were changing in their attitudes to the game and I was starting to feel alienated from them. There was something about joining the throng on the way to a sporting encounter that had always appealed to me. Parking the car in an unfamiliar town when City were playing, I would always look eagerly for signs of other supporters to reassure myself that I wasn't too far from the ground. There is something about supporters hurrying towards a football ground that is different from spectators sauntering to a cricket ground in midsummer. L. S. Lowry captures it perfectly in his portrait of Burnden Park called 'Going to the Match'. His familiar stick figures are all bent forward slightly as if drawn towards the ground by a magnet or huddled against the bitter wind or more likely by the awareness that they are late and need to hurry if they are to get into the ground by kick-off. It would come as a great surprise to the artist, who died in 1976 when the average footballer probably earned between £100 and £200 a week, that the painting was bought in 1999 for nearly £2 million by the Professional Footballers' Association. As a symbol of the changing times it could hardly be a better example.

As a teenager in the 1960s, I would walk from home up to the bus stop at Grand Lodge from where the number 75 bus departed and meet my three friends with whom I shared the experience of so many City home matches. On to the bus, as it clanked its way south, shoppers would get on and get off as they disappeared into the centre of Manchester but they would be replaced by men and boys, it was invariably males in those days, with blue scarves and hats, until the bus was heaving with excited chatter and the anticipation of the match. Getting off at Claremont Road, the trickle become a stream and then, if the match were big enough, a flood of supporters would sweep towards the ground, anxious to hear the click of the turnstiles behind them before the fearful rumour 'They're closing the gates' could be heard.

Attending any football match now offered few of these delights. Everyone had a ticket, there were no cash admissions on the day, so there was no point in hurrying. The spectacle had become formalised in a way I found soulless. The Kolpak players of Lancashire County Cricket had their equivalents in City's Premier League team. They weren't all bad players, some of them were adequate enough to do the limited job they had been signed to do – Michael Tarnat, Paul Bosvelt, Albert Riera, Claudio Reyna, Antoine Sibierski – but I wouldn't cross the road to see any of them if they

175

weren't wearing a blue shirt. That's not to be taken as a statement of xenophobia – the English players were no more exciting; Ben Thatcher and Danny Mills, Trevor Sinclair and Darius Vassell were incapable of setting the pulses racing.

The 2005–6 season, in which I began my slow climb back to join the rest of the human race, was a particularly undistinguished season to rival if not surpass the previous undistinguished season. Shaun Wright-Phillips, who had been the shining light of 2004–5, was unsurprisingly sold to Chelsea in exchange for more than £20 million of Roman Abramovich's personal assets. We could hardly blame the City board for selling at that price but in addition to little Shaunie, Schmeichel, Anelka, Benarbia, Berkovic, even the ever-smiling Shaun Goater, had now all left and their replacements were poor and filled me with a sense of frustration. The goals that had to be scored in order to keep City up were now going to have to be scored by Vassell and the superannuated Andy Cole. Neither of them got into double figures. A painfully accumulated £6 million was lavished on the Greek striker Georgios Samaras, who joined in the January transfer window but, perhaps predictably, turned out to be the proud inheritor of the Biggest Waste of Money label previously bestowed upon Lee Bradbury and Jon Macken. Within two years he was off to the heights of the Scottish Premier League.

I retained brief hopes for two of the successful City youth team of 2004 whom I had seen while researching my book about the City and United youth teams of 1964. I had chosen the forward Lee Croft and the midfield player Willo Flood as the likeliest candidates to make the grade into the first team from the academy. There is something very rewarding for my generation of supporters about watching young players come through the system of youth teams and into the first eleven. Under the management of Kevin Keegan, City had, to my regret, turned away from this policy, despite the remarkable and consistent success of Jim Cassell who ran the City academy. Cassell was as successful as anybody in the game at the difficult task of guiding young players through the junior ranks. Keegan wasn't greatly interested, though. Nothing for him matched the attraction of the open cheque book. One of Stuart Pearce's qualities, it seemed to me, was that he brought to the job of manager the experience of two or three years working with the youngsters at City and I hoped that he might be prepared, unlike Keegan, to encourage them with first team opportunities; although, in the former manager's defence, I have to admit that Flood had not distinguished himself on the few appearances he had made for Keegan.

I saw Lee Croft score the City goal at Craven Cottage in a 2–1 defeat. The defeat itself hardly surprised me, though the seeming inevitability of it depressed me. It wasn't that I expected Fulham to lie down and roll over but that they played with an *élan* and a belief that I thought we might have matched but didn't. I had hoped that the first team appearances of Croft and Flood, along with Nedum Onuoha and Micah Richards might herald the start of a youth-inspired revival. I was at Highbury to see the first appearance of Micah Richards, who I think was sent on up front, but he just appeared that day to be another big lad in the style of Ishmael Miller who had also sparked some hope recently. City tried hard but Arsenal were always going to win, even though Thierry Henry and Robert Pirès decided to pass the ball to each other from the penalty spot instead of scoring, which afforded enormous enjoyment but of a very brief duration. The defeats mounted and relegation threatened but, though my spirits were low, I had no cause to doubt my fundamental loyalty at this time.

*

At some point during February 2006 the *Daily Telegraph* asked me to write a travel piece on the state of Wyoming, where *Brokeback Mountain* was set, to coincide with the almost inevitable coronation of the film as the winner of Best Picture at the Oscars at the end of the month. Unfortunately, part of the deal was that I previewed a cowboy holiday, which I am sure would have been lots of fun in the sunshine of the summer but which in the sub-zero temperatures of February was a lot less inviting.

Still, I had never previously been part of a cattle round-up and, though to my amusement it was partly done in these enlightened times by quad bike, the horses still did most of the business. GMT being six hours ahead of Central and Mountain time in the USA, I was herding cattle on horseback (dressed entirely inappropriately in a long, purple, rainproof jacket I wore for filming on cold locations and a Manchester City bobble hat without the bobble) when City's home game against Charlton Athletic was in progress.

I took some comfort in being not only the most stupidly dressed cowboy in the history of the Wild West (certainly the only one to be wearing a City hat rather than the *de rigueur* Wyoming Stetson on a cattle round-up) but I thought back to John Wayne and James Stewart and Gary Cooper. I wondered if any of those heroes of the Old West had spent much time, saddle sore and weary after hundreds of miles on horseback driving cattle from the plains of Texas to the Missouri railhead, worrying about a match against Charlton Athletic. Maybe they just contemplated the absurd sum City had lavished on Samaras.

This brief trip to the coldest place I had ever been was the first time I had been back to America since Lynn's death almost exactly a year before. I was curious to see if my attitude to the country had changed but it hadn't. I still had no interest in revisiting California but I enjoyed much of what I saw of Wyoming from the interior of a heated car. What I was conscious of mostly was my sense of being alone. If I had managed to achieve this broadsheet commission in previous times I would have enjoyed talking to Lynn about a part of her country she had rarely visited. This was now denied me, so what would have been a conversation became instead an internal monologue. That was the situation in much of my life. The children had grown up and found partners, which was only to be expected. I was becoming stuffed to the earlobes with unspoken conversations.

The 2005–6 football season finished in the same downbeat manner that too many other seasons had finished. Of the twelve matches that followed the spirited 3–2 win over Charlton when I was riding the range and clinging on to the horse's neck like grim death, City managed to win two and lose the other ten. It was a nothing team going nowhere.

I suspect the two reasons why Stuart Pearce retained his post for the start of the 2006–7 season were firstly that they couldn't afford to sack him, hire a new manager and buy the players that new manager would have demanded, and secondly because City had performed creditably in the two derby games. Despite the fact that we finished a lowly fifteenth, we had taken four points off United. There had been a 1–1 draw early in the season in which the City goal had withstood a fearsome battering but heroic defending by Dunne, Distin and James had kept out the Reds. At Eastlands in January, United had played particularly poorly and the *coup de grâce* in a 3–1 win had been applied by Robbie Fowler. The former Liverpool striker, with his last goal for City before returning for a romantic but brief interlude to Anfield, had celebrated by racing round the perimeter of the pitch and waving five fingers at the stunned United supporters, which we were informed was supposed to remind them of the five European cups Liverpool had won compared to United's paltry three. To me it seemed like one of those convoluted explanations in the Haggadah, the prayer book used at Passover, when the youngest male child present asks the Four Questions to which every rabbi in history appears to have a different answer. Who cares? United got thumped. Amen.

On the credit side there had also been a Cup run which had awakened our enthusiasm. We hadn't won the Cup since 1969, hadn't even reached the semi-final since 1981, so the hard-won victories over Scunthorpe United, Wigan Athletic and, after a replay, Aston Villa inevitably aroused memories of Tony Book holding the cup aloft and Paul Power's memorable extra-time free kick in the semi-final against Ipswich Town at Villa Park in 1981. City were drawn at home against West Ham United in the sixth round and ahead of us, if we dared to think that far, Liverpool would play Chelsea in one semi-final while the winners of the City v West Ham match would face the much less threatening Middlesbrough side. The twin towers would have beckoned had they not been demolished and the final was scheduled to be played at the Millennium Stadium in Cardiff.

I had never been to the Millennium Stadium and still haven't because in their televised big opportunity City fluffed their lines badly. They gave a dreadfully disappointing display, losing to a resurgent West Ham side 1–2 and embarking on that final run of seven defeats in the last eight league games. Dean Ashton scored twice and City lost Sun Jihai, the mildest of men, to a flailing arm which Howard Webb, to the bemusement of all, deemed worthy of a red card. It was a decision that somehow chimed with the frustrated mood of the supporters. Although I saw the West Ham tie stretched out on the sofa, I recall the bad-tempered, sickening feelings which accompanied the defeat; a real irritation with the way in which they had tossed away the chance to redeem this unimpressive season. It reminded me slightly of 1993 when City had been beaten at home 2–4 by Spurs in a sixth-round tie at the end of a Cup run which had briefly ignited the blue half of the city. Going out of the Cup still meant something to me in 2006. It doesn't mean half as much now.

The 2006–7 season arrived shortly after yet another bad-tempered Test series against Pakistan, culminating in Darrell Hair taking off the bails in the middle of the final Test at The Oval and awarding the match to England as the opposition remained sulking in their dressing room. It was one of the few Augusts that I didn't mind the arrival of the football season because surely watching City couldn't be worse than watching an empty ground at The Oval. In fact it was a close-run thing. City achieved the remarkable record of failing to score a single goal at home after New Year's Day. It was gratifying that they no longer expected the goals to come from Andy Cole and Darius Vassell because we could all have told Stuart Pearce there was not going to be much coming from that quarter.

Instead Pearce proudly unveiled his latest capture, the Italian striker Bernardo Corradi, signed from Valencia for what was termed 'an undisclosed fee', later suspected to be one pound four shillings and seven pence plus a tube of Rolos. Corradi made his debut in the first match of the season at Chelsea, which ended in a 3–0 defeat. Corradi himself ended his participation early, hastened on his way by a red card after a clash with Michael Essien. The match was played on a Sunday afternoon and I remember looking at the league table in the Sunday morning papers and seeing that after 0 games producing 0 points we had achieved a sort of mid-table respectability based entirely on alphabetical order. I knew then, hours before the kick-off at Stamford Bridge, the lights were going out all over Eastlands.

Bernardo Corradi eventually scored his first goal for Manchester City against Fulham in the middle of November. The following month he was sent off again, this time for diving at Old Trafford, much to our manager's publicly stated disgust. Corradi finished the season with a grand total of three goals, which actually represented more than 10% of the team's total. On that basis, and possibly on the basis of acquiring an extremely attractive blonde girlfriend which caused much comment from at least one of my friends, he must be accounted a success. He lost his place to a Belgian loan signing called Émile Mpenza and was returned to Italy in a large crate with 'Not Known At This Address' heavily stencilled on the side. His girlfriend, I should imagine, travelled first class. On his reappearance in his native land he was almost immediately sent off in one of his first matches for Parma. Recalling the sultry image of his girlfriend, Corradi presumably wished to spend more time with his family, even though as yet he had no children.

Now I know City are not the only club to have bought unwisely. All clubs have a history dotted with the names of the incompetent, the overpriced and the frankly embarrassing. Supporters, however, look at other clubs signing Francis Jeffers or Juan Sebastián Verón or Diego Forlán or, at the time of writing, Fernando Torres and Andy Carroll and smile, maybe smirk, but essentially shrug their shoulders and thank Whomever that at least it wasn't their club that erred so disastrously. It's not their own money that has been wasted but looking at poor old Torres you can't help feeling that Roman Abramovich might have done better to have kept his money in the building society even at current rates of interest.

It's hard to look back on any of the seasons from 2002 to 2007 as a golden time and, despite my current feelings about what was to come, I wouldn't want any reader to imagine for a moment that this is the sort of thing I'd like to go back to. 2006–7 was another nervous season, anxiety tugging constantly at the frayed nerves of players, supporters, manager and board of directors alike. Pearce had been a fine player, in many ways an admirable one, and it was hard not to want him to make a successful transition to management from his playing status as English Bulldog number one. He had the most remarkable way of pulling out a win at exactly the moment he needed it to save his job. After the first seven away matches had produced exactly one point, City went to Villa Park and cruised to a very impressive 3–1 victory, clinched by a goal from Sylvain Distin in which he brought the ball elegantly out of defence like Bobby Moore, exchanged passes with Georgios Samaras and scored with the aplomb of a Bernardo Corradi or indeed a Georgios Samaras. Ah yes. Mr Samaras, the Greek bearing gifts of goal-scoring potential. Well, his mobility wasn't anything like as good as that of the Trojan Horse, which at least had been pushed around the walls of Troy a few times, and his goals tally didn't quite match that of Signor Corradi. The two he scored against Everton on New Year's Day were the sum total of his season's output in the Premier League. Nevertheless, those two goals appeared to be regarded so highly by his colleagues that the entire team refused to sully the memory of them by scoring again at Eastlands until August.

The victory against Everton was the last in three consecutive wins over the holiday period which had followed three consecutive defeats and rumblings of discontent with the players and their manager. Pearce's job was safe again. However, the goalless displays at home matches, witnessed in endless profusion for the rest of the season, reawakened calls for the sacking of the manager who had marked his first few games in charge with that dramatic gallop towards Europe. I travelled to Manchester for the match against Liverpool which, predictably, turned out to be a buttock-numbing 0–0 draw. I had no idea as I left Eastlands that, on a point of principle, it would be the last time I would attend a City home game, but looking back on the occasion now it was somehow a predictable match and result, much as the last match at Maine Road against Southampton had ended on a discordant diminuendo. Secure in my ignorance of what was to come, I was at Vicarage Road a couple of weeks later in the bright spring sunshine to watch an equally meaningless 1–1 draw against a Watford side already doomed to relegation.

City ended fourteenth in the table, clinging on to their cherished Premier League status and finishing the season in the style they started with three successive defeats, including handing Manchester United their latest championship after a 0–1 defeat at home in the penultimate game. John Wardle and David Makin, whose JD Sports money was essentially keeping City going at this time, were finding it impossible to compete with the new spending authorised by Abramovich and other wealthy and almost invariably foreign owners in their quest for glory. They were understandably fed up. We were certainly fed up. We had scaled to the heights of fourteenth place by virtue of the failings of others. It was no way to run a sweet shop, let alone a publicly quoted Premier League football club. Wardle agreed, sacked Pearce to no protest at all and ensured that the For Sale sign was prominently displayed outside the City of Manchester Stadium. Whatever happened to City, whatever happened to me, whatever happened to my relationship with City, what was to come must surely be better than what we had all just endured.

Chapter Eleven

I'VE ALWAYS ENJOYED THE COMPANY OF WOMEN. DESPITE all the sport that crowds my life on all the televisions in my house, despite the recognition that my early life was spent in the unreconstructed north of England at a time when men permitted themselves a social latitude they did not permit women, thus inevitably colouring my expectation of future partners, I have always liked women and found their company something to be desired. I was never really a pub man, having a medical allergy to cigarette smoke and a cultural aversion to alcohol. 'No,' confirmed one of the women I particularly liked, ' I see you as more of a tea shop man.' I can't say that I disagreed with that dubious accolade.

After Lynn's death I needed time to heal before I considered myself ready to re-enter the fray. Even when eventually I considered that I was fit enough, I realised very quickly that I wasn't coming back on to the pitch having been off since February 2005. I was coming back after having been off since May 1972 and not only was I not the player I was then but the pitch wasn't where it used to be either. I had very little knowledge of what to expect as I warmed up on the side of this intimidating arena where new romantic and sexual encounters took place.

The dating world had changed and I was set in my ways. Did I really want to change my daily routines which I suppose might be considered mildly eccentric? I don't respond well to change so it was with some trepidation that I stuck my nose out of the front door. I was surprised by much of what I discovered 'out there'. My daughter told me that she was expected to contribute 50% of the cost of any date she was invited on. That had certainly not been the case in 1972 and it made me uneasy. Much as I have applauded the way in which women have made their impact in the workplace in the past thirty years, I found their newly acquired sexual confidence slightly intimidating, even if this was a highly general observation. I hoped that when I started 'dating', a horrible term but one which conveys the nature of the activity perfectly well, I would find that my instincts were still regarded as chivalrous rather than unemancipated.

Gender politics was still a new term in 1972 and I wasn't entirely sure how they were now going to impact on the little courtesies Lynn had always taken for granted. She was always very keen that I walked on the outside nearer the kerb even if the origin of the custom was to enable the man to draw his sword quickly in the event of an attack on the woman and it rarely happened on Muswell Hill Broadway. Opening doors for women and letting them precede you, ensuring they had the choice of seats at a restaurant table, these had always been automatic responses to standard social situations. Should I continue to behave in that fashion and risk ridicule or ignore them and risk being regarded as boorish?

I couldn't help noticing how social manners had changed on public transport. In olden days I would have found it impossible to sit down while a woman near me was standing. It required little in the powers of observation to see that this was no longer a general rule and that, by and large, women didn't seem to expect it any longer. However, on the increasingly rare occasions when I have risen gallantly and offered my seat, usually to a woman older than I am rather than one who was simply attractive which would have been the determining factor before I reached sixty, I couldn't help noticing the rather relieved smile of thanks she flashed. It was as if she were grateful but equally socially embarrassed.

Before I could determine how widely this new approach to the time-honoured game of flirtation and romance had spread, I had to find somebody to go on a date with. Sitting at home writing all day interspersed with a daily tramp across Hampstead Heath was unlikely to provide me with the sort of opportunities offered to Mr Bingley and Mr Darcy at the Netherfield Ball. However, I wasn't so far removed from reality that I was unaware of the astonishing growth of internet dating, but it demanded a technique for spotting fraudsters that took me a little while to develop.

As a writer I thought I had an advantage. After all, an epistolary relationship, much in the manner of eighteenth-century or nineteenth-century gentlemen and ladies of leisure writing to each other two or three times a day, ought to be something that would suit me and my lifestyle perfectly. What I hadn't realised was that the slightly formal, gradual unfolding of a relationship that might have characterised the novels of Fielding or Trollope was not really what was on offer in an age of instant communication and text speak. The idea of responding to a dating website profile with a courtly but delightful formality as in:

Dear Ms Smith,

    I was both charmed by your photograph and captivated by your delightful handle . . . etc.

was not possible when most of the messages I received started and finished, 'Hi, Pls snd photo x'. I doubt that even the impulsive Lydia Bennet communicated with Mr Wickham in this manner and quite what that 'x' was supposed to indicate puzzled me, though you can't help feeling on re-reading *Pride and Prejudice* that their relationship would certainly have flourished on Twitter had it been around at the time. Back in 2007 I was fully prepared for 'Thks. Not interested. **** off x'.

There was certainly a degree of double standards in my initial refusal to attach a photograph to my profile, given the fact that I was only searching for women who had attached a photograph to their profiles. My plan, which was about as cunning as anything Baldrick might have concocted for internet dating, was to avoid depressing my female correspondents too early on in the game by showing them my face and I hoped that would allow me at least to get to half-time with the game still scoreless. My dogmatic view of women, and indeed part of my high regard for their intellect, was that they were far less trivial than men, far less inclined to make judgments on the basis of what they saw rather than what they heard or read. Logically, that should have allowed me to post a photograph with no anxieties about what might follow but I soon discovered that the anxieties were greater than my confidence and I happily skulked in the shadows of visual anonymity.

Women who laughed easily or read widely would, I had supposed, be more amenable to seduction by words. That was indeed true of the women I ended up with but decidedly untrue of most of those whose flirtation lasted precisely three exchanges of one-line messages. It didn't take long for me to get fed up with the many thousands of women who stated that they liked long nights in and short days out (or possibly vice versa), who were as comfortable in an old pair of jeans as a designer dress, who liked long walks in the country and theatre, ballet, music, reading and the Arts. They were devoted to their animals but they still had room in their intellectually full and emotionally fulfilling lives to share a little portion with the man of their dreams. This rather desperate scattergun approach had the effect of making me feel like an even more boorish, testosterone-fuelled, aggressively male chauvinist than Jeremy Clarkson could supply.

Eventually I decided that answering honestly the same boring questions that every website posed would open me to a similar charge, in which case the best thing I could do was to write to amuse myself and if it attracted women that would at least mean they shared my sense of humour. At first I called myself 'Ron Obvious' which was a small bow in the direction of *Monty Python*, but that produced no recognition at all and I dare say many women thought that really was my name and had no desire to become Mrs Obvious.

My first stab at the profile was for a website whose clients had to be (or possibly just had to claim to be) university graduates. The photographs of women who looked very attractive might have been ten years old but a woman with a bright mind ten years before would still have it and that had to be the right place to start. Accordingly, I answered the question 'Describe the sort of woman you are looking for' with what I considered to be a response that would be different from anything else on the site:

> I am looking for a partner to accompany me on a series of armed robberies I am planning to make on rural sub post offices. I am starting small, holding up postmistresses who must be in their seventies and no taller than 5 feet 2 inches but I think if I can find the right partner and we can garner enough postal orders we will be able to expand into white collar crime which I am particularly keen on because it saves

189

on laundry. I see a time a few years hence when my partner and I will be able to sell all our collars to a nice firm called Enron and maybe go legit. The woman I am looking for should have the body of Marilyn Monroe and the mind of Arthur Miller — that worked out very well between 1955 and 1957. Anyone with the body of Arthur Miller and the mind of Marilyn Monroe need not apply.

I was pleased with what I had written. I had no idea if anybody else would be but it would surely deter the women who were looking for long nights in and short days out. In answer to the question 'Describe your perfect journey', which I supposed was designed to bring out the romantic in their clients but which sounded to me like another dull series on BBC2 presented by Michael Portillo, I wrote:

> I would like to lie in a punt and be poled slowly along the hard shoulder of the M1 by Greta Garbo, stopping off at Junction 24 to admire the water cooling towers at Kegworth.

The question which offered the chance to expand most imaginatively was 'Describe your hopes for the future, yours or the world's' to which I responded:

> I believe I am the reincarnated spirit of Warwick the Kingmaker. Admittedly I was born in Manchester and live in North London but I have a strong affinity with the mediaeval warlord. I am particularly irritated with Shakespeare who allowed Edward IV the smarty-pants line 'Wind-changing Warwick shall change no more'. I hope to make the Earl of Warwick a United Nations Ambassador to Africa alongside Posh Spice.

The trick, I felt, was to write something surreal and possibly amusing while at the same time slipping in enough genuine information to placate the rather angry response which complained that my profile was worthless because it told her nothing about myself. However, I received enough similarly outraged responses along these lines to realise that my plan was not exactly foolproof, though it did have the negative benefit of ensuring I didn't initiate a correspondence with a woman with no sense of humour.

On the reasonable assumption that everyone else was doing it, I knocked a couple of years off my age. I was getting a bit close to sixty and, however young I thought I looked and however irrelevant I hoped it might be to the woman with whom I would share an overwhelming sexual charisma, the fact remained that sixty might have been the new forty but it was still too old to be pretending I was twenty-three again. I made this shocking discovery when I put myself in the position of the woman on the other side looking at my profile (don't forget no photograph was available) and seeing my proximity to sixty years would surely delete me into the recycling bin of history.

Of course like most men I was looking for a woman younger than I was, possibly by up to ten years or so. Glancing through the photographs of the women displayed on these websites I could not avoid the conclusion that the women whose faces I found attractive were aged pretty much in their late forties and early fifties. I wasn't particularly proud of the fact that I was joining the ranks of all those men who constantly sought regeneration in the charms of younger women, even though I was comforted by the fact that, as I remembered my adolescent reading of the Old Testament, King David had been subject to similar tendencies. Even when he was very old, the wise Elders of the Kingdom of Judea were helpfully guiding attractive young women into his bed. As far as I could remember, my synagogue, the Prestwich Hebrew Congregation, did not offer this same service, which was a shame because it might have increased their membership subscriptions rapidly, particularly in the 14–19 age group.

At Maureen's birthday party I began a conversation with a very beautiful woman in an elegant white trouser suit. As we talked it became clear she was or maybe had been an actress, which allowed me to start asking questions about previous productions which would enable me to work out how old she was. As the conversation progressed I became very excited to realise that she was about sixty-one or sixty-two. I was thrilled. Not only did I find this woman very attractive but she was certainly older than I was by a few years and still, to my inordinate pride, I was interested in her. How about that for selfless behaviour? I realised that in the circumstances this extraordinarily attractive woman almost certainly had a husband in tow and was probably not circulating the room looking for chance encounters but I was still sufficiently intrigued to inquire of Maureen the identity of the woman who had so spectacularly caught my attention.

Maureen confirmed that the woman in question was married to the well-known theatrical impresario Duncan Weldon which came as no surprise. The man clearly had good taste. I asked whether the woman had indeed been an actress. 'That,' smiled Maureen broadly, 'was Ann Sidney. She used to be Miss World.' Of course she was. She was Miss World in 1964, the year when Ann Packer won the gold medal in the 800 metres at the Tokyo Olympics. She was Miss World in 1964 when everyone watched the Miss World competition on television and felt no shame or self-loathing. She was Miss World in 1964 when I was fifteen years old and shame and self-loathing were fairly constant companions. I slunk away into the Mayfair daylight. It now transpired that, despite the fact I was myself approaching sixty at a speed usually seen on an Italian autostrada, any woman over the age of sixty to whom I was prepared to offer a second glance had to be at the very least a former Miss World.

Around this time I was of the opinion that I would marry again. I was the marrying kind and I have always been profoundly respectful of the domestic virtues. The appeal of bachelorhood struck me as being of limited emotional satisfaction, although there was one time when I was lying in bed late on a Sunday night and watching cricket in Australia on one channel and switching between balls to the Superbowl on another channel when I marvelled both at the miracle of modern technology on the one hand and the realisation that I would probably not be permitted to do this if a recumbent female form were lying next to me. Having a woman back in my life on a full-time basis would mean a return to watching cricket from Australia in the middle of the night lying on the couch downstairs and covered by an inadequate blanket. This chivalry might appeal to the woman I was looking for, but I knew perfectly well that an obsession with stacking the dishwasher properly which I shared with Jack (and, I was later to learn in a shock *News of the World* revelation, with Sven-Göran Eriksson) was probably not something a woman wanted to be confronted with immediately. I thought perhaps I should lead up to this announcement on the third or fourth date.

The other conviction I held back in 2007 was that the woman I ended up marrying would be Jewish. It wasn't that I was specifically demanding that any woman I dated had to be Jewish, I just had this feeling that after thirty years with a blonde California *schickse* there would be a sort of perverse logic in choosing a nice dark-haired Jewish girl probably from Hampstead Garden Suburb with a shared interest in Jackie Mason and chicken soup with *kneidlach*. My daughter, the fount of all knowledge in this area, encouraged me to join a Jewish dating agency called, with admirable bluntness, JDate. I decided to change the approach from outright surreal comedy to a suggestion of humour carefully tailored to appeal to the Jewish appreciation of culture. Now I called myself *Nonpiuandrai*, after the aria sung by the eponymous servant at the end of the first act of Mozart's opera *The Marriage of Figaro* (which aroused no comment or recognition whatsoever), and I described myself extremely accurately with sufficient obsessions to discourage the puzzled and intrigue the companionable:

> As Michael Palin might say in the Spanish Inquisition sketch, 'Among my passions are: music (passionate 1760–1830), books, theatre, movies (passionate European & American cinema 1925–69), cricket, football, tennis, golf (all active), fell walking in the Lake District, concerts in Salzburg and Vienna, British and American history and politics, Central European culture, the sight of a beautiful woman, the presence of a loving woman, the touch and proximity of a sweet-smelling woman who is both beautiful and loving, comedy (passionate about American Jewish comedy) and the taste of chopped liver on a fresh bagel.' Enough already.

As for the question about the location of a first date I thought I might add a little observational humour:

> I apologise in advance for suggesting the most conventional if practical of evenings. In other words a film, play or concert where there is a chance to sit sideways on to the other person and take odd squints at her with the occasional sniff to discover whether or not I am allergic to her perfume. A pleasant dinner out would be fine but sitting sideways in a restaurant might look rather odd.

I sense a feeling of irritation creeping in when I am asked about my ideal relationship:

> One that is deeply unsupportive, profoundly cynical, probably with a lot of spousal abuse and financial fraud.

There seemed to be an awful lot of women on this site whom I dismissed as likely to spend too much time at the Brent Cross shopping mall. Lynn had travelled from St Albans (where we were living when the children were born) to Brent Cross precisely to get a feel of Southern California retail therapy but I felt that I didn't want that any more.

I knew that I had found Lynn's blonde, California, sun-bleached looks particularly attractive not just because she was so beautiful but because it was so far removed from what had been on offer when I was growing up in virginal seclusion in Prestwich, north Manchester. Even as an adolescent I knew that my life would not be bounded by the city limits of Manchester and the chances therefore were great that I would find my life partner elsewhere. Manchester was too parochial and the Jewish girls of my early acquaintance did not fit in with my dreams of the exotic or more accurately the dreams that were shaped by exposure to too many Hollywood films where the stars I lusted after – Ginger Rogers in her Fred Astaire days being the most enduring – were almost invariably blonde, American and Gentile. I thought that at fifty-eight I would no longer be subject to those adolescent fantasies and that I would be comforted by acceptance back into the bosom of Jewish family life. It was one of many illusions with which I comforted myself. I remembered a notorious, presumably comic, list of Jewish singles that did the rounds on the internet. One that stuck in my mind was:

> Female graduate student, studying kaballah, Zohar, exorcism of dybbuks, seeks mensch. No weirdos, please.

I decided not to apply for that one, nor to advertise myself as somebody did thus:

> Torah Scholar, long black coat, black hat, long sidecurls, thick glasses. Seeks similar in woman.

I did find someone on the site but it was quickly apparent that we were destined to become friends and not lovers. In fact, as a general observation, nearly all the women I met on these dating sites, the ones who survived the first meeting that is, were women with whom I could easily envisage a lasting friendship if not an enduring romance. At one point, I began successively to see three or four Jewish women, mostly because of that insistent feeling that the next wife was going to be Jewish and if she were going to be Jewish the best place to start looking for her was on a Jewish dating website. It took me nearly a year to discover the blindingly obvious fact that being Jewish was not anything like the most important quality that the woman I was going to fall in love with would possess. I was adopting a very scientific, rather academic, approach to the search when what I was really hoping for was another chance to fall in love. Friendships could work on the basis of shared interests. Romance, particularly a romance that endured (otherwise it was simply a refusal to acknowledge lust for what it was), would find me if it was going to survive as I hoped it would.

The point of the search was to find the enduring romance and it quickly became evident in the initial sparring that followed those many first meetings that, however desperate I was to find someone to fill the emotional void in my life as fast as possible, most times I knew it wasn't going to work within minutes of that first meeting. I would try to convince myself that whoever I was meeting was going to be The One but there remained a little voice inside my head saying, 'It's not right and you know it.' I would counter this irritating Jiminy Cricket who sang 'Always Let Your Conscience Be Your Guide' as a constant refrain by doing my damnedest to ignore him. However, being a smallish chap, even wearing a top hat and carrying a rolled umbrella, he managed to insinuate himself past all those defences and into my brain.

I did not feel my checklist of desirable attributes was either too long or too unreasonable. I wanted a woman who was sweet-tempered and kind, a woman with whom I could create a domestic environment that would nurture me, a woman who would accept and like my grown-up children who remain such a significant part of me. At the same time, she had to be attractive enough to satisfy my vanity and desires, and bright enough to enjoy the intellectual banter that would inevitably form part of much of our conversations. I was offering a bruised, vulnerable heart, a body starting to accept the fact that it was shortly to start its seventh decade on earth and a professional mind that had been suffering a slump in its recent exploits.

On the other hand, I had achieved some significant targets prior to the slump; I had an active, inquiring, challenging mind which shouted at the screen during *University Challenge* and I continued to plough on relentlessly on my exercise bike, tramp across Hampstead Heath and, in short, try every physical means possible, with the exception of curtailing my intake of chocolate, to defy the ravages of time with what I considered estimable fortitude. In other words, I admired myself inordinately while at the same time being too frightened to leave the house. A winning combination, I think you'll admit. Alone in the bathroom I was a fearsome sight. Arriving at the restaurant I was as confident as Bernardo Corradi or Georgios Samaras in front of an open goal.

Drama has always revolved around conflicts over money and sex. The difficulties aroused in human relationships by these two elements can be found in plays back to the time of the Greeks and stories back to the times of the Bible. We can disguise them but we can't ignore them. I was amused by the woman who wrote on her profile that she was looking for 'a man without baggage'. Presumably what she meant was that she was looking for a man without a personality, since our baggage, so-called, is the sum total of who we are. Returning to the dating pitch in the 2007–8 season, I knew I was being waved on while carrying so much baggage I'd have to leave it in the net behind the goalkeeper otherwise I could scarcely run.

I was no longer the callow youth of twenty-three I had been when I had met Lynn. Although we had our disagreements, as all married couples do, we almost never argued about money. I didn't want to start a new relationship by comparing bank statements but I didn't want this new relationship to be the cause of denying myself the supreme satisfaction of handing on to my children the fruits of my years of labour. Women considerably richer than I was would have caused a similar problem because I could see myself sitting at the back of the plane next to the toilet while my inamorata was ordering champagne in first class. I also knew that I would inevitably end up staring at the meter ticking away on the taxi, hearing my parents shouting at me from beyond the grave. I needed someone of reasonably comparable financial status.

Sex was even more problematic and it reflected the confusion in which I existed. I might have lived through the most sexually liberated years in modern history but I was born at a particular point in history when morals were loosening, even if it was only apparent at one remove in place and time. Despite being younger than Larkin I shared his sorrow that he had been born too late for sexual intercourse, which he alleged began in 1963, the year I always recall for City being relegated from Division One, JFK's assassination and the Profumo Affair. The latter two, of course, had a wider impact on Western society but, from a personal point of view, being relegated after a 6–1 defeat at West Ham was by far the most profound experience. The girls I met in my adolescence were less affected by the sixties in which we lived than the fifties in which we had grown up. Sunday colour supplements told us that there was sex happening all over the place but I never saw much evidence of it in north Manchester. Not when I was around, anyway. Maybe they all waited till I left the room.

Maybe it all happened in the following decade when 'nice girls' saw sex and the freedom offered by the pill as sound reasons to enjoy themselves. In the 1960s it was all too new and the sort of girls I met were still influenced by the equation drummed into them by their mothers that sex = marriage. When I was at university as an undergraduate at the end of the decade, living away from home for the first time, there were ten men for every one woman. The fact that I found a girlfriend with whom I had a brief but intense relationship was a source of major satisfaction both emotionally and physically. It ended in disaster and merely re-emphasised that novels like *Tess of the D'Urbervilles* and *Saturday Night and Sunday Morning*, which told of tragic consequences following hard upon the feelings of sexual pleasure, were realistic transcriptions of life rather than works of the imagination.

I rebounded from one website to another, taking in *The Guardian* and *The Times* as I veered from wanting a woman who voted as I did, to wanting a woman who brushed her hair in the morning. Much as I tried to avoid judging my correspondents too harshly and too early, in the end it was clear to me that if they weren't articulate, it was never going to happen. I had noticed a tendency in myself to become intolerant of poor grammar in a way I hadn't when I was younger, which I suspect is not uncommon. My son, who is one of the brightest people I know, doesn't like this tendency because he is dyslexic and has fought hard all his life to triumph over this adversity. My complaint wasn't about spelling *per se*, it was about an ability to express oneself in writing. You expected people after a while to lie in the manner of someone 'improving' a CV, so what became important, beyond what they actually wrote about themselves and what they were looking for, was the way in which they wrote it. I never had cause to doubt a decision not to carry on writing to someone when I detected something in their emails which caused concern. The times I came unstuck tended to be when I made decisions to proceed simply because the woman had a pretty face.

Over the course of three years from 2007 to 2010 I launched a number of relationships which developed faults immediately after take-off, keeled over and disappeared into the sea. It was extremely frustrating to bounce from pillar to post in my search for emotional intimacy with the ideal partner, for ever seeking that perfect combination of intellect, sensitivity and a desirable figure. As each mission failed I began to lose even more of the small amount of confidence with which I had started. Was it me? Was it them? Was I doing something wrong? Was I too forward or too passive? Was I too old? Was I too demanding? Did I disappoint them more than they disappointed me?

I did not go looking for what I was now thinking might turn out to be nothing more than a figment of my imagination with quite the zeal that Manchester City displayed in their search for a new owner. John Wardle, the chairman, was like so many other rich local businessmen who in previous years had managed to sustain their local football clubs out of a mixture of civic pride and personal ambition. He couldn't now give his manager anything like the amount of money necessary to compete in the marketplace with the clubs who won the trophies. Wealth, pure cash reserves derived from whatever source was available, was virtually the sole determinant of success and local millionaires were being replaced by foreign billionaires as British sport, particularly football, aped much of American sport, particularly American football. During the late, unlamented 2006–7 season, Manchester City could be seen lifting her skirt like a nineteenth-century street-walker looking for a quick time with any gentleman in a cutaway coat and a top hat with half a crown in his pocket, a raging lust and no fear of the clap. Increasingly desperate to unload themselves into the arms of the first taker, the best they could find turned out to be a man with a dubious financial history and a human rights record that should have given both the sellers and the supporters far more pause for thought than it did.

It was reported that Manchester City passed into the hands of Thaksin Shinawatra, the former prime minister of Thailand, for a sum said to be £81.6 million. I can certainly attest to the £32 that was my share of the loot, having had my shares compulsorily purchased. I was surprised that the sale had been so difficult considering the ground, the fan base and the fact that we hadn't been relegated since 2001. I always felt that we were a sleeping giant and I found it incomprehensible that we were finally knocked down to a man whose name had become a byword for disreputable behaviour. All the mistakes of the past in terms of buying players, appointing the wrong managers, suffering under the egotistical ineptitude of Peter Swales for twenty years, were as nothing compared to what had now happened. We weren't Manchester City any longer. We had been taken off the market and we were now just a possession owned by a man who knew not Bill Leivers nor had watched the traumatic 2–0 defeat at Shrewsbury in 1979 under the Second Coming of Malcolm Allison.

Oddly, nobody cared. I would like to think in retrospect that I was uncomfortable right from the start of the Thai ownership but honesty compels me to admit that it took me some weeks before I realised the true nature of this new owner. At first I was simply disconcerted because the club was no longer in the hands of someone who had grown up in Manchester, knew the traditions of Manchester City and understood what it was to be a Manchester City supporter. This wasn't blind xenophobia. Shinawatra had previously tried unsuccessfully to buy Fulham and Liverpool, whose board had given him short shrift in those far-off days when the Liverpool board still commanded respect. I did not think that Shinawatra had any real interest in Manchester City. His interest was Thailand and what he wanted was a football club, quite frankly *any* football club, that could be exploited to further his ambitions in Thailand, from where he had fled charges of financial malfeasance.

I knew we couldn't continue in 2007–8 the way we had miserably finished 2006–7 but Shinawatra was not the sort of owner who should have been welcomed with open arms. At first I expected some suspicion to be manifested. After all, this was a major step for the club and its supporters and shouldn't supporters go through some version of due diligence of their own? We were handing our precious club over to a man whose history we did not know in detail but whose reputation was certainly not that of the much sought after White Knight. Unfortunately, Shinawatra did not get the forensic examination he should have received. Instead, the red carpet was rolled out for him. It was palpably obvious that few knew this man's history. If they did, they certainly didn't care about it and indeed why should they when the famous former

England manager and sex god Sven-Göran Eriksson was appointed to manage the club in succession to Stuart Pearce? Eriksson predictably brought with him his assistant known as Tord Grip, a name which to me always sounded like some kind of sealant for putting round the bath and which could be bought at Ikea.

My first thought was that Sven was facing his ultimate humiliation. Desperate to get back into the game after his high-profile, high-salaried pay-off from England and having already smilingly dismissed on television the idea of managing Manchester City, he had finally accepted the poisoned chalice that had frightened off the more sensitive candidates. Whom the gods would destroy they first make the manager of Manchester City. The visceral hatred that Sven-Göran Eriksson had evoked in much of the country through his apparent greed and quarter-final defeats was about to find its supreme expression. The Swede with the roving eye and the famously laid-back temperament seemed set-up to receive a punitive sentence of such soul-destroying cruelty that even Judge Jeffreys would have thought twice before delivering it. Steve Coppell, Phil Neal, Mel Machin and Frank Clark must have been captivated by this new successor. For them and certainly for me, the prospect arose of Sven losing his Grip and being chased down the M6 by an angry mob carrying pitchforks and icons of Colin Bell and Mike Summerbee.

In the event and to my surprise, Eriksson, who had been out of the game for a year, had an impressive Filofax of telephone numbers, which included not just the women with whom he was invariably being associated in the tabloids. In the first few weeks of his managerial regime he secured the services of Rolando Bianchi, Martin Petrov, Valeri Bojinov, Gelson Fernandes, Vedran Ćorluka, Javier Garrido and Geovanni and Elano, who being Brazilian had no need of first names. We hadn't heard of many of them before they showed up but we were dazzled initially by the quantity rather than the quality of the new signings. You couldn't go to the toilet without coming back to discover City had signed some unknown Croatian.

I did wonder whether this was real money he was using rather than a series of HP agreements but to speculate in this fashion publicly seemed churlish in the face of the renewal of optimism that I welcomed. My initial response to the arrival of Dr Thaksin Shinawatra was one of suspicion and caution and it took me a few weeks to find out for myself quite what a loathsome individual he was reputed to be. Certainly, I was never going to be queuing up outside his surgery but Sven seemed so happy and initial results were so promising I decided initially to swallow any anxieties. As in the dating game, I thought perhaps it was all my fault that I didn't particularly care for the new owner whom nearly everyone else seemed to welcome with open arms. If, by Christmas, it all started going wrong, I could rely on the City crowd to chase the Swedes away with those pitchforks. In which case, maybe the Thais, not being of this parish, would not have the bloodyminded-ness of Peter Swales and hang on despite the hostility. I am ashamed to say I waited too long for others to indicate their dissatisfaction. I am not proud of myself for failing to take a public stand against the Thai invasion the moment it happened but I suppose I wanted to see how long the miraculous start to the season could be sustained.

An impressive 2–0 win away at Upton Park was followed in the next few days by two 1–0 home victories, the first against Derby County and the second a somewhat fortuitous but no-less-welcome triumph over Manchester United, courtesy of a goal scored by Geovanni, who might have been known to his mates as 'Don' but I suspect wasn't. Within eight days of the start of the season we were top of the table with maximum points and an eagerly prized derby victory. For the next two months, City maintained a position in the Champions League places so it was never going to be possible to tell fans that the club was now in the hands of a man who was on the Most Wanted List published by Amnesty International. When I learned that piece of news my attitude towards the club's new owner began to harden into one of implacable opposition, but the idea that anybody could tell fans whose club was suddenly successful and whose message boards were full of the words 'fairy tale' that really they would be better off returning to the miseries of the past few seasons was patently absurd. The fans would never listen.

Halfway through the 2007–8 season, my moral reservations about this man who had simply bought my club and made it his own property were starting to cause me considerable anxiety. I concluded that if anyone at all, however morally suspect, had arrived promising to deliver everything that football supporters ever wanted, not too many of them would be clearing their throats and wondering whether the compromise required was truly worth the winning of a trophy. The desire for success in football is so overwhelming that common sense and any kind of moral sensibility has long since departed.

Meanwhile the men who were supposedly charged with ensuring the probity of Premiership football culpably abrogated their responsibilities. In a sense, the real blame for the way the Premier League has become a vehicle for rich men to satiate their personal desires belongs to Scudamore and his gang. These people who were supposed to stand as guardians of the health of the game simply stood aside and waved men like Shinawatra, Abramovich and those heroes of Anfield Road, Hicks and Gillett, through to the top table, elegantly laid with crisp white linen and expensive silverware. Indeed, to extend the metaphor, it was almost as if they also pulled back the chairs and spread the napkins across the laps of these interlopers.

We had all heard of the 'fit and proper person' test which was designed to filter out those potential owners whom the Premier League considered to be unsuitable. This test must have been based on the scene in *Life of Brian* when Graham Chapman, the eponymous Brian Cohen, is selling half-time refreshments at the sparsely attended Gladiator Games and realises his customers are the People's Front of Judea, a terrorist gang he longs to join. John Cleese curls his lip in the way that only John Cleese can and dismisses his application scornfully. 'Listen, if you want to join the PFJ you have to *really* hate the Romans.' 'I do,' says Brian earnestly. 'How much?' 'A lot.' 'Right,' pronounces Cleese, 'you're in.' Presumably the Scudamore interrogation of Thaksin Shinawatra was conducted along similarly forensic lines.

The Premier League always seemed to me to have been designed to make greedy men richer but many of us disempowered supporters clung on to the hope that someone somewhere might have looked at all the snouts that had shoved their way into the same trough, and stopped and thought about the higher interests and values of the game. Possibly Sir Dave Richards, the august chairman of this distinguished body, intended to perform this highly moral and necessary act when, in a speech at a hotel in Qatar in March 2012, he accused FIFA and UEFA of 'stealing' the game of football from the English who had invented it. It seems unlikely, however, that the contentious historical argument was significantly validated when Sir Dave followed it by stumbling into the hotel's water fountain from which he was fished out by Phil Gartside, the chairman of Bolton Wanderers. This pratfall, which gave such pleasure to so many people all over the world, seemed to sum up the refined elegance of the Premier League. Not that the comically inept Richards was alone in his myopic buffoonery. Any pretence my club might once have maintained to rise above the unedifying spectacle presented to the rest of the world by the selfishness of the Premier League had disappeared for ever.

There were honourable exceptions. Simon Hattenstone in *The Guardian* and an old acquaintance Bill Borrows who founded *Blue Print*, one of the first City fanzines and who was now writing for *Esquire*, both made admirable statements expressing their disgust at what had happened to the club, but they were as voices crying in the wilderness. United supporters had put up a far better show of resistance when the Glazers bought their club but, such had been the misery in which City supporters had wallowed for so long, they had no resistance left in them. If this man were prepared to take over the debt-ridden club, inject funds, buy players, hire a top manager and generally perform CPR on a rapidly dying organisation, then those of us who had strong doubts were powerless to intercede.

Thaksin Shinawatra became known fondly as Frank Sinatra and jolly good fellow that he was, he let it be known that he could take this kindly ribbing in good heart. It might have been the case that this jollity wasn't shared in Thailand. The human rights group Human Rights Watch alerted the Premier League to allegations that, during his time as prime minister, Thaksin caused to be killed large numbers of his own citizens using the war on drugs as a cover for his murderous intentions. But who cares? The village idiot who posted his mundane and predictable thoughts on City's internet newsletter began one of his match reports 'It was good to see Frank back on Saturday' after the owner had been absent from the ground with better things to do for a few months. Fortunately, someone wrote fiercely in the following issue 'In what sense was it "good" to see Frank back?' and proceeded to let other fans know that he, too, had strong reservations about Shinawatra. It didn't bother the village idiot and the rest of them as they joined in the happy birthday tributes to the King of Siam. It would have been better if they'd launched into the sing-along version of Rodgers and Hammerstein's *The King and I*. At least we'd have listened to a decent musical score. As far as 99.6% of the crowd were concerned, though, what really mattered now was that we had Elano, whose Brazilian skills immediately placed him in a select group alongside Georgi Kinkladze and Ali Benarbia. A photograph appeared on the web of the statue of Christ on the hill overlooking Rio de Janeiro. It was clad in a City shirt with the name Elano on the back. Frank couldn't possibly be a murderous dictator with an appalling record in human rights abuse. He was a genius.

They couldn't see it, they really couldn't. On the City website the new owner (how I had already come to hate that word) now declared openly:

> I will do my best to make Manchester City a global brand which in the future will also incorporate Thai products.

You couldn't fault him for honesty in this regard but it ran counter to everything I believed in. Manchester City belongs to Manchester. If football fans in other countries want to look favourably upon us that is very gratifying but it is about as relevant as my telling you, quite truthfully, that I like going to concerts in Vienna so I always support Rapid Vienna in any European competition in which they appear. I do not expect any Rapid Vienna supporters to be much impressed by my so-called support of their club. In any case what exactly were these Thai products our new owner was promising? Were the bars at the City of Manchester Stadium to cancel their orders for Thwaites and Boddingtons and serve nothing but satho, a traditional rice wine from the Isan region? Or were the pies to be replaced by that well-known Lancashire favourite tom yam kung nam khon? Then the names of Thai players started appearing on the club's website. I would have thought that Sven would not have been thrilled that he was now also expected to be the unpaid part-time manager of the Thailand youth team, but the Swede's legendary smile and willingness to keep his well-paid job until he was offered another even-better-paid job was not going to prompt him to make any public refusal. Outside of food and drink and young players I wondered what other 'Thai products' this pernicious owner intended to foist on us.

Thaksin Shinawatra might have wanted Manchester City to become a global brand but I certainly didn't. The reason I supported Manchester City was I was born in Manchester and it was my local team. I was fortunate that I was born in a big city and I have always been delighted that I was born and raised as a Mancunian and that my cricket and football teams played their home games a short bus ride or a long walk away from where I lived. I did not want to feel that the principal object of my club was to tart herself up so that she could attract 'supporters' who could watch City matches on their mobile phones while walking down Kuala Lumpur High Street. This is the sort of stupidity for which Manchester United had been rightly pilloried. I did not want to see photographs of people in Beijing and Uttar Pradesh wearing City replica shirts and grinning at the camera. It was, however, the stated purpose of the club's owner and, to their everlasting shame, seemingly also the principal interest of Scudamore and his wretched cabal who should have been protecting English football against exactly these sort of rapacious robber barons.

I think this was the starting point for the disillusion that was to gather pace over the next few years. I had always been a

Manchester City fan. I had always found in Manchester City fans elements of humour and self-awareness which I greatly admired. I had revelled in their disparagement of Manchester United and its global obsessions. We were different. We lived in the real world. Unlike United supporters we knew that you sang 'Always Look on the Bright Side of Life' ironically when you were losing at home to Everton, not when you were winning. As a football club our recent results didn't match up with those of United, of course, but as supporters, as people, we were better than they were because we knew what life was about. We'd stared into the abyss and survived and we knew that what mattered was being us, being sure of our identity which would never change, whatever the vicissitudes surrounding the club on and off the pitch. Then along came Frank and a few new players and all my long-cherished ideals about City and its supporters started to fade. The hard truth was that we were no better than anyone else. We were just like the rest. It was shattering but it was true.

Chapter Twelve

THE PAIN THAT ACCOMPANIED THE REALISATION THAT MY club was changing in ways that not only was I powerless to resist (I had never been anything else) but of which I morally disapproved was partially assuaged when I started work on my fourth and what I had supposed at the time would be my last book on Manchester City. I had already written a book on my time as a young fan in the 1960s (*Manchester United Ruined My Life*), the next being a biography of the Summerbee family (*Fathers, Sons and Football*). The last, which sold the fewest copies but which received the best reviews, was the story of the boys who had played in the two legs of the 1964 FA Youth Cup semi-final between City and United and the men those players subsequently became (*George Best and 21 Others*).

I had recently read *The Damned Utd* by David Peace, his account of Brian Clough's forty-four days in charge of Leeds United in 1974. The irony was that although I usually squirm at historical inaccuracies in books, such was the compelling narrative power of Peace's writing, it never bothered me when I read *The Damned Utd*, though, rather perversely, it did when I saw the film that was eventually made of it. The portrait of an alcoholic Brian Clough which runs through the novel's sections set in Leeds is contrasted with the bright young enthusiastic man who, in partnership with

Peter Taylor, transformed first Hartlepool United and then Derby County. The fact is, as we can see quite plainly from the famous television interviews Clough gave to Yorkshire Television with Don Revie and shortly afterwards to Michael Parkinson on his eponymous chat show, he was nothing like the broken-down figure of David Peace's imagination. Those television programmes reveal a Clough in his late thirties, bright-eyed, self-confident and charming, far removed from the drink-sodden depressive on the edge of a breakdown who was depicted in the novel.

However, Peace's inaccurate portrayal of his leading character did not in any way affect my enjoyment of his book. As soon as I had finished reading it for the first time I started again at the beginning. Not many novels have caused that reaction in me. The idea that one could write football history in the form of a novel with all the freedom that the genre affords the novelist was intoxicating. I had already written one non-fiction novel, so I hoped, in the wake of the triumph of Peace, that I could interest a publisher in the story of Joe Mercer and Malcolm Allison to be written in similar fashion, particularly as I had been afforded a ringside seat when the two City managers spectacularly fell out with each other. They had been the best of friends for five successful seasons but in the end Malcolm's ambition and Joe's refusal to compromise led to the irretrievable breakdown of their relationship. I called the book that eventually appeared in 2009 *The Worst of Friends*.

I was always a 'Joe man' and had regarded Malcolm's over-weening ambition as one of the prime causes of City's decline (as well, of course, as their spectacular rise as soon as he took charge of the coaching), so I expected the research I would do in and around the club would confirm my prejudices. In fact, it did the reverse. In the early months of the 1971–2 season when Joe had given me permission to train with the first team squad and generally stick my nose into most areas of the club's operations, Malcolm, perhaps understandably, had seen me as a spy sent from Joe's headquarters. His treatment of me was brusque and unsympathetic to the point of rudeness. This inevitably coloured my perception of the two men and the way power was distributed at the club. It was therefore to my surprise that, on deeper examination, Malcolm turned out to be a much more sympathetic character than I had suspected. Writing about Malcolm and his excesses gave me a much more tolerant view of his activities and made me understand why he had despaired of Joe ever fulfilling his promise to let him have full running of the club.

The research took me back to the club I had been in love with for so long. I spoke to many of the key figures who had been around in the Mercer/Allison era including Eric Alexander, the chairman and Bernard Halford who had taken over as secretary from the old-school, unbending figure of Walter Griffiths who had certainly been a Joe man rather than a Malcolm man during Malcolm's brief, unhappy first spell as manager. It was also a pleasure to reminisce with Peter Gardner who had been the *Manchester Evening News*'s indefatigable City reporter since 1965, Sidney Rose the distinguished surgeon who had been appointed a director of the club in that same year and who was still going strong in his nineties, and Ian Niven who had fought his battles with Peter Swales over the course of his time as a director. All of these men had given years of service to Manchester City and their affection for the club was as deep and as sincere as my own. Talking to them made me feel what a small tight family Manchester City had been and how attractive that was compared to what confronted us today. Many of them had made their peace with what had happened. It frustrated me that I couldn't join them.

Nevertheless, I thoroughly enjoyed researching and writing *The Worst of Friends*. I knew that era, the 1960s and 1970s, so well because I'd lived through it. Looking at photographs and television programmes from the time I was struck not so much by the old-fashioned nature of the filming but the picture of Manchester that they revealed. Manchester wasn't the thrusting dynamic cool city of recent years, of course, but I remembered it as vital and progressive. I was wrong. Manchester in that era was still displaying in those grainy images the last remnants of Cottonopolis, the soot-blackened buildings, the predominance of an urban poverty that had vanished. It was useful to have those images and the contrast with what was to follow as a parallel to the way the two men saw the world and the way they were perceived.

Joe Mercer and his contemporaries, particularly the board of directors he found at Manchester City when he arrived in 1965, belonged in a way to the 1930s, when Malcolm Allison was still in primary school, when the world had been a drab black-and-white affair. Maybe that was why they felt so comfortable with Joe Mercer. They had seen him play before the war, and they had seen him continue his career into his fortieth year, a veteran in the early 1950s. Malcolm belonged to now – to a world of pop music and champagne and nightclubs, to a world of flowered ties and girls in miniskirts with long straight hair, to a world of television and advertising, to a world suffused in bold primary colours. That was my world, too, and maybe I was now the Joe Mercer and Thaksin Shinawatra and his like were the new Malcolm Allisons?

I knew that both men, for all their contrasting ways, would have taken jobs under Shinawatra or Abramovich had they been offered them. Mercer and Allison were men I had admired inordinately yet I was quite sure that Allison would have hung on to his job at all costs and would probably have had exactly the same battles with Shinawatra as he had with Swales. He would have wanted the money to spend on the players he coveted and he would have done whatever was necessary to ensure that when Saturday afternoon came he had those players at his disposal. It was the certainty of this knowledge that prompted the writing of my favourite part of the book.

It was, after all, a novel. I was making up dialogue which readers knew was my own invention, just as Peace had. Allison was on a tour of North America with his championship-winning side in June 1968 when he disappeared for a few days. That much I could factually confirm. It was not a great surprise to anyone. Allison made a habit of disappearing; once, famously, telling his then wife that he was just going to the chip shop down the road and not coming back until the next day, having obviously found *en route* a diversion more attractive than a bag of chips.

In Atlanta, where City played a match, I decided that he would go off with the very attractive wife of the owner of a radio station. Allison had enormous physical charisma and it wasn't difficult to believe the chip shop anecdote, so I led him into the bedroom of this attractive woman and let them get down to business. The woman is besotted with the charms of the Manchester City coach, unhappy in her marriage and on the verge of a divorce and a consequently large financial settlement. She offers some of it to Malcolm in an attempt to keep him in Atlanta and adds a further incentive by dropping to her knees in front of him and 'performing' as they always say in prurient tabloid journalism to my amusement 'an unnatural act'. It always calls to mind Woody Allen's response to Diane Keaton in the brilliant science fiction comedy *Sleeper* when she asks if he wants to perform a similar act on her. 'I don't think I'm up to a performance,' responds Woody with typical comic self-deprecation, 'but I might manage a rehearsal.' Anyway,

Malcolm's mind races as the woman consumes him. With the sort of money this woman is talking about, he thinks, he could buy Wyn Davies from Newcastle United because Francis Lee who had played with the Welsh centre-forward at Bolton was always telling him how well they would work together at City.

That struck me as the perfect example of what you could do in a non-fiction novel that you couldn't possibly do in a sober biography which demanded adherence to very strict rules of historical accuracy. Given Allison's character it seemed entirely consistent with his behaviour patterns and illustrated that even at moments of supreme physical ecstasy the thought of a transfer deal or a change of attacking formation was never far away for a true football man. It therefore depressed me when I was rung up by a friendly journalist who was reviewing the book who told me that he simply could not get his head round the fact that this was a novel and not a normal sports book. The conversation that followed reminded me of the delicious story Michael Parkinson has told of his early football match reports in his home town local paper when his somewhat arcane reference to F. Scott Fitzgerald was replaced in the final edition by Scott of the Antarctic. When he asked why, he was informed brusquely that in Barnsley nobody had ever heard of Scott Fitzgerald but they'd all heard of Scott of the Antarctic, particularly as the film of the same name starring John Mills had been recently released.

Working on *The Worst of Friends* restored some of my feelings for City, although the nature of the ownership of my club still caused me sleepless nights. On the pitch there was one famous victory in the second half of a season that in the end brought little but disappointment. It was presumably a computer rather than an individual with a sense of mischief that sent City to Old Trafford on the weekend of the fiftieth anniversary of the Munich air disaster. The build-up to the game was almost entirely focused on whether the 3,000 City supporters who had acquired tickets for the game would behave themselves during the one minute of silence that would precede the kick-off. In the event not only did the supporters distinguish themselves by their restraint and decorum to my enormous relief but the team actually won at Old Trafford for the first time since that blessed day in April 1974 when Denis Law had back-heeled United into the Second Division.

I did not realise it at the time but I had already watched my last Premier League City match live. If I had, I might have chosen something other than a rather mundane 2–1 defeat by Tottenham Hotspur at White Hart Lane with which to depart the scene. It was certainly getting harder and harder for me to arouse the enthusiasm to open my wallet and hand over a lot of money to an owner I thoroughly despised. I know I was supposed to think that the owner was irrelevant and that my support for the team was such that I should have been able to put my anxieties to one side. I agreed. I should have done – but I couldn't even though I rose to my feet to acclaim the third of the four goals that Rolando Bianchi scored for the club. This was a magnificent thumping header from a corner that brought to mind Dave Watson's last-minute winner against Ipswich thirty years before that was still fresh in the memory. Bianchi, who had been signed for £9 million during the summer influx, was shortly afterwards loaned back to Lazio for whom he was sent off in the first five minutes of his first match, thereby maintaining a consistent record of City players getting sent off in such circumstances. At White Hart Lane, Bianchi's equaliser was followed twenty minutes later by Stephen Ireland being sent off and Defoe winning the game for Spurs to leave me with that familiar sensation of not greatly enjoying life. There was a certain amount of ill luck in that the first goal was palpably both handball and offside, but dear Mark Halsey was in no mood for confirming his position as my favourite referee that day.

The derby win at Old Trafford was pretty much the only memorable moment in the last three months of the season. We could, of course, count the last match, away at Middlesbrough, which we contrived to lose 8–1 as memorable but for all the wrong reasons. However, objectively one would have to admit that based on what had preceded it, 2007–8 was a reasonable season. We were never in danger of relegation, we beat United twice, even though they went on to win the Premier League, and we had signed a lot of new players which tends to keep supporters relatively content. It was clear, however, from the rumours leaking out of Eastlands well before the end of the season that Sven was indeed losing his Grip. Strangely it was one of the first times I can remember that the manager's position was threatened by his employer before it was threatened by his club's supporters.

Contrary to my belief twelve months earlier, Sven's insecure tenancy was not going to result in his being chased down the M6 by fans carrying pitchforks. His problem was that the owner fancied the idea of running the club himself. It was like watching the young Charles Foster Kane taking over the *New York Inquirer* against the advice of Mr (rather than Mrs) Thatcher, his childhood guardian and early financial adviser, and declaring, 'I think it would be fun to run a newspaper!' Mr Thatcher counsels against it, rather as one supposes Sven would have done to Kane. Shinawatra, like Kane, was not to be thwarted by mere sensible advice. He had been humiliated by the 8–1 defeat in an Oriental loss of face sort of way, and not in a Mancunian way, which involves banging doors, kicking domestic pets, shouting at the children and insulting the wife's new hair-do. Oh and a fair amount of Boddingtons and Thwaites bitter.

Instead, Shinawatra dug up the Swedes and tossed them out of Manchester, hiring in their place Mark Hughes and his Welsh mafia. There was a muted welcome for the former Manchester United player, partly because Sven had given us the eagerly prized season of two derby victories and partly because Hughes *was* a former Manchester United player. The previous ex-Manchester United player who had managed Manchester City had been Steve Coppell and he resigned after just thirty-three days in charge at Maine Road, knocking eleven days off Brian Clough's record at Leeds. Coppell claimed he had to leave on medical grounds which caused widespread mutterings and scepticism until he emerged blinking into the Manchester rain looking as though he had been asked to build the bridge on the River Kwai singlehanded using only Georgi Kinkladze as raw materials. Within six weeks he had obtained a doctor's sick note and had been sent back to manage Crystal Palace until he recovered.

Hughes, despite his chequered playing history, had earned respect as manager of Wales and Blackburn Rovers and his appointment at least had the immediate effect of stopping the threatened haemorrhaging of good players. Over the few days of the interregnum the email inboxes and telephone lines of City supporters had been filled with references to the possibility of Richard Dunne, Micah Richards, Joe Hart, Michael Johnson and Stephen Ireland all leaving Eastlands. At least with Hughes as the manager they wouldn't depart without receiving the sort of kicking he gave to defenders for twenty years.

Already, though, the impatience of the owner was clearly evident in the casual and contemptuous way in which he had dismissed Eriksson. He had no real understanding of Manchester or

Manchester City or English football but his position of power allowed him to affect our lives. Indeed, such were his ridiculous expectations, we thought it entirely possible that written into Hughes's contract would be the understanding that unless he won the Premiership and the Nobel Prize for Literature by the end of the following season he would be deemed a failure and would be following Sven and Tord down the M6.

The first signing after Hughes had been appointed confirmed my fears. The mantle of Manchester City's Most Expensive Waste of Money was now to be bestowed on a Brazilian who went by the name of Jô. This was not Jo as in Joe Hayes from Kearsley near Bolton who scored the opening goal in the 1956 Cup final. This was Jô as in João Alves de Assis Silva who had played football for Corinthians and CSKA Moscow before joining City for £19 million, as opposed to Joe Hayes who had worked in a cotton mill and down a coal mine before joining City for a £10 signing-on fee. Jô scored precisely six goals in forty-one appearances for City. Joe Hayes scored 152 goals in 363 appearances. I think you can tell which one I have more admiration for.

Amid the excitement generated by the signing of this £19 million dud was the small detail which one only noticed on going back to look at the deal a few years later. Jô's agent/adviser/close friend and constant companion was a man called Kia Joorabchian, who had been involved in the third-party ownership of the two Argentinian footballers, Javier Mascherano and Carlos Tévez. In future months Joorabchian was to wreak as much damage to the fabric of English football as the lassitude of the Premier League and the Football Association would combine to permit. It wasn't the fact that football was now Big Business that caused the major concern. It was the fact that the bigger the business, the greedier these men were to generate profits for themselves, the more irrelevant became the football *qua* football. Joorabchian was a slicker operator than most so his meddling caused more damage than the simpler, cruder demands of the agents who were mostly interested in the money and didn't care who paid it.

Shinawatra's reign was a disaster for Manchester City. The people who now entered the club were far removed from the pleasant, easy-going, mostly local people who I knew and who had been around the club for years and had made it a warm, friendly, family concern. It had been announced that Shinawatra was going to hire a chief executive to run the club in his absence, which was likely to be extended given the fact that the courts in Thailand had sentenced him to two years in prison and that the British government had refused him asylum. He was now being referred to in the press as an 'international fugitive terrorist'. It was more embarrassing to support a club that was owned by such a man than to support a club that could lose 8–1 to a Middlesbrough team that had managed to score only thirty-five goals in its previous thirty-seven games. Seeing the man who owned my club accused of Crimes Against Humanity made me nostalgic for the old days when footballers with neatly brushed centre partings and enormous toecaps aspired to no more than a packet of Woodbines, a pint of bitter at the local and the odd spot of breaking and entering during the close season. This criminal activity was on a scale that even Maurizio Gaudino would have been unable to comprehend.

Gaudino was, contrary to the expectations aroused by his name, a German footballer who, in 1995, City had signed on loan from Eintracht Frankfurt. Only after he arrived at Maine Road did we learn that he had previously been arrested for insurance fraud but we could tolerate that. After all, as Graham Chapman playing a liberal psychiatrist in a *Monty Python* sketch reminded us, 'Who at one time or another hasn't wanted to burn down a great public building?' Gaudino produced a few goals and some decent performances during his time with City and he helped us to stay up in 1995, thereby postponing relegation for a year but the idea that we had been reduced to employing a player with his particular history made me concerned back then that the club was turning itself into a laughing stock. What Shinawatra was doing didn't bear comparison with Gaudino's exercise in petty criminality.

Just before Sven was sacked, Shinawatra announced the name of his new chief executive to replace Alistair Mackintosh, a thoroughly decent and competent man who had been supportive to me during Lynn's illness and whose departure for Fulham I regretted. Alistair's successor turned out to be an unknown marketing chap from Nike. My first reaction was to roll my eyes. My patience for most things to do with marketing, an entirely bogus operation raised to the level of an art by American business and depending largely on cute packaging of euphemisms, exaggerations and possible untruths, was distinctly limited and the fact that Garry Cook, City's new chief executive, came from that background, although originally from the Midlands, and had been appointed by a man of such dubious morality, aroused still more fears for the future. I wondered if the arrival of this new executive and the sudden callous removal of Sven followed by the arrival of Mark Hughes were not in some manner connected.

The signing of Jô did not comfort me at all. He struck me as precisely the sort of player for whom Mark Hughes would have no time at all; a fancy Dan to make Joe Royle's toes curl, and a stark contrast to Christopher Samba and the kind of players that Hughes had brought to East Lancashire and made Blackburn Rovers a difficult team to beat. Was Hughes changing his nature now that he had more money to spend? It seemed unlikely. What seemed more likely was that Shinawatra and Cook, who between them clearly knew less about football than F. Scott Fitzgerald and Scott of the Antarctic put together, were now having a worrying input into player transfers. City supporters had longed for a white knight and they had ended up with an international fugitive terrorist. Was our dream of being in Europe again going to end up with a visit to watch the owner and chairman standing trial at the International Criminal Court at The Hague? On 1 September 2008 we all knew the answer.

Chapter Thirteen

BEFORE 1 SEPTEMBER 2008 I HAD NEVER GIVEN MUCH thought to Sir Thomas More, or indeed to any religious martyr, Catholic or otherwise. I had a fairly standard response to More, being principally in favour of the way he educated his clever daughter Meg and dubious about his biography of Richard III which was a fairly one-dimensional view of his subject, designed not so much as to win the Whitbread Prize as to elicit murmurs of approval from the son of the Tudor monarch who had brought about his downfall. On the other hand, the portrayal of More by Paul Scofield in *A Man for All Seasons* was irresistible and, though I sympathised with More's dilemma in refusing to acknowledge the Act of Supremacy and Henry VIII's establishment of the Church of England after the break from Rome, I could not empathise with it. All that changed on the day that the Royal Family of Abu Dhabi bought Manchester City.

Thomas More and I now shared a belief that somebody had realigned the planets. Prior to the Reformation even More might have admitted that the Roman Catholic Church had a few flaws, like the selling of indulgences, but did the King of England really need to start an entirely new religion to deal with them? I wish More had been around in 2008 so we could have had a jolly good chat about it but unfortunately the King had chopped off his head in 1535 so I will never know if he would have been as sympathetic to my plight as I now was to his.

Manchester City allegedly changed hands for a sum reported to be in the region of £200 million, giving the rapscallion Shinawatra a profit of £120 million, a return of 150% over twelve months. The sale was without doubt a relief of sorts. Whatever the new owner's political stand it would have to be an improvement on what had gone before. However, before the day was out I had already come to the conclusion that we had leaped from frying pan to fire.

Admittedly, this bunch weren't anything like as controversial as Shinawatra was alleged to have been but it took only two clicks of a mouse to discover that a number of academics who had made polite and respectful representations for some form of democratic representation had been thrown into prison without trial. Women had no legal right to object to physical abuse perpetrated by their husbands. We were back in the hands of another brutally repressive autocratic regime but let's ignore that and talk about something really important like football.

It was a fine day in late summer when the news of the sale was released to the media and the telephone started ringing off the hook. It had been a day I had been looking forward to – my last visit to the Proms for the 2008 season. Great music always lifts my spirits and that night Sir Colin Davis was conducting the Gustav Mahler Jugendorchester in the Symphony No. 2 by Sibelius, and Nikolaj Znaider, a bright, young, talented violinist, was playing the Beethoven violin concerto. I met fellow music lover and City supporter Michael Henderson outside the Royal Albert Hall and confessed that, glad as I was to see the back of the Thai Rack, I did not much care for the way in which City were being sold like a toxic mortgage debt, quickly passed on to some unsuspecting bank by Lehmann Brothers, a scenario that was to become only too evident a few weeks later. Hendo shared my reservations but the glory of a late summer evening and the anticipated enjoyment of the concert postponed a detailed analysis of the implications of what had just taken place at Eastlands. We simply agreed that the ludicrous overpayment as indicated by the announced sale price suggested that the new owners had more money than sense. By midnight this suspicion was confirmed.

It was the last day of the transfer window, the day for which Sky Sports News waits all year as tired, hungry, young reporters, thrilled to be allowed to stand in front of a television camera, chatter excitedly into the microphone that whichever ground they have been standing outside since 6am is completely deserted and if there is any activity going on they can't see it. So desperate become the television presenters that they are forced to speculate live on air about the shadow they can vaguely see in an upstairs room flitting against a venetian blind and whether it might be that of Dimitar Berbatov – or possibly an office cleaner. 'Yes,' declares the intrepid reporter with commendable bravery and no sense of irony, 'I can definitely confirm that there is nothing happening here. Back to the studio.'

It was into this atmosphere of breathless excitement that the Abu Dhabi millions were first unleashed on the football world in the profligate manner to which we were soon to become accustomed. First we heard that the Brazilian Robinho was leaving Real Madrid for Manchester City for a fee reported to be in the region of £32 million and then we got wind of an even bolder move. Manchester City were trying to hijack Manchester United's move to bring Berbatov from White Hart Lane to Old Trafford. It wasn't clear if there were fisticuffs at Manchester Airport as the unsuspecting Bulgarian got off the plane but City were allegedly happy to pay even more money to Spurs than United had offered, which was already up around the £30 million mark. It was like an unseemly tussle over a house which the purchaser had thought was settled until, on the day that contracts are to be exchanged, a new prospective buyer emerges determined to gazump the man who had already ordered the building society survey. In the end, based on the fact that Berbatov clearly had no interest at all in going to Eastlands, City had to settle for the acquisition of Robinho. The new co-executive chairman announced that the signing of the Brazilian international superstar was a statement of intent by the new owners.

We were all a little confused at first by who the new owners actually were. At first it was thought to be the Emir, Sheikh Khalifa bin Zayed Al Nahyan. It was going to be difficult to match the classic clean lines of 'Swales Out' if this was to be the bloke taking the heat for future disastrous home defeats. Then it appeared that the deal had been done by Sulaiman Al-Fahim, who was going to be chairman of the new board. Mr Fahim was soon removed from view quicker than Steve Coppell from the manager's office and the new chairman was to be Khaldoon Al-Mubarak, who was very rich but not, we later learned, rich enough or possibly insane enough to have bought both Berbatov and Robinho on the same afternoon.

The man whose money was actually being sprayed about in all directions like the Dreaded Batter Pudding Hurler of Bexhill-on-Sea was called HH Sheikh Mansour bin Zayed Al Nahyan so we could all rest easy. Except that in the one photograph that most City supporters have ever seen of this vastly rich man he looks so young that he could be mistaken for a twelve-year-old child. I started to wonder if the new owner was buying City as some kind of GCSE Geography project at school, enabling him to become very familiar with Manchester rivers (the Irwell, your Highness) and levels of rainfall (bring an umbrella and a mac, your Highness) to the satisfaction of the examiners. Well, no wonder pass rates continue to soar if this is the sort of dedication schoolboys now demonstrate.

Once my suspicions were aroused that City's new owner might be a twelve-year-old schoolboy, an entire scene arrived in my head. We all write our scripts in different ways but for me the starting point has always been one scene, sometimes, as in this case, one image. Twenty years ago I wrote and produced for Thames Television (that'll show you how long ago it was) a six-part serial about the life of the young Charlie Chaplin. It originated entirely from a description in Chaplin's autobiography in which he describes the moment that his mentally-ill mother has to accept that she can no longer look after Charlie and his brother Sid, their feckless father long having disappeared, and that they will have to go into the Lambeth workhouse. Men and women are divided into separate living areas so at the door to the workhouse the two screaming children are dragged away from their heartbroken mother. It was this one image that haunted me and began the creative process.

That photograph of Sheikh Mansour impacted on me similarly and sent me off on a flight of creative fancy. Where would a kid of twelve get the money to buy a Real Madrid player? From his dad, obviously, and not necessarily with his dad's knowledge. I was aided by the memory of the research I had done for *High on a Cliff*, whose plot turns on the twelve-year-old hero buying an airline ticket with his father's credit card. The following scenes take place in the royal palace in Abu Dhabi.

SCENE 153 INT. SHEIKH MANSOUR'S DAD'S STUDY – DAY

DAD is looking through the post and muttering to himself. He is dressed not in traditional Arab garb but as a Lancashire working man of the 1950s with braces and a cloth cap.

                              DAD
Bills, bills, bills. Virgin Media? I don't think so.

He tears up an envelope without bothering to look at the contents then slits open the next one. He scans the bill briefly and then lets out a roar. We can see an item on the bill to pay Real Madrid £32 million. He goes to the door and shouts up the stairs.

                              DAD
Mansour! Get yer arse down here. Now!

SCENE 154 INT. SHEIKH MANSOUR'S BEDROOM – DAY

The twelve-year-old SHEIKH MANSOUR is sitting at his desk with his headphones on playing a computer game. His room is decorated with the usual teenage paraphernalia – posters of pop stars and pin-ups with one of the Beckhams in the centre. DAD storms into the room and is clearly angry that his son hasn't bothered to answer his call.

                              DAD
Mansour! Oy! Cloth ears!

The boy finally clocks his father's presence, knows instantly he is in trouble and tries to smile winningly. He takes off the headphones.

MANSOUR

You told me to wear them if I wanted to listen to music.

DAD

(*waving the credit card bill*)
Did you just buy bloody Robinho without telling me?

MANSOUR

(*clearly lying*)
No!

DAD

You bloody did. You stupid little twerp. Right that's it. I'm taking one of your oil wells away.

MANSOUR

You can't do that. They're my oil wells.

DAD

I can do what I like. I'm your dad.

MANSOUR

That is SO unfair!

DAD

Who gave you the security code on t' back of t' card?

MANSOUR

Mum did.

                         DAD

Remind me again. Which one's yer mum?

                       MANSOUR

The one with the blonde highlights.

                         DAD

Oh her! I might have known.

                       MANSOUR

We thought you'd be pleased. It was like an early birthday present.

                         DAD

Robinho! You've been listening to that crap music too long. Your brain's gone soft.

                       MANSOUR

The kids in my class said Robinho was cool.

                         DAD

I suppose you know you've just spent £32 million of my money on a twerp who thinks he's signed for Manchester United.

                       MANSOUR

I'll pay for him then. There's my Abu Dhabi Post Office account . . .

                         DAD

You're not touching that fifty million. That's for your university fees. I wonder if I can persuade Barclaycard to take Robinho back? I'll tell them it's a fraudulent transaction. Anyone who's seen Robinho play would understand.

MANSOUR goes over to his DAD and gives him a hug. For a moment it's like a US TV family drama.

MANSOUR

I love you, Pop.

DAD

Don't start with all that crap. Just don't do it again.

MANSOUR

I won't.

As DAD starts to leave the room . . .

MANSOUR

Dad . . . Have you ever heard of a player called Carlos Tévez?

With the sudden realisation that they were now the richest club in the world, Manchester City began the 2008–9 season in a style familiar to us but deeply disturbing to anyone who had just plonked down a cheque for £200 million. Before the Premier League had even started, City's European hopes for the season sustained a serious dent when they were beaten at home in front of 17,000 spectators by the Danish minnows FC Midtjylland, a team owned by a local carpenter – not in the sense that Jesus Christ was a carpenter but a real carpenter, a man who worked with wood and charged VAT.

In the first league match of the season at Villa Park things disintegrated still further even before the kick-off when Valeri Bojinov, who had missed the previous season in its entirety after being signed by Sven, snapped an Achilles tendon in the warm-up and was ruled out for another six months. A 4–2 thrashing on the back of a Gabriel Agbonlahor hat-trick then followed and we assumed we would be in for yet another relegation battle. However, this being City (are you still there, Mr Royle?), we beat West Ham at home 3–0 and won impressively at Sunderland by the same scoreline, aided by two goals from the returning hero, Shaun Wright-Phillips. This came a few days after we had scrambled into the first round proper of the UEFA Cup courtesy of a fortuitous own goal in the ninetieth minute in the away leg at Midtjylland and a victory on penalties after extra time. Would the foreign owners who were to take over three days later understand that this was normal behaviour for Manchester City?

The first match under new management was delayed for nearly two weeks by the intrusion of the early September international weekend which merely heightened the expectation for the debut of Robinho which would take place in the home match against Chelsea. It was a memorable start, the Brazilian scoring with a direct free kick after thirteen minutes, only for Ricardo Carvalho to equalise three minutes later which rather took the wind out of our sails. In the second half, goals by Lampard and Anelka established a comfortable superiority for the visitors who ran out easy winners despite having John Terry sent off. The new owners who had shown up to wave at the crowd and sit back to watch the goals flow must have been surprised to say the least. There is no way they could possibly have realised that anti-climax was Manchester City's closest blood relation. Back in Abu Dhabi the whole population must have grabbed the Football Pink off the newsagents' counter and been equally devastated – or, as I rather suspect, completely uninterested.

Normal public service was resumed in the next match when City hammered a poor Portsmouth side 6–0 with most of the team featuring on the score sheet including Robinho, Richard Dunne and even Jô. We all wondered how many it would have been if Samaras and Corradi had still been there. At last, they must have thought throughout the UAE, 'our' lads were doing the business, or whatever the appropriate Arabian slang was. In fact, it was more like another good British tradition with which the good people of Abu Dhabi would have been unfamiliar – the pantomime. City proceeded to lose five of the next seven and when they went down 2–1 at West Bromwich Albion just before Christmas 2008 'the richest club in the world' had slipped into the relegation zone. Then they battered Hull City 5–1 on Boxing Day, causing Phil Brown to reprimand his players on the pitch at half-time in full view of the crowd as if they were naughty children, thereby detonating his own career with a performance worthy of Brian Blessed as Widow Twankey.

In one sense I was strangely comforted by this bewildering see-saw of results. Despite the idiotic supporters dancing around Eastlands on 1 September with dishcloths on their heads welcoming the new dawn, City had refused to change the habits of a lifetime and had continued to delight and frustrate in equal measure. At the end of the season that was supposed to usher in a revolution we had won fifteen matches, lost eighteen matches, acquired fifty points and finished tenth. It was respectable, it wasn't boring, and it was still (just) recognisably Manchester City. It was a state of affairs the co-executive chairman was desperate to change. Although he certainly had his fans even among the City supporters who regarded his maladroitness with an amused tolerance they had not extended to Richard Edghill or Ian Bowyer, it was my conviction from his first day 'in charge' that Garry Cook was a disaster for the club.

Only Manchester City could head hunt a chief executive whose avowed task was to show the world what a smart modern club we now were and appoint a man who made Peter Swales look like Isaiah Berlin. He was, I thought, Thaksin Shinawatra's last black joke for it was the good Doctor who had found him in the Nike marketing department in Portland, Oregon and inflicted him on us. You take a £120 million in profit over twelve months by buying and selling the club like a commodity and to add insult to injury you thumb your nose at us by leaving us an executive that will make us a laughing stock.

When, in his first jaw-dropping public interview, Cook revealed himself in his full glory I started to wonder why, if these people who had just bought us were such smart businessmen as it had been alleged, they left this unwanted inheritance to blunder about. You could argue that Shinawatra's departure came so soon upon the heels of Cook's appointment that it would be hard to make a judgment. They needed only to have picked up *The Guardian* a week before they signed off on the deal to take over the club to have read an interview that would have given any halfway intelligent board of directors food for thought. In this interview Cook revealed himself to be stupid, ignorant and insensitive, which presupposes that there is no Arabian phrase that equates to 'due diligence'. It was this interview above all else that told me that Manchester City were in the wrong hands and we would all suffer.

The only conclusion to be drawn in Cook's favour was that he was 'refreshingly open'. To be open when dealing with people in the normal course of events is indeed refreshing. On the other hand, to be refreshingly open with a journalist when you are telling him stuff that makes you look like a clown is just plain stupid and Cook started as he clearly meant to carry on, by trumpeting his plans for world supremacy while revealing himself to be a man of little intellect and no sense of propriety.

The reporter, Daniel Taylor, wanted to ask Cook about his relationship with Shinawatra who, a week before his departure, was still arousing controversy. Cook did the journalist's work for him by interviewing himself and providing the answers:

> Is he a nice guy? Yes. Is he a great guy to play golf with? Yes. Does he have plenty of money to run a football club? Yes. I really care only about those three things. Whether he [Thaksin] is guilty of something over in Thailand, I can't worry. I have to be conscious of it. But my role is to run a football club. I worked for Nike who were accused of child-labour issues and I managed to have a career there for 15 years. I believed we were innocent of most of the issues. Morally, I felt comfortable in that environment. It's the same here.

Cook then went on to talk about his ten-year plan (which a week later got abbreviated to a two-year plan) to become a 'global empire' and bringing in a box-office signing. He was clearly not convinced that Mark Hughes was the man to sign and manage a superstar. 'I've talked about this a lot to Mark and he sort of understands. China and India, 30% of the world population, need a league to watch and we want Manchester City to be their club. To do that, we need a superstar because, no disrespect, Richard Dunne doesn't roll off the tongue in Beijing.' Richard Dunne, at this point, had given four or five years of outstanding service as a central defender to Manchester City. For Cook to make a statement like that showed more than disrespect. It revealed the mind of a man who had no idea what Manchester City stood for and no idea how every player at the club, never mind Richard Dunne, might feel to hear an honest Irish professional slighted in this way.

The interview continued with Cook demolishing everything in his path like a runaway combine harvester. The next target on his list was the manager. Now bear in mind Cook had been, at the very least, partly responsible for getting rid of Sven and Tord and bringing in Hughes from Blackburn ten weeks earlier. So far City had played under Hughes precisely one league game but Cook seemed already to have come to the conclusion that a mistake had been made – not his, of course:

> Mark is adamant he wants Premier League experience because that is what let us down last season. Mark's a homegrown lad, very old school. He'd rather sign players he knows, even overpay. That's an endearing piece of what he's all about. He doesn't like the unknown because it takes him out of his comfort zone. He jumps out of his comfort zone when we say to him, 'Hey, you've got to change this up a little bit.' But he can't have Roque Santa Cruz so now he's back in his 'uncomfortable zone', which is that he will have to bring in someone new and develop them.

Reading this interview again and again I started to experience a sinking feeling worse than anything that Swales had given me in his twenty years of mismanagement of the club. Not only did this twerp not understand City, despite being English he didn't even understand English football as the interview went on to demand an end to the idea of promotion and relegation and the institution of a Premier League with 10–14 clubs in it, not one of whom could ever be replaced, it appeared. In other words he wanted to turn English football into Major League Baseball or the NFL. This 'visionary' was bent on destroying football and he was going to use my club to do it. He signed off with a flourish, complaining bitterly about the Manchester City Masters team that had recently won a tournament and had not asked his permission to take part and had even been congratulated for winning in the club's programme. This article had clearly escaped his eagle eye until after publication.

You could argue that some of the players who had achieved so-called 'Masters' status would have been playing for City in the 1990s and you would then have to query whether there wasn't a case to answer under the Trades Description Act, as some of the players who wore the shirt in those days were clearly somewhat short of 'Masters' status. However, the idea that a team representing Manchester City composed of players who had actually played for Manchester City should arouse the wrath of the co-executive chairman of Manchester City to this extent by winning a tournament in front of delighted fans caused me to wonder if this man was actually Karl Power – the prankster from Droylsden who walked out of the crowd at Headingley to bat in an Ashes Test match and who stood next to Andy Cole for a Manchester United team photograph before a Champions League game against Bayern Munich. The truth was actually the reverse. Power looked like a player but was a fraud. Cook appeared to all intents and purposes to be a fraud but, terrifyingly, actually held real power.

Just over a week after this mind-numbing article appeared in *The Guardian* Shinawatra gave way to Mansour, and Cook, instead of following his hero round the pitch-and-putt course at Heaton Park or wherever the former prime minister of Thailand was hiding, was re-appointed by the new owners and actually allowed to play with real money. For Mark Hughes this must have been a mixed blessing. At Blackburn Rovers he had, by all accounts, done an excellent job in stabilising and slowly improving the club by signing players of whom Garry Cook had presumably never heard because they wouldn't have rolled off the tongue in Portland, Oregon, where Mr Cook had been living, let alone in Beijing. The fact that they rolled off the tongue in Blackburn was all that mattered to the club's genuine fans. Hughes had travelled to Eastlands because he knew a bigger challenge awaited him there and, apart from the players and fans of Blackburn Rovers who were sorry to see him go, nobody could blame him for wanting to further his career as he saw it.

The problem with Hughes is that, apart from the purely parochial view that he played for Manchester United, he is a difficult man for fans to warm to. He might possibly be the life and soul of the party in private, doing hilarious impressions of Nick Clegg and Fabio Capello but in public the only word that ever comes to mind when looking at him being interviewed is 'dour'. All managers are guarded because they are literally guarded by PR people and there is a formula for expressing dissatisfaction with the referee, the opposition, the press and discontented fans which managers are expected to observe. The reason the press love successful managers like José Mourinho and even less successful managers like the eccentric Blackpool manager Ian Holloway is that they always sound as though they are actually answering a question without having run it past their Director of Communications first.

Hughes never managed to give the impression that he was speaking from the heart so that even though, as the season progressed, I sympathised with what I am sure was intolerable pressure lumped on him by Cook, it was hard to feel too passionate in his defence. Hughes might have been Cook's choice (I doubt Shinawatra spent much time looking at Blackburn Rovers' results or reading the *Lancashire Telegraph*) but he wasn't the choice of the new owners whom Cook was desperate to please. Hughes did well to survive that first season with eighteen defeats and a mid-table finish. It became apparent after he was dismissed in December

2009 that Cook had been lining up Mancini for some time and, even though he strenuously denied it, the truth soon came dribbling out. Cook's denial of an event, that turned out shortly afterwards to be revealed as the truth, became something of a *modus operandi* for the co-executive chairman.

So now Hughes had money but he clearly didn't have control of its spending on players. Robinho would hardly have been the first name on Hughes's shopping list but Hughes wasn't Alex Ferguson, he hadn't been in charge for more than twenty years and he was faced not with the possibility of absolute power but the reality of political compromise. Actors and directors during the days when the Hollywood studios ruled the film industry more completely than they do today used to make a similar compromise. They would make films because the studio thought these movies would make money and they wanted to be seen to be cooperative so that next time round the studio would indulge them and permit them to make the film they really wanted to make. 'Two for them, one for me' became their watchword and it led to some decent films and a durable career in an insecure profession.

Robinho, however, was the only name (apart from the mysterious £19 million Jô) that stood out as being the choice of somebody other than the manager. The rest of the incoming players during the close season – Pablo Zabaleta, Tal Ben Haim and Shaun Wright-Phillips – all looked as though they had the manager's stamp of approval.

The decks were starting to clear from previous regimes as the Swedish goalkeeper Isaksson, the willing but limited Sun Jihai, 'Don' Geovanni, the fearsome strike twins Corradi and Samaras, as well as Mpenza and the old hero of '99 Paul Dickov all left the club, in Dickov's case for the second time. The only departure that seems to have been unsuccessfully resisted by Hughes was that of the Croatian defender Ćorluka who was sold to Tottenham Hotspur on that never-to-be-forgotten transfer deadline day. In Cook's defence, Ćorluka had made it clear that he wanted to go and join his compatriot Luka Modrić who had recently arrived at White Hart Lane. It must have been as Ćorluka was driving south that the news of the takeover was released and I couldn't help wondering, impoverishment being the fear of every Premier League footballer, that he must have been sorely tempted at the cost of three points on his driving licence to make a skidding U-turn on the M6.

The strangeness of the 2008–9 season was reflected in my private life as I started behaving, at the age of fifty-nine, like a teenager, or so I liked to think. In fact, as a teenager I had very little success with women and no problems with my lower back or knee joints. At the age of fifty-nine I suddenly started flitting from woman to woman in a progress that was hindered only by moral self-doubt and pain in my knee joints. Deeply etched in my memory is that seminal first time when I discovered that I could no longer bend from the waist to pick up the post that had been pushed through the letter box on to the floor in the hall. I sank, humiliated, to my knees to retrieve the junk mail and the bills only to find that I couldn't stand upright again without clutching the wall for support. It became such an agonising movement that I wondered if there was something else I could usefully do while I was down there. Praying was all I could come up with but the prayer wasn't particularly spiritual. 'Dear Lord, permit thy humble servant to get up again without those shooting pains in his knees', didn't strike me as the sort of prayer the Almighty would spend much time on.

Watching rugby on television and marvelling at the speed with which those seventeen- and eighteen-stone bodies hurled themselves at each other I now couldn't help thinking about a match in which everyone was aged sixty. One tackle and that would be it. All thirty players would be on the floor groaning, holding various parts of their anatomy while their children stood over them offering no sympathy at all and asking in a pained voice, 'Isn't it about time you stopped pretending you were young and accepted the fact that you're not?' I'd given up playing cricket and football with reluctance. It was a decision based solely on the unwillingness to countenance my own diminishing performances and therefore become the worst player on my own team.

I still remember the way in which teams were chosen in the primary school playground when we played with boys who were older than we were. Everyone lined up against the wall and the two best players became captains and chose alternately until all the players were assigned to one team or the other. The fear of being the last to be chosen ('Oh all right, I'll have him, then') caused me disproportionate anxiety but at the age of seven I had the feeling that mere growth would make me a better player. Now the only way I was growing was going to make me even slower. Football went first, hastened by the onset of asthma. Cricket went slightly later. Having missed the whole summer of 2004 because of Lynn's illness I found in 2005 that, as a widower with no worries about abandoning a wife to cricket, I no longer wanted to play if it meant that I missed catches which previously I would have snaffled and that when I walked to the wicket a fight would develop among the opposition's worst bowlers to grab the ball and have a go, sensing that any straight ball would be too good for me. I had seen it happen to others who insisted on continuing to play on into their late sixties or early seventies and becoming the butt of their own team's scorn. I retired with few regrets. I'd had some great days out there as well as some miserable ones but there was no way I could do anything after the age of fifty better than I could do the same thing under the age of forty. Frantic activity on the sports field would have to be replaced by decadent afternoons in the bedroom.

Of course it never quite worked out that way because by the time I got to the stage in life when I could devote myself to this form of strenuous activity, I had developed enough moral qualms and performance anxieties to stop me. Despite these hindrances, though, I was aware that the physical side of my relationships still featured strongly in my never-ending quest for female companionship if not perfection. I was told by one woman in her fifties that she had found men of her own age or slightly older to be 'rather dusty', which I think was a rather charming euphemism for a libido in permanent decline. I had plenty of problems but that wasn't one of them, as she acknowledged. What had clearly moved on since 1972 was a recognition by the women I met who were also looking for a serious relationship that sex was on the agenda much earlier than it had been in our respective youths. I suppose that when you get past the menopause it's hard to use the standard responses of 'I don't want to get pregnant' or 'I'm saving myself' – who for? Has she been watching *The Seventh Seal*? 'I'm sorry, I can't do this. You see I'm just about to start a game of chess with the Grim Reaper.'

Although all my relationships were those of what is now called a serial monogamist, I was constantly cross and disappointed that none of them were giving me that unique fusion of physical desirability, intellectual companionship and emotional maturity for which I was so desperately seeking. As each relationship foundered, the fear that I would never find this particular Holy Grail grew proportionately. Most of the relationships ended sensibly with each of us admitting that it wasn't working and agreeing to go our separate ways. It helped that after thirty years of marriage these relationships were of relatively brief duration, disproving the lyrical allegation that breaking up is hard to do. One of the Jewish ones lasted about a month, although in that time we had two reconciliations and three break-ups. My desire for a life of spiritual serenity was not going to be satisfied in that partnership and though she called it a day, I left with some relief.

I usually preferred it when the other party made the final decision because it preserved my battered sense of chivalry. The only time the decision left me in a rage was when I was sent off on the twenty-ninth floor of the Crowne Plaza in Times Square, a hotel I am not enthusiastic about checking into again anytime soon. It wasn't the red card itself that bothered me but the manner in which it was produced. The relationship had seemed all right flying into New York one Friday afternoon. I took her to the Carnegie Deli on Seventh Avenue to eat that night, an appropriate way to spend Friday evening given we were in Jew York City as H. R. Haldeman used to refer to it. Who could possibly resist the Carnegie's notorious pastrami sandwiches on rye bread, so enormous that they had to be stapled together with a large toothpick? Well, she could. From that moment on things began to go downhill. I was accompanying her on business so I was the one patiently waiting in the hotel bedroom for her to come back to the room between meetings. Only, she never came. All week I waited in that room but there was always one reason or another why she didn't return.

On both weekends of that trip I travelled up to Boston to see David and Susie, who was now heavily pregnant with my first grandchild, but I would go alone. The conversations with the prospective father were not easy. It was impossible not to think back to the time of David's own birth in 1977 in the close season after Tony Book's blue-and-white army had finished second in

Division One, a point behind the all-conquering Liverpool. It seemed from my perspective in 2008 to be a golden age. I was twenty-eight, was producing my first television serial and was already the happy father of a delightful two-year-old daughter. I had it all. I don't suppose if I could have transported myself back in time I would have felt the same way but I was living in 2008 and all I could think about was how happy I had been then and what a bad place I had now been inhabiting for what seemed like many years.

Looking for some kind of compensation when I got back to the Crowne Plaza was a mistake and as the gnawing sense of betrayal became a conviction of some certainty, I forced a showdown on our last day in New York. It wasn't easy to do. At least Gary Cooper knew that the train carrying the Miller brothers was going to arrive at High Noon. I had no idea when she would come back. I had arrived from Boston at about 10.30am and I just sat in the room reading until 7pm when, to her horror, she came in and found me still there. She knew exactly when I was coming back because I had left numerous notes to that effect so she found it easy to avoid me by staying out of the room. I have no doubt that she supposed, as had been the case the whole of the previous week, that I would give up in the end and go to the theatre since we were situated next to Broadway. By the time the play had finished she was 'asleep' in bed with the light off.

The staged confrontation resulted in her admission that it was all over so at least my suspicions had not been paranoid fantasies. Unfortunately, we then had a day of packing and travelling which is not the easiest thing to do with someone who has just dumped you in fairly difficult circumstances. It hurt for a few weeks but this is the only relationship I have written about in any detail simply because the manner of its ending was so painful.

With each successive failure I careered wildly into another one. I went from an actress to an academic, from a rich widow to a poor teacher, from blonde to brunette, from Jew to *schickse*. Why was I so desperate, or more correctly, why was I behaving in this desperate manner? I had been effectively living on my own since 31 July 2002. I was perfectly capable of running the house, of working, of going out with friends. I wasn't nineteen and in the grip of a hormonal frenzy. I suspect it was because I had a destiny in mind. I knew there was someone out there for me and with each failure I began to panic, berating myself for mistaking the one I was seeking for the one I had found and let go.

Eventually, in the mid-summer of 2009 I got to the extraordinary age of sixty and though there was someone around at the time she didn't wish to be identified to my friends who came to my party as having any claims on my affections so I dutifully obeyed her request. I seemed to be very good at choosing women who didn't want to be with me. Fortunately, the celebration took place on 4 July and coincided with the first visit to his father's birthplace of my grandson Oliver who had been born in Boston in June 2008. It allowed me to send out invitations to our joint sixty-first birthday party, all dressed up in the language of the Declaration of Independence.

David, aided and abetted by his father and his sister, had ensured that the baby was born into his Manchester City birthright. It had meant a lot to me to have my children imbued with a sense of their belonging to Manchester City. David, in particular, had taken a fair amount of abuse at school in London when he was growing up in the 1980s and 1990s. Neither of them had wavered in their steadfast support and I was very proud of them for it.

Now there was Oliver and whoever followed him. He was quickly dressed in Manchester City finery and, thanks to the miracle of satellite television, he has already been acquainted with 'his' team for some time. I don't know in what sense that identification will mean anything to him but I do know that his father grew up in London and could not have been distinguished in his enthusiasm from a lad brought up in Manchester. I have, therefore, some hopes that Oliver will follow the family tradition, even though I recognise that being brought up in North America rather than England will present him with a new set of problems. In London, David the outsider was reinforced in his support for City by the constant barracking coming from his Chelsea-, Arsenal- and Spurs-supporting peers. In North America, Oliver won't even have the consolation of being persecuted for his beliefs, and the triumphs that will surely follow in the wake of the unlimited investment the current owners seem willing to provide will not resound greatly in a land where the Patriots and the Red Sox rule the playgrounds and back yards.

I have no problem with American sports. I have always liked baseball and think it is a grand game; not as grand as cricket certainly, but it's a pleasure to spend an afternoon in the sun in a family atmosphere watching sport, even if the food appears to take precedence over the sport, just as the popcorn appears to be the main feature of an evening at the cinema in America. If you look at the crowd during a baseball game there is a constant flow of traffic towards the concession stands in the concourse. Baseball, like cricket, is a game with a lot of pauses interspersed with moments of dramatic action. The food consumption never seems to recognise that occasionally it's a good idea to watch the game.

That, however, is a price I'm willing to pay if it means an end to the violence that still simmers in the cauldron of football. In April 2011 David flew over from Boston so that we could go to the FA Cup semi-final against United together. Whatever my feelings about New City, my desire to beat United never wavers. It was a decent game, obviously wonderful for us because we won and Scholes got a long overdue red card for raking his studs down Zabaleta's leg. Whatever his considerable skills as a player, there is a streak of nastiness in Scholes that tends to be excused because the genuine skills combined with his irreproachable behaviour off the pitch have created a respect from referees and journalists that seems to preclude his being ordered off for tackles that Joey Barton wouldn't have dared to make.

It was a memorable afternoon, made better for me by the presence of a decent United supporter in the seat behind us. After two dreadful Berbatov misses in the space of a minute, he tapped me on the shoulder and said in a voice like Al Read's, 'You can have Berbatov for 50p.' 'You'll have to take Balotelli in part-exchange,' I replied. 'No bloody chance,' he remarked and we smiled at each other. This was how it should be between the two teams' supporters. At the end of the match we shook hands and he wished us well for the final. I wished him not so well for the Champions League but we parted amicably and David and I waited in the stadium for as long as we could to soak up the atmosphere of such a momentous win and to let the idiots depart on the tube from Wembley Park station before we made our way to the exit.

However, when we emerged from the stadium an atmosphere of incipient violence hovered in the air. There were flurries of action as small groups of rival supporters clashed and were separated by the police. I had been to matches throughout the 1980s, a decade cursed by hooliganism, and much as I despised the gentrification of modern football I had assumed that one concomitant blessing would have been the disappearance of exactly what we witnessed on that spring evening when United supporters should have slunk away and City supporters should have celebrated without the need

249

to engage on a physical level with the opposition.

David observed that he would never bring Oliver to a match at the age of three the way I had taken him to watch City play Spurs in 1980 for his first match when he was three. I could hardly dissuade him. If I had been Ollie's father rather than his grandfather I would have made the same decision. New owners, new money, new silverware, new players, new glories. Same old brain-dead stupidity. The idiots I saw at White Hart Lane venting their fury at the award of a throw-in to the opposition, were no different from the idiots I saw taunting each other on Wembley Way. It's a great game but it's not always a great experience.

Chapter Fourteen

THE 2009–10 SEASON WAS THE YEAR IT STARTED TO SLIP away from me, as far as football was concerned, and yet it turned out to be the year of my salvation from the sense of despair that had enveloped me since Lynn had left. The players arrived at Eastlands thick and fast, the cash registers rang all over Europe and the sponsor on the front of the shirt changed from a company that on a bad day might strand holidaymakers in the desert, to a company that flew hardy holidaymakers to and from the desert. As Etihad Airways signed a deal with Manchester City reported to be worth £400 million for sponsorship and naming rights, we were asked to believe that it was all somehow a coincidence and that the owners of Manchester City had no influence over the commercial decisions of the national airline. For those who wanted to see it, the evidence of financial bullying was becoming increasingly clear.

As we had all foreseen from the day he signed his contract at Eastlands, Mark Hughes got his way with the £18 million signing of Roque Santa Cruz in what must have been an arm-wrestling contest with Garry Cook. As it turned out, Cook was right to have resisted but not for the reasons he thought he was right. Gareth Barry, on the other hand, was a reasonable signing from Villa for a mere £12 million, to be followed by the signing that rather defined the new mood that was abroad at City. Carlos Tévez, a man who earned more than the gross income of the combined population of Lytham St Annes and Blackpool, despite the odd situation of not actually owning his own economic rights, was signed from Manchester United for a fee reported as anything from £25 million to twice that amount, with wages approaching £200,000 a week. Like many others I suspect, I wondered if someone could be persuaded to own my economic rights – particularly when the gas bill arrived. City fans, delighted by the idea of nicking United's striker after Ferguson refused to pay the equivalent of the gross national debt of Argentina, hung a banner with a portrait of Tévez across Deansgate. Beneath it was the slogan: **Welcome to Manchester**.

Inevitably, the manager of Manchester United who appears, in public at least, to have no sense of humour at all especially when it is directed at him, was extremely angry. He really doesn't understand that, if you are being teased, the only way to stop it is to laugh and smile. The predictable outburst of rage simply confirmed to everyone that he couldn't take a joke and the laugh was once more on him. For a man who is lauded as being an exemplar among managers, there are kids aged seven who could teach him a thing or two about 'mind games'. For the season to follow, Tévez was a dedicated professional whose goals kept City's season afloat. His fall from grace was spectacular but it was in the future. For now he was just a key part of the jigsaw that was being assembled so expensively.

The money continued to pour out but for every good but pricey signing there was a bad and equally expensive signing. Emmanuel Adebayor cost a mere £25 million and was, quite predictably, trouble as soon as he arrived. Was this a Cook signing or a Hughes signing? It was getting to be an interesting parlour game. At that time Wenger simply never lost players he wanted to keep, which was what made me slightly suspicious of the £15 million transfer of Kolo Touré which followed a few days after the Adebayor deal, but it was widely believed that the Alsatian professor was unable or more likely unwilling to match the wages Manchester City were now offering. He had been thrilled to palm David Seaman on to us the year after Peter Schmeichel retired because he knew that Seaman was finished. Indeed he was, but it cost City considerable money to pay up a contract the former Arsenal goalkeeper could not fulfil after sustaining a career-ending injury at Fratton Park.

If Adebayor was leaving the Emirates Stadium it must have been because his manager thought he was more trouble than he was worth. The Arsenal fans were glad to see the back of him, too, so it became perfectly obvious that Adebayor was trouble. Fans don't usually turn on their own players without a good reason. Richard Edghill never seemed to me to warrant the abuse that he attracted from the City faithful and Ian Bowyer, who was also wrongly hounded out of Maine Road, ended up winning the European Cup at Nottingham Forest but I can't remember too many other players who left the club with the sound of disapproval ringing in their ears for no good reason. In a team of conflicting large egos it took no kind of perspicacity to see that Adebayor was a liability. It was, however, a perspicacity unknown to Cook or possibly to Hughes.

It took just four games for the trouble to manifest itself. Having won their first three matches impressively, City were due to face Arsenal at home in a match that would indicate the distance they had progressed since the previous season's mid-table finish. In the event the match was won 4–2 but nobody remembers this game for the score. Adebayor saw to that. After heading the ball past Almunia with ten minutes to go to make the score 3–1 and seal victory, Adebayor shrugged off the congratulations offered by his new team-mates and sprinted ninety yards to the far end of the stadium where the Arsenal fans were congregated. The explosion of anger that greeted him was presumably exactly what Adebayor had wanted. The idea that he might follow the convention which Robbie Keane, Craig Bellamy and others in a similar position also follow, of not celebrating against a team for which he had previously played, obviously didn't occur to Adebayor or if it did it was cursorily dismissed. Just to round off the afternoon he stamped on the head of his former close friend Robin van Persie and was banned for three matches.

Is it important that we like the players who turn out for our team? I think it's important that we admire them and admiration has only a peripheral relationship with talent. Adebayor is a skilful, talented footballer but I did not welcome his arrival, I was not surprised by his crass stupidity and I was pleased when he disappeared on loan the following year. He seemed to me to be symptomatic of the team that was being hastily assembled like an expensive marquee with some basic central support poles still missing. It was the manner in which the next player arrived that left a bad taste in the mouth when it had become obvious that financial bullying was the new *modus operandi* at Eastlands.

Joleon Lescott was a competent enough player for Wolves and Everton but few would have looked at him and sighed for his presence in their team. Richard Dunne had been an honest and faithful servant for City since 2000 and after a difficult first couple of years, during which he had been suspended for breaches of club discipline, he seemed to have straightened himself out to the extent that he had become the fans' player of the year in the 2004–5 season. His name didn't roll off the tongue in Beijing, though, and for City's co-executive chairman this constituted grounds for dismissal. We would all be interested to know how easily the name Joleon Lescott rolls off the tongue in Beijing but we were never vouchsafed that information. Everton didn't want to sell Lescott and Dunne didn't want to leave City but for the mighty steamroller of the Abu Dhabi petrodollars, these were minor irritants. Lescott was coming and Dunne was going. Get over it.

My sympathies were more with Dunne than with David Moyes, who certainly made a fuss, but I was never sure if that was because he desperately wanted to keep Lescott or because he knew that, if he kept complaining, the City offer would keep going up until it reached its position of maximum incredibility and went 'ping', which it did when the price got to £22 million. It was a truly absurd sum to pay for a player who was, by any standard of comparison, not worth over four times as much as the man he was replacing. The determination of the owners to have the toy they wanted no matter what it cost or, more to the point, the toy they were told they would enjoy playing with, meant that after a couple of weeks of name-calling in the press, Lescott came to join the other millionaire players with their snouts in the trough and Dunne went down the M6 to Aston Villa. It came as no surprise that, when he scored the Villa goal in a 1–1 draw on City's visit there only four weeks after he had been unceremoniously evicted from Eastlands, the former City centre-back refused to celebrate, in marked contrast to the behaviour of the reprehensible Adebayor.

The inevitability of Dunne's departure and Lescott's arrival being dictated only by how wide they felt they had to open the chequebook in Abu Dhabi reminded me of the summer of 2002 when Manchester United decided that they wanted Rio Ferdinand. It was completely irrelevant that Ferdinand had signed a contract to play for Leeds United. We all knew he was going to Old Trafford no matter what the club that held his registration thought and the timing simply depended on when it was convenient for the purchaser to go to the ATM and withdraw the cash. Financial bullying was now regarded as standard practice, for money was the sole arbiter of life in the Premier League.

My sense that the time was out of joint gathered pace. I was now embarrassed by my club not because they lost games but because they had become an ugly club. I had become used over the years to the losing of games. I didn't like it but it happened to everyone and there was no need to be more than temporarily upset. There would be another game in a few days and we would all be able to seek salvation again. This sense of distaste for the behaviour of the new owners and their acolytes was much more insidious and worrying than a string of bad defeats. These people were changing the culture of the club and were proud to proclaim it because they thought, in their naïve blundering way, that it simply meant a change from a losing culture to a winning culture. They didn't mind being despised because they were rich. In a climate of envy, rich people are always despised. What they were palpably incapable of understanding was that not all their supporters believed that success was worth the price of the embarrassment that they were being asked to pay.

They employed people to spread the word that Manchester City was under new management and all the dreams of their supporters would be realised because they now had the means to realise those dreams. What these people could not grasp (and presumably did not wish to since it flew in the face of their job description) was that for people like me good opinions were not for sale. Their assumption would be that 'not for sale' was a bargaining position like that of Everton when Lescott was being auctioned off. For me 'not for sale' meant exactly that. By now I despised these new owners for a different reason from that which had caused me to despise Shinawatra.

It is important that I clarify why the words 'foreign owner' are a problem for me. 'Foreign' is far less problematic than 'owner'. Who would I prefer to see as the public face of my club, Nelson Mandela or Peter Swales? Right first time. I might prefer to see an Englishman as the manager of the national football team but if Arsene Wenger wanted the job I would be thrilled. When the FA blundered into the appointment of the Englishman Steve McClaren, I was not. I am an old-fashioned left winger, a believer in Clive Colbridge and Tony Coleman, a *Manchester Guardian* radical with an instinctive anti-capitalist bias.

On that basis, the very word 'owner' is a problem for me. Why do people want to be owned? A slave is owned, an animal is owned, inanimate objects are owned. I have no desire to be owned. 'My owner is richer than your owner, therefore I will defeat you.' It was like the old playground taunt of, 'I've got a big brother who's bigger than your big brother.' It was the reverse of romance. I had always loved football for its romance. No owner wants romance. Owners want certainties; capitalism wants guarantees of financial profits. That's why there are 'bankable' stars in the movies. I don't want to see a film with a bankable star. I want to see a film that makes me laugh and moves me to tears. A big budget and a bankable star does not automatically deliver that. Sport offers or should offer the chance of the unexpected, the unpredictable, but everything about football in recent times has conspired to cheat us of that vital element of unpredictability.

American football in particular tries to deal with the unwanted element of unpredictability by creating enormous squads of players for every conceivable situation. Its playing squads are so large that they can be divided into offensive and defensive units.

When the defensive unit secures the ball, off they all trot to be replaced by players who can only travel in a forwards direction. The Cup finals of the 1950s and 1960s were frequently ruined by injuries which became known as 'the Wembley hoodoo'. In 1965 each team was allowed to nominate a substitute who could be utilised if a player was injured. As a piece of entirely pointless trivia it has always stayed in my mind that Roy Cheetham was City's first-ever substitute, coming on when Mike Summerbee was sent flying by a Wolves defender over the touchline and into the stand at Molineux where he collided with one of the pillars holding up the roof. His face was badly cut open and blood poured out of it as if in a Tarantino film. A pregnant female spectator who witnessed it lost consciousness. All this extraneous detail was supplied by the injured party nearly forty years after the event, which is why I remember City's first substitute.

Cheetham coming on in that fashion as Summerbee was taken to the local hospital could hardly be anything but a good thing. However, managers soon learn to exploit any loophole in the law if it gives them a miniscule advantage over the opposition and they had no scruples about telling players to fake injuries so the authorities were forced to permit substitutions for tactical reasons. Eventually, instead of one substitute, three were allowed and so the 'professionalisation' of the game continued. The numbers of players on the substitutes' bench increased to five and then to seven even if only three could be used. The important thing was that managers should have more and more choice so that if any player was injured or was having a stinker there were always two and possibly three choices of substitute available. In addition, pitches are no longer mud heaps in the winter and spring, with a small strip along the wings the only evidence that the game is normally played on grass. Shirts and footwear are streamlined, balls are lighter so centre-backs and centre-forwards won't die from heading heavy leather balls soaked by the rain and weighing the equivalent of a small cannonball. Jeff Astle, it was reported in his obituary, was supposed to be one player whose premature death was attributed to this phenomenon.

Is all this progress entirely to be applauded? One of my favourite games was a match against Derby County played at Maine Road towards the end of the 1990–91 season. Tony Coton was sent off for bringing down Dean Saunders and was replaced in goal by the crowd's permanent favourite, Niall Quinn, who then proceeded to save Saunders's penalty, receiving an ovation from all concerned. Down to ten men and with our centre-forward in goal, we hung on to win 2–1. It was a hugely satisfying victory in the circumstances and it was entirely the result of the heroics of The Blue Niall. Nowadays it is rare that among the platoon of substitutes who litter the benches behind the manager there isn't a goalkeeper. A substitute goalkeeper can spend an entire season warming the bench.

When City had two of the best goalkeepers in the Premier League, Joe Hart and Shay Given, Hart had to be sent out on loan to Birmingham City. He couldn't play reserve team football as in the Olden Days and he was too valuable to waste on the bench. That job went to Stuart Taylor, a free transfer signed for that purpose. Ironically, City ended the season with a goalkeeper from Hungary between the posts after both Given and Taylor were injured while Hart continued to gain experience playing for Birmingham City. We got the unpredictability I liked in an entirely unpredictable manner.

The self-incriminating interview Cook gave to *The Guardian* mentioned the idea of scrapping promotion and relegation. He isn't alone in the crassness of this demand. It was rumoured that

Venky's, whose ownership of Blackburn Rovers is a constant warning against the folly and ignorance of overseas ownership, were unaware when they bought the club that there was a possibility that their new investment could be relegated to a lower division where revenues were much smaller. For owners like these and the Americans raised on the franchise system, the whole idea of promotion and relegation is anathema. They are running a business not a crapshoot and how can they be expected to plan properly for the years ahead if they can't even be sure of the division their team will be playing in?

I wish to make it perfectly clear that I have absolutely no desire to turn the clock back to 1968 or any other past era, so anyone who dismisses this argument as the ravings of an old man lost in the nostalgia of his youth needs to think again. Yes, I fully admit that I am a romantic and football in 2012 doesn't exactly welcome romance but as a professional historian I have written books and made programmes about recent history in which I have striven hard not to advocate the primacy of the past over the present or the future.

In 2007 I wrote and presented an hour-long programme for BBC4 which was supposed to coincide with the fiftieth anniversary of Harold Macmillan's speech in Bedford, which included the fateful phrase 'Some of our people have never had it so good'. Thanks to good old-fashioned BBC scheduling ineptitude, it went out five months too late so it missed the anniversary by some distance. I tried as best I could within the fifty-eight minutes that the programme actually lasts to present a cross-section of British society in the year 1957. I did not start out with the conviction that it was all so much better in 1957 than it was in 2007. There were plenty of things that we had to tolerate in 1957 that nobody would wish to reinstate, ranging from fatal childhood diseases that have now been eradicated to the treatment of gays, divorcees and the mentally ill. What became apparent, though, was that for all the uncertainties of life in 1957, particularly the idea that we could all be involved in a nuclear war at any time and the whole world would be destroyed in an hour, people were more optimistic about the future then than they were fifty years later, for all the economic and other benefits conferred by 'progress'.

I feel much the same about football. The swish new stadia, the world of instant communications, the high level of skill displayed in a game that has never been played at a faster pace than it is today are all evidence of this same progress. It was wonderful to be sitting on a horse in Wyoming at the time that Manchester City were playing a home match against Charlton Athletic and yet be able to fall inelegantly off the horse, dash into the farmhouse and, through the miracle of technology, learn that we had won the game 3–2, seconds after the final whistle had sounded eight thousand miles away. Does it make me happier? I suppose you could say that finding out that they won three days later would make me happier than knowing instantly that they had lost. Now that I know I can find out instantly, if I am within range of a computer with an internet connection, it would be frustrating if I were then forced to wait.

There was, however, something quite interactive about going to the big overseas news-stand on Las Palmas Street just off Hollywood Boulevard when I was living and working in Los Angeles in the 1970s. The English newspapers would generally be on display a day late so that I wouldn't get the report of Saturday's match until after the Sunday papers arrived on Monday. The Sunday papers were also extremely expensive for a student living on a tiny grant (whatever that was) so I had to try to open the *Observer* sports section unseen by the news-stand owner and read the results and City report without being spotted by the eagle-eyed man whose primary interest was stopping impoverished students from illicitly devouring the porn magazines.

On the other hand, money was money and a man stealing the result of the Tranmere Rovers v Stockport County match was technically as guilty of theft as the man wanting a free look at photographs of young attractive women who had mislaid all their clothes as well as all sense of decorum. I had just worked out a way of committing my theft inconspicuously and successfully, when the newsagents of America invented the enormous 'super staple'. This horrible thing skewered the precious newspapers shut so that all that was visible was two quarters of the front page. Pretty soon after this technological disaster I decided to ring fence the two dollars it cost to buy the English newspapers.

When I was staying with Lynn's parents in Riverside it meant a journey of sixty miles each way to that foreign news-stand. In the summer months the Lancashire cricket scores took the place of the City scores of the football season and it was heartbreaking to travel all that way, hand over the two dollars of blood money to read the brief but traumatic entry:

Colwyn Bay. Glamorgan (1pt) versus Lancashire (1pt).
Match Abandoned. Rain.

On the other hand, the disappointment and the inconvenience were partially compensated by the dedication. Following City and Lancashire frequently dominated my waking thoughts to a possibly unhealthy degree but it was a love that I felt was reciprocated by Clive Lloyd and Harry Pilling, as it was by Joe Corrigan and Mike Doyle. The trouble that I took to follow their endeavours reinforced my support for the teams they played for. In an age when all is revealed by the click of a mouse, loyalties cannot possibly be forged to the same degree. I wouldn't necessarily choose at my advanced age to return to these travails of my youth so I merely observe that each element of progress contains within it a counter movement of something that is being sadly lost.

The one thing that has remained untouched by the passage of time is the feeling I get on derby day. I have profound misgivings about City to the extent that most matches now arouse little beyond a polite interest but if you line up eleven blue shirts against eleven red shirts something quite primeval starts to happen. Somehow a City v United match returns me to my natural state and no match revealed this more than the game that was played directly after the miserable Arsenal match in which Adebayor disgraced himself. It was the Old Trafford derby and it was, the result notwithstanding, as memorable a game as I have seen. Sometimes the tension of derby matches is so great that, like many a Cup final or semi-final, the result is a game of mind-numbing negativity with each side too frightened to risk anything for fear of being caught and ridiculed.

In late September 2009, New City went to Old Trafford with hopes of a result that would demonstrate the swinging of the pendulum from red to blue. Admittedly we had won there in February 2008 under Sven, but that had been the fiftieth anniversary of the Munich disaster, an odd day on which the football seemed to take second place to the momentousness of the occasion. The win, however satisfying, did not feel like the end of a red era and the start of a blue one and nor was it. This time, though, we had decent players like Carlos Tévez, Kolo Touré, Gareth Barry and Nigel de Jong, instead of Sven's patchwork quilt of Darius Vassell, Mwaruwari Benjani, Dietmar Hamann and Martin Petrov.

The odd thing about United is that I don't think they've had much of a team since Roy Keane was hustled out of the club with a blanket over his head like so many others who have said or done something to upset the tender sensibilities of the manager. Even the team that day sported John O'Shea, a very average full-back and a midfield containing the ageing limbs of Scholes and Giggs, which were still more effective than those of Anderson and Park who made up the rest of the middle four. The increasing girth of Wayne Rooney and the wildly ineffective Berbatov should not have made any newly acquired City millionaire shiver in his expensively sponsored boots. However, you can't deny that they have something beyond talent that is extremely difficult to quantify. The manager has instilled in his team an enviable belief in their own invincibility. It's a good place for any professional to exist, but to the analytical mind it always looks like one of those cartoon characters like Road Runner who keep running over the edge of a cliff and seem to hover in the air for a few seconds entirely unsupported by anything under their webbed feet until the inevitable plunge downwards. Occasionally United get what they should have received many times in the past few seasons – a 1–6 pasting at home by City or a 2–3 humiliation at the hands of relegation candidates Blackburn Rovers, a just reward for their arrogance and complacency. In most matches, however, this enduring aura of invincibility accounts for any opposition that displays the merest glimpse of mental frailty.

It was certainly much in evidence during that derby match in September 2009. Rooney put United ahead after just two minutes which should have induced a familiar sinking feeling, but didn't, because you hoped that these new players might not carry with them the expectation of defeat as previous City sides seemed to do when running out at Old Trafford. Sure enough, a bungling attempt to clear by the erratic Ben Foster resulted in his losing the ball to Tévez who unselfishly (a word that now appears like an oxymoron when in close proximity to the Argentine) rolled the ball across to Gareth Barry who carefully side-footed it into the unguarded net.

Tévez should have given us the lead just before half-time but missed badly, much to the delight of the home supporters who unaccountably did not appear to welcome the return of one of their former heroes. The second half began like the first, with Fletcher putting United ahead early on, only for the outstanding Bellamy to equalise, this time with a spectacular Roy of the Rovers shot across the helpless Foster and into the far corner. United knew they were in a game now and responded with verve but, for all their possession, they could not find a way past the indefatigable Shay Given until ten minutes from time, when Fletcher headed home from a Giggs cross. This was deeply frustrating and I was feeling every moment of passion in this passionate game as much as I ever had, so when Bellamy robbed Ferdinand out on the left-hand touchline near the halfway line and set off for goal leaving the tiring England defender gasping for breath in his wake, I was hoping for a last-minute miracle. He ended up on the United goal line near the edge of the penalty area, and somehow he managed to squeeze the ball under the diving body of the culpable Foster for an entirely unexpected but thrilling equaliser.

A share of the points was the least we deserved and it stunned the 72,000 majority of the 75,000 crowd. However, as we all knew, this game wasn't over. What we now had to face was a referee, in this case Martin Atkinson, who appeared to us to have decided he was going to permit play to continue until United scored. Again it evoked memories of ten-year-old boys playing football at David's birthday party and my deciding as referee and father, that the game would only end when the birthday boy's team were ahead, preferably with the birthday boy scoring the winning goal. Having said that, we still shouldn't have given them the satisfaction but in the ninty-seventh minute, after three equalising goals, Michael Owen stole the winner to end a memorable seven-goal thriller as it was inevitably termed. The final indignity was supplied by the sight of the unwelcome, unused substitute figure of Gary Neville provoking the crowd and then mendaciously claiming he was 'just warming up'.

I have welcomed the decision of Sky Sports to choose this 'Mini-Ferguson' to take the place of the unlamented Andy Gray because whenever I hear his voice I reach instantly for the remote control and watch the game with the sound switched off. I can thoroughly recommend the experience, by the way, and not just in attempting to create a Gary Neville-free zone in life generally. Simply by removing the irritating hysteria of most of the commentators in this manner it enables viewers to concentrate exclusively on the game itself. It's great. Try it! *The Artist* won the Academy Award for Best Picture at the 2012 Oscars. Maybe it will start a trend for silent football matches on television thus obviating the need for commentators at all.

City recovered from the defeat at Old Trafford to win convincingly 3–1 at home to West Ham United but then came a string of seven consecutive draws that ultimately proved to be the undoing of Mark Hughes. The first draw came at Villa Park, the game that was distinguished by the grace of Richard Dunne in not celebrating his goal. It was clear from the body language displayed by the manager and from the unsubtle hints dropped into the lap of the press by Cook, that Hughes's time at City had a finite span and it was shortly to reach its unnatural conclusion.

I was puzzled by my own reaction to these events. For years everything about supporting Manchester City had been straightforward, sometimes blessedly so in a life that was complicated, as many of our lives are. I was a City supporter and, to a degree, that defined the person I was. Anyone meeting me, say, at some kind of reunion after twenty-five years would remember me as that ridiculous Manchester City supporter and some kind of City-related conversation would break the ice as we surreptitiously compared expanding waistlines. Usually I blustered something inconsequential in reply to a question about my reaction to recent developments but it was starting to get too complicated to be able to summarise succinctly in a trivial conversation.

All I could really trust were my own fundamental emotions. The pleasure I felt at the sight of Bellamy's two goals at Old Trafford was as intense as anything I had experienced when Francis Lee or Colin Bell had scored at Old Trafford. They were marvellous goals, they shut the Red supporters up if only briefly and they lifted my spirits in the way all City goals used to do. Conversely, when Owen scored the winner in the ninty-seventh minute I was as devastated in that familiar stomach-churning way I remembered only too well.

I had filmed a short interview for ESPN the day before I left for Boston to catch up with the progress of my fourteen-month-old grandson Ollie. It was comforting to be sitting on the couch holding the baby and looking at my son — three generations of City fans with the youngest now setting out on his own path as a boy in blue. When ESPN rang for a reaction for their Monday night programme, I was holding Ollie under one hand with the telephone receiver in the other. I looked at my grandson whose life I was going to blight in the way I had blighted that of his father. I had already told ESPN that our conversation might be interrupted by the small child I was looking after, so Mark Chapman was primed to ask, 'And how did your little grandson take the result?' I looked at the innocent face in front of me. 'He said he was very disappointed with the refereeing,'

I replied. I thought he might as well get used to the language of these occasions sooner rather than later.

After the raw excitement and disappointment of the derby match it was back to my emotionally neutral stance, which was only coincidentally paralleled by those seven consecutive draws. I tried hard to recapture the passion that had been reawakened during the game at Old Trafford but it wouldn't come. Drawing at home to Fulham, Hull City and Burnley, three clubs we should have dispatched without a second thought, I felt none of the usual gnawing pangs of frustration. What I was faced with was a horrible realisation that, with the exception of any game that involved Manchester United, I no longer cared if City won or lost. Losing didn't hurt, winning gave me no sense of exhilaration. I was bereaved. My club had been taken away from me and transformed by the riches of foreign owners whom I neither respected nor trusted into an entity with which I could no longer sympathise let alone empathise.

My next trip to Boston was for the Christmas holiday season. Leaving London in the middle of December enabled me to spend time with Ollie and his parents before the rest of both sides of the family arrived for Christmas. The day I got there, City lost badly 3–0 at White Hart Lane. Mark Hughes was a dead man walking. Thanks to the miracle of David's satellite television subscription I could watch the matches that kicked off at 3pm on Saturdays live and so we sat down to watch City win 4–3 in an entertaining mistake-strewn match at home to Sunderland. By the time the game started, Hughes knew his fate and stood impassively in the technical area, probably as bemused as the rest of us as to why the incompetent Cook had chosen the moment of a predictable victory to lower the axe when he might have done it to wider popular acclaim after the poor performance at Tottenham Hotspur on the Wednesday.

Shay Given and Craig Bellamy were reported to have led a deputation to the boardroom to complain at the treatment meted out to a manager they liked and respected but it was the press that did their work for them. They descended on Cook and his employers and ripped into them for the cack-handed manner in which they had handled the situation. There were comprehensible arguments on both sides that Hughes should or should not be given more time to supervise the new signings and ensure they integrated better than they had done so far. I was torn myself. Hughes had not particularly endeared himself to me as a supporter either by his robotic manner on television or by the apparent failure of some of his big signings, particularly Santa Cruz, Adebayor and Lescott. On the other hand, the appalling manner of his removal reminded me of the legend of the death of Mary Queen of Scots whose execution apparently needed half a dozen attempts before the man with the axe managed to strike her head from her shoulders.

Apparently the owners were both astonished and annoyed that they were so roundly and justifiably criticised in the press. Clearly, they believed they had bought the club, they had spent a large sum of money on re-equipping it and so they could do with it whatever they wanted. If they wanted to change the manager they could do so and the very idea that the press or the supporters might have a different point of view which they might wish to articulate seemed to them to be insufferably disloyal. If you have been raised in the tradition of absolute monarchy it is quite difficult to get your head around the concept of rule by parliamentary democracy. As far as they were concerned, they had lavished a fortune on this 'project' and we supporters, I am sure, were seen by them as ungrateful children.

The bad press they got for the sacking of Hughes was

compounded when Cook held a press conference in which he tried to explain with sweet reasonableness his side of things and, predictably, simply exacerbated matters. Somehow he managed to convey that only after the seven draws was the possibility of Hughes being removed raised. In language better suited to the marketing department at Nike in Portland, Oregon, it was explained that Hughes was expected to achieve a total of seventy points by the end of the season. His latest results, when plotted on a graph, suggested he was falling below the line that indicated ultimate success. That was why Hughes was dismissed. When someone revealed that it was well known that Cook had approached Guus Hiddink's agent at the start of the season, the marketing unflappability disappeared. More comical was the fact that the urbane, sophisticated new manager Roberto Mancini openly told the assembled media that he had met the chairman Khaldoon some weeks earlier. One of them was badly 'off message' and it continued to spiral downwards.

Asked why he had not simply informed Hughes on the Wednesday night that he was being replaced by Mancini, Cook blustered that the chairman wanted to sack Hughes in person but unfortunately couldn't get a seat reservation on a plane until Saturday morning, which left Hughes to get through the public humiliation of the match against Sunderland knowing that his P45 was already inside his jacket pocket. Cook had transformed Manchester City, all right – from a club that couldn't win a trophy to a club without dignity, class or honour. Cook and his mean-spirited, arrogant employers deserved every column inch of the vituperative criticism they received.

In previous years, incompetence in the executive offices produced the standard response of 'Sack the Board', demonstrations outside the front entrance of Maine Road and angry letters in the

Manchester Evening News Football Pink. The directors might claim to be unmoved by this public display of disaffection but they couldn't ignore it and their wives couldn't ignore it either in the hairdresser's or at their charity coffee mornings. If you live in Abu Dhabi there is no limit to the number of angry letters in the *Manchester Evening News* that you can comfortably ignore. Hughes didn't inspire supporters to go to the wall in his defence, like Brian Clough had achieved when he was sacked by Sam Longson at Derby County in 1973. Mark Hughes did not inspire affection like Joe Mercer or Malcolm Allison.

There was a perception among many City supporters that he had been badly treated but he was yesterday's man now and, as the executives at Manchester City knew perfectly well, a new manager, a new transfer window and an upcoming run of relatively easy games that promised a series of solid victories would ensure that Mark Hughes and the Welsh mafia, presumably well compensated for their humiliating departure, would go the way of Ron Saunders, Mel Machin and Brian Horton. The chances were that City's new 'supporters', the people Cook really cared about, those fanatics who were desperate for news of 'their' club on their mobile phones in China and the Far East, had never heard of Saunders, Machin and Horton and did not care to learn. Who was the next £30 million player and when was he coming? That was what these people cared about.

It was becoming increasingly hard for me to define what it meant to be a Manchester City supporter in the twenty-first century. The club was executing a sharp turn to the right and I was being left standing at the bus stop, although plenty of other supporters were hopping on board without a care in the world. When City went to Stamford Bridge in February 2010 and won 4–2, completing the double over Chelsea, I should have been ecstatic. In the early 1990s I was in the old West Stand because I could only get a ticket among the Chelsea supporters when Mike Sheron scored a fine goal there. Instinctively I rose to my feet, arms aloft and was told pretty sharply by a policeman to sit down again and revert to my previously inconspicuous status. The Deputy Governor of the Bank of England as I think he was at the time smirked gleefully in the seat next to me. Like Howard, I had loved the club with all my heart for nearly sixty years, yet now I had reached the stage where an outstanding victory at Chelsea raised not much more than a resigned shrug of the shoulders.

What was especially galling about that particular win in February 2010 was that I had shared the widespread belief of many football supporters that Abramovich's purchase of Chelsea had been bad for the game and to see Chelsea overturned at home by my team should have been the occasion for sticking up a middle finger at the owner's box. Morally I could not do this. What was the difference between a billionaire from Russia buying the Premiership and a billionaire from the UAE doing exactly the same thing? I suppose you could argue that at least Abramovich showed up at Stamford Bridge fairly often because he liked to watch this particular investment into which he had poured some intemperate emotion. The man whose money had bought and transformed Manchester City into the footballing equivalent of a seven star hotel in Abu Dhabi couldn't even be bothered to show up at Eastlands. Well I had no interest in staying at seven star hotels. My natural instinct is to take my holidays in a small hotel in the Lake District from where I can set out each morning to climb Great Gable, Skiddaw or Helvellyn. The gap between where I was and where the owners wanted to take Manchester City was growing wider every day.

I did not suffer their muddle-headed stewardship of my club in silence. BBC Radio 5 live invited me on to a programme with David Bernstein in which we would discuss in sound bite chunks the impact of the new ownership of our club. The programme was called, somewhat predictably, *The Abu Dhabi Blues*. Insofar as it was possible to do so in between the news headlines, the weather and traffic reports and commentary from a cycle race in the velodrome, I set out, in as calm a voice as I could muster, some of the doubts that had assailed me since 1 September 2008. The following day the assistant producer on the programme rang me to say that the woman who sang under the title of Director of Communications at Manchester City had been dismayed by my negative comments. Perhaps, it was suggested, I would like to attend a match as a guest of the club so that in the future my comments would be considerably more positive in tone. I replied with what I thought was commendable calm that the woman who complained should be given my telephone number and I would be happy to explain to her in person why my tone was perceived as negative, although I did think that if she had actually listened to what I had said, rather than reacted instinctively, she would have to agree that I was making valid points.

As I replaced the receiver I was suddenly overwhelmed by the futility of it all. Did this woman really think that for the price of a free seat, a cup of tea and a chocolate digestive biscuit at half-time I would instantly dismiss all my reservations about what had happened to the club? It bothered me that this was the woman who was now charged with conveying the image of my club to the public. I could only presume that she had been acting under the orders of the new marketing regime that had been installed by her boss who had so memorably welcomed Uwe Rösler to 'the Manchester United Hall of Fame'.

*

Manchester City had always been the crutch on which I had leaned when my emotional life was in turmoil. Now I looked down to see the crutch lying in pieces at my feet. Returning from Boston shortly after the Hughes debacle and the installation of Roberto Mancini and Giuseppe Mazzini in Manchester, I came to the end of yet another short-lived relationship. She was a nice woman but like all the other nice women I had met she wasn't the woman I needed or wanted. January and February were the months in which I spent a lot of time teaching and lecturing so I deliberately stayed clear of internet dating sites which could be extremely time consuming and ultimately, as I had found to my cost over the past couple of years, quite unrewarding.

At the suggestion of a friend I decided in March 2010 after the end of the Lent term to try another approach, this time based on my love of music. Classic FM ran a dating site she said, why didn't I try that one? I demurred, explaining that, much as I liked listening to the music the station played, I wanted to exterminate the jovial and mostly uninformed presenters and that I had always loved Alan Bennett's description of Classic FM listeners as Saga Louts. She replied tartly that since I listened to it I must be one of them, a logic with which I could not disagree. In truth though, I felt that I was essentially a Radio 4 and Radio 3 listener. Why didn't *they* run internet dating sites? Lovers of *Composer of the Week* or *Money Box Live* would be bound to be drawn to one another.

By now I was an old hand at this game of filling in the profile so instead of writing another variation on the Warwick the Kingmaker joke, I would try an entirely different approach. It wouldn't find me a partner but it would amuse me while I worked on it. Eventually I settled on the handle of 'Alexander Portnoy'. *Portnoy's Complaint* was my *Desert Island Discs* book so any intelligent lover of classical music might also realise that I was Jewish and that I liked the novels of Philip Roth.

No long evenings in and short days out were visible as my target female audience was confronted by the following description of myself, disguised in what I thought was an original way:

He screwed back the top of his haemorrhoid ointment and zipped up his trousers. 'Wouldn't it be nice,' he sighed, 'to find someone who would always be around to find the haemorrhoid ointment. Someone who ... oh, I don't know, maybe had something wrong with her. Nothing major, of course, just something irritating like laughing whilst chewing a mouthful of peanuts and spraying bits into the four corners of the room.'

He went over to the window and looked out, noting the leaves on the trees that had started to turn red and flutter to the ground. Another autumn was upon him, gripping him in its annual melancholy. He had to do something to arrest the onset of his profound sadness. A woman to soothe the ravages of his mind was all he wanted. 'I know,' he thought, 'I'll start dating online. The people who do that are all mad, desperate and with a poor standard of personal hygiene – and that's just the men. I'll find someone there.'

He typed away diligently, sending details of his credit card to a suite of offices in a remote Caribbean island. He was surprised, when writing longingly of his passionate desire to meet a beautiful, intelligent, sophisticated woman in her early 50s who could reproduce the melody from the last movement of Sibelius 2 in the manner of Le Pétomane, to be greeted on his computer screen by photographs of men in a state of remarkable arousal. 'I think,' he said to himself sadly, 'I might more profitably read *Women in Love* again.'

As before, there were plenty of clues there to the real nature of the author – low comedy, slapstick, a tendency towards melancholia, desire both intellectual and physical, a love of music and literature and an anxiety about trusting the internet with my credit card details. The form continued with details of likes and dislikes and concluded with a request for the description of my perfect date. I decided to set the bar rather high:

> My ideal match would be able to multi-task. She should be able to perform a root canal operation whilst doing the hoovering, cook an elegant six course dinner whilst reading *The Gulag Archipelago* in Sanskrit and achieve orgasm whilst on the phone to her mother. This sexy, smart, intellectual, emotionally literate elder sister of Buffy the Vampire Slayer should ideally have served two terms as president of the European Commission and have had her sense of humour surgically removed by the Director of Human Resources for the Taliban. She doesn't have to have opened the batting for England but she does need to know how to spell and where to place an apostrophe.

By now you will recognise the style. By now so did most of the unattached female population of the country. Two women made it through the qualifying stages to reach the dating finals. Both were in their mid-fifties. One was a high-flying academic, the other was the polar opposite – a woman who had trained as a dancer with the Royal Ballet but who had left to take up a modelling career, working (so she said, of course) with photographers like Duffy, Bailey and Donovan. The academic had teenage children; the ballet dancer had grown-up children. Each lasted precisely one very 'successful' date. I liked them both. To all intents and appearances they liked me. The academic who had written very un-academic emails before we met was charming, delightful, attractive, witty, interesting. 'I've told the babysitter I'll be back at twelve thirty,' she said within five minutes of meeting me. 'Fair enough,' I thought. It was a perfectly reasonable stance to adopt even if doing it in quite that manner at that early point in the relationship felt a little abrupt.

Nevertheless, the evening proceeded apace and ended at exactly the time she wanted. It seemed, as I drove her back to the station, that we had both had a good time and I looked forward to the next occasion. Admittedly, we had a slight disagreement about our voting intentions at the General Election which was due to take place in three weeks' time but I thought no more about it. The following day was a Sunday. By the time I had stirred and stretched and worked myself into a state where I could turn on the computer, a letter from her was already waiting for me in my inbox. Owing to our being at different stages in our lives, she wrote, it would be better if we didn't see each other again; particularly since she intended to vote Conservative which I clearly was not going to do. I was, for that entire Sunday, terribly upset, cursing our different attitudes to 'tax and spend' fiscal policies which seemed to be at the root of a thwarted romantic encounter.

Five days later, the striking photograph of the ballet dancer–model floated across my consciousness and I seized on it eagerly. This time I felt fairly sure there would be no fundamental disagreements on political or socio-economic matters. I didn't know what sort of pillow talk she had previously engaged in, given her interestingly bohemian lifestyle, but I was pretty sure it didn't extend to a detailed discussion of Gordon Brown's immigration policy which was that week's hot topic. Again, the encounter seemed to be mutually beneficial. It was a lunch on a warm April day at a pub overlooking the river and as we wandered along the street back to the station we discussed our next date. It was going to be lunch in two days' time at my house.

I busied myself, ensuring that both the house and the householder were in their best state. I went shopping for the most delicious delicacies Tesco could provide. Meanwhile, she had written in high excitement that according to the AA website it was a distance of 18.1 miles between our respective dwellings and the journey should take her no longer than 39 minutes. I had set the table, opened the wine and mounted the stairs when I heard the beeps indicating a text message had arrived. I assumed the message was telling me she had just set off at the start of her 39-minute journey. When I came down, appropriately attired and perfum'd, I opened the text. It began, devastatingly, 'You will know by now that I am not coming.' I stared at the phrase before moving on to what I felt instinctively and correctly would be no real explanation. My attempts to elicit one went unrewarded. I now felt cursed, marked for life as unlovable, doomed to wander the earth as an outcast from romance. These rejections all hurt, not because they were from women I was madly in love with, but because they kept ripping off the scab from the same wound that had only recently started to heal.

That's it, I thought, I've had it with internet dating. Period. Classic FM has disappointed me in this area, just as it does when its presenters talk down to me. My month on the site is nearly up, I'm going back to Radio 4 Extra or Radio 7, as it was then called, so I could comfort myself with endless re-runs of *The Goon Show* and *Take It From Here*. On 1 May I was going to pay my regular springtime visit to Boston to play with Ollie, who by now was nearly two and managed to make the words 'duck', 'truck', 'sock' and 'dog' all sound indistinguishable from one another. Lancashire were setting out on their annual quest to win the County

Championship outright for the first time since 1934, although in reality our ambitions were limited to ensuring that they avoided relegation to Division Two. I had no need of a woman or indeed of a date, certainly not now and possibly not at any time in the future.

A couple of days before departure I found a note in my inbox from Classic FM. Instead of deleting it in a stupid fury I decided to open it because in the subject box it contained the phrase 'Free Offer' – two words which, in direct juxtaposition to each other, I find irresistible. The free offer turned out to be a free extra week now that my paid-for month had expired. It had only been a few days since I had sworn off the site for good. It seemed unlikely that Ursula Andress or Julie Christie or any of the heroines of my adolescence had joined the Classic FM dating site in my absence. A swift trawl through confirmed that to be the case. Then the mouse saw a profile headlined 'Accidental Soloist' and it hovered.

Chapter Fifteen

I CAN'T REMEMBER THE DETAILS OF THAT PROFILE AND ITS composer refuses point blank to help me, attributing my ignorance to reprehensible neglect. I remembered that she said she liked going to Italy and interestingly, dry-stone walls. The dry-stone walls did not involve building them, impressive as that would have been, but admiring them in the Yorkshire Dales, from where the paternal side of her family had originated. I suppose, superficial male as I remain, that it was the photograph that had probably made the mouse pause. It showed a delightful face; it was pretty, warm, sympathetic, smiling, revealing neatly cut, shoulder-length hair. 'Accidental Soloist' was much cleverer than 'Alexander Portnoy', which probably only provoked thoughts of sexually obsessed American Jews. 'Accidental Soloist' evoked the novel *The Accidental Tourist* by Anne Tyler and a clever play on words from a woman who had not expected to be on her own in her late fifties. It was a pleasing start but recent events had combined to make me cautious.

It soon became apparent that Accidental Soloist could write exceptionally well. We embarked on an old-fashioned epistolary courtship, she in West Molesey near Hampton Court, me in Auburndale in the suburbs of Boston. Every day I looked forward eagerly to those elegant email letters in which she expressed her emotions so fluently. We had both lost our spouses, a parent in our teens and our best friends in recent years. Those statements of fact started to forge a bond. We then slowly exchanged those pieces of information in which we truly reveal who we are. For the first time since I had begun this whole internet dating process I was writing not in a flirtatious way and not in a way designed to show off but with a genuine desire to get to know this remarkable woman. Accidental Soloist was unlike anyone else I had met over the internet. I had such a clear picture of her that when she told me that her name was Katherine I felt as if I should have known it.

Like Victorian lovers, we wrote once or twice a day, each exchange of correspondence building a picture of each other that proved more and more attractive until the one that arrived with the piece of information that simply stopped me dead in my tracks. I knew that Katherine had a son and a daughter who was about to give birth to her first child. This grandchild would be named Oliver, another bond of coincidence. However, the email which arrived midway through my stay in Boston informed me that Katherine also had another child, a son, William, who had died in an accident at the age of eleven, some seventeen years before. It was a shocking piece of news. I knew other parents who had lost children and of course it immediately raised memories of Amy's cancer when she was twelve. Katherine and I shared so many of life's blessings and misfortunes but this one overwhelming tragedy was something I could never begin to measure.

I wrote back immediately, unwilling to trust myself to think about how to compose the perfect reply. Whatever I wrote came directly from the heart and must have passed whatever test had been set because Katherine thanked me for writing sensitively and understandingly (though who could not in such circumstances?). By the time I flew back from Boston to London I was keenly anticipating our first meeting. Usually internet dating led to a meeting after a brief flurry of emails over a few days. On this occasion, simply because I was out of the country, we had been forced to take things more slowly. I thought it almost certain that when we did actually see each other face to face for the first time we would be at ease in each other's company.

We decided to meet on the South Bank for an afternoon concert at the Royal Festival Hall. It made me smile to see that the programme included the infamous Sibelius 2, which by coincidence I had written about on the dating website profile, as well as Dvorak's sublime cello concerto. It was the penultimate Sunday in May 2010, the football season was thankfully over, the Champions League having been won the previous night by José Mourinho as he was passing briefly through Milan. The day was hot and I sat in the cool interior of an Italian restaurant, unwilling to swelter outside with the sun worshippers. The Victorians knew a thing or two about staying out of the sun as well as the attractions of a love affair conducted by the exchange of formal correspondence.

In the event I arrived early and Katherine's South West Trains service was late. She texted me this unsurprising news and I replied that there was no rush and she mustn't race over from Waterloo Station. I still had my head down looking at the screen of my phone, screwing up my eyes because my vanity did not permit me to bring my reading glasses when I heard a soft 'Hello'. I looked up to see the smiling face that I had only ever seen before on a computer screen. It was both a pleasure and a relief.

We talked easily with none of the anxiety and guardedness I had experienced on previous first dates. After lunch, before the concert started we walked along the South Bank licking ice creams as fast as we could before the strong May sun turned them back into liquid. For the record I can state that the Dvorak cello concerto was beautifully played by Alban Gerhardt, and Esa-Pekka Salonen conducted the Philharmonia Orchestra perfectly in the Sibelius. The rest I shall draw a discreet veil over. The Victorians knew a thing or two about that as well.

Chapter Sixteen

IN THE YEAR THAT I WAS BORN, 1949, EALING STUDIOS made *Passport to Pimlico*, one of its best comedies. It is a charming, whimsical story of a fourteenth-century document unearthed on a bomb site that appears to prove that the area of London near Victoria called Pimlico still 'belongs' to the mediaeval Kingdom of Burgundy. The expert, played by Margaret Rutherford, gives evidence in court that the people of Pimlico are not Londoners and Englishmen, as they had all previously supposed, but Burgundians. 'Blimey,' says a bewildered policeman, 'I'm a foreigner!'

It's a charming film which appealed to its initial delighted audience because it prompted the fantasy of a life free from rationing and all the petty bureaucratic restrictions of the age of austerity in which they lived. That line of the policeman, however, always echoes in my mind. It was funny because, in 1949, the very idea that a Cockney copper could be a foreigner was in itself comic. We live now in a society so multi-cultural that the line has lost its power. Today's Metropolitan Police is nothing like the police force of 1949. The England of *Passport to Pimlico* has gone with the wind. The England that I was born into simply doesn't exist any longer, yet my attitudes to life were shaped by growing up in Manchester in the 1950s and 1960s and I can't really change them.

It's not that I decline to embrace change, although I have chosen not to embrace either Facebook or Twitter. I do have an extremely intelligent and highly cultured friend who refuses to buy a computer and won't condescend to use email so I receive letters in the post typed on a battered old typewriter which appears to be the same one he used in the 1970s. That's a charming eccentricity but it doesn't occur to me to imitate his lifestyle. I can, after some patient coaching from my children, download podcasts on to my MP3 player. I have three DVD players, two digital televisions and an iPod. I shop and bank online. I have embraced as much of modern life as might be considered reasonable for a sixty-two-year-old man. Why then do I continue to resist the blandishments of the Premier League and the bright shiny future for Manchester City so selflessly purchased for me by the club's latest owners?

In *The Mikado*, written in 1885 by W. S. Gilbert and Arthur Sullivan, Ko-Ko the Lord High Executioner of Titipu, sings of his 'little list' of people he finds deeply offensive and who comprise the names of the heads he'd like to chop off. Among them is 'the idiot who praises with enthusiastic tone/Every century but this and every country but his own.' I hope with all my heart that this is not the way I am perceived, for in truth I envy those of my friends who have managed to make the adjustment necessary to find the new Manchester City as attractive as the old Manchester City. To them remains the vision of the Promised Land. To me remains a significantly diminished life, devoid of those moments of ecstasy and even those of despair. Famous victories and desperate defeats are the stuff of life for a supporter but if I can look at a City defeat and a City win and treat those imposters just the same then I am not a man, my son, I am in fact an ex-supporter.

That does not mean, of course, that I spend my Saturday

afternoons oblivious to what is happening on the football fields of England. I do not wander round department stores, a lost soul, impervious to the deeply irritating shouts of the Sky Sports *Soccer Saturday* team who are embarked on the ludicrous task of watching television screens on behalf of the viewers who are forced to pay a monthly subscription for this service. I am relieved that occasionally matters are lightened by Jeff Stelling's dissolution into a pool of liquid around 4.45pm, caused by his stage-managed hysteria or by the original pronunciation of the name Thierry Henry by Robbie Fowler as 'Terry Enry'. I am perfectly aware of City's progress, as ever I was; it's just that their wins don't thrill me and their rare defeats don't depress me. Lynn would be astonished and frustrated that she had to live the entire length of a thirty-two-year marriage with a man whose moods were dictated by eleven men in blue shirts kicking a ball about. 'Why are you in such a bad mood?' she would ask me at 5.15pm on a Saturday afternoon after City had just lost 3–1 at home. Even after thirty-two years she couldn't understand.

It's taken me the duration of this book to try to explain how that fanatical devotion to the fortunes of my home town club has dissipated in the years since control of it passed into the hands of a former prime minister of Thailand. The problem is not so much that he was from Thailand rather than Rochdale or that the current owners come from Abu Dhabi and not Failsworth. Heavens above, Joe Smith who bought the club in 1972 ran his Weatherseal company in Oldham and his purchase of Frank Johnson's shares for £110,000 was the start of the bad times in the boardroom. It's not so much the fact of foreign ownership that lies at the root of my unease as the money that it now requires to run a football club automatically excludes most rich local men because they are not rich enough. I thought Jack Walker's purchase of Blackburn

Rovers, of Sutton and Shearer, of Dalglish and the Premier League, was altogether a jolly good thing, particularly as it deprived Manchester United of the title on the last day of the season, even though Blackburn lost at Anfield to a free kick by Redknapp in the last minute. It was a romantic story because Walker was a Blackburn lad, a true and faithful supporter of his home town club, a man who chose to spend the proceeds of his life's work in the steel business on the club on whose terraces he had stood as a kid. There was still room for romance in the Premier League in 1995. It's gone now, I'm afraid; vanished like that joke in *Passport to Pimlico*. It's the money that's done it.

You don't have to be a Marxist or even share my instinctive suspicion of capitalism to decry the influence of money in English football. The Premier League is 'a great product' or so the Premier League consistently tells us. Marks & Spencer's 'Salmon en Croute' is also a great product but when I am not buying it, cooking it or eating it, I don't give it a moment's thought. I give Manchester City plenty of thoughts and mostly they are of the variety, 'Please can I have my football club back?'

I return to Gilbert and Sullivan because *The Gondoliers*, their affectionate satire on monarchy, still contains more than the odd line which is relevant to our contemporary world. I was introduced to G & S at a very early age and as a party piece I used to be able to sing, tunelessly, some of the songs which I had learned almost phonetically without the slightest understanding of what the words actually meant. One of the songs concerns the story of a good-hearted king who, in a policy born of kindness, spreads his riches before his grateful people. Unfortunately, the king finds that his largesse leads only to social chaos and an increasing lack of appreciation as the law of diminishing returns kicks in.

The end is easily foretold/When every blessed thing you hold/ Is made of silver or of gold/You long for simple pewter.

When you have nothing else to wear/But cloth of gold and satins rare/For cloth of gold you cease to care/Up goes the price of shoddy.

It's a song that I have been singing, as tunelessly as ever with increasing frequency since the day a bewildered Robinho landed in Manchester or, as he seemed to indicate by his distracted behaviour, on Mars.

City won the FA Cup in May 2011 for the first time since 1969. It was the club's first trophy since 1976. I had been to Wembley to see the semi-final victory over United but I felt no such compulsion to repeat the exercise for the final against Stoke, even though David was back from Boston, so he and I and Amy and Adam Rosenthal watched it together on television in the living room. It was a poor game, Stoke seemingly having expended all their energy on beating Bolton 5–0 in their semi-final. When Yaya Touré's goal went in, I was transferring the clothes from the washing machine to the tumble dryer. I didn't feel deprived at having missed it. When the players went up to receive the trophy I was elsewhere in the house having already lost interest.

When City win the Premier League and when they follow that triumph with victory in the Champions League final, I shall be watching on television and dropping my eyes down to the book I will probably be reading at the same time. The more money they spend, the more predictable will the games become and the more meaningless the results and the consequent prizes, exactly as that Victorian lyricist had once foretold. When the team holds up the trophy on its open-top bus tour round the UAE it will not be for my edification. Deep in my heart where my love for

Manchester City resides there is a small vacuum. It's only small because I have a lifetime of memories of Manchester City that fill most of the ventricles.

When City won the FA Cup in May 2011 Lancashire were already top of the LV County Championship. Their last outright Championship pennant had been won in 1934, the same year that City had won the Cup for the second time in their history, an encouraging omen. I had seen too many summers when Lancashire had chased the winners all the way to the finishing post to end a gallant, unlucky second, to become too excited by their perfect start. The idea that City and Lancashire would achieve another double seemed even more unlikely.

However, as the summer progressed and, despite the two defeats to Durham and a desperate collapse at New Road to give relegation-threatened Worcestershire an easy win, something was clearly stirring in Lancashire CCC. They were winning games they had no right to win. They scored 121 in 14.2 overs to beat Yorkshire with just four balls left to play. In the penultimate game of the season at Aigburth, Simon Kerrigan took 9–51 on the last afternoon to beat Hampshire with three minutes left. The tenth wicket partnership of Neil McKenzie and James Tomlinson had batted through 21 excruciating overs before Smith caught McKenzie at slip. The last match of the season was against Somerset in Taunton. Katherine had renovated a terrace house in Frome. I could stay there and drive to Taunton each day. I hadn't seen every day of a Championship match for years but I had always fantasised about being present on the day Lancashire won the Championship and, even though Warwickshire would still win the title if they beat the hapless, already-relegated Hampshire, I just felt that it was worth the gamble.

For the past few seasons since the retirement of the team of Atherton, Fairbrother, Hegg and Martin, Lancashire had relied far too much in my opinion on overseas signings, inter-county transfers and foreign Kolpak players who were permitted to play county cricket through a loophole in the European employment laws. As an example of what I mean, when the long-serving Warren Hegg finally retired, instead of giving a chance to Gareth Cross, the young reserve team wicketkeeper from Bury, the coach Mike Watkinson signed Luke Sutton from Derbyshire so Dominic Cork could have a friend to play with.

In 2011, Lancashire were involved in a bitter legal dispute with an implacable rival over their development plans without which they would be unlikely to survive as a financial concern. The Jarndyce versus Jarndyce nature of the English legal system drained the coffers and there was no money left for the new coach Peter Moores to spend on expensive signings. Out of necessity he was forced to promote young players from the second eleven. Under the wise guidance of the veteran captain Glen Chapple and the indefatigable, balding, slow left-armer, Gary Keedy, the youngsters blossomed. There were no stars, everyone played for each other, took pleasure in each other's performance and contributed whatever he could. It was everything I wanted City to be – local, youthful, unglamorous, talented and successful.

We all knew that, on that flat Taunton pitch, bowling out Somerset twice was not going to be easy but every time it looked as though the match was going to run away from them, Lancashire responded. On the first afternoon Somerset were 259–3 before Lancashire gritted their teeth and took the last seven wickets for the addition of only another 121 runs. When their own first innings bogged down at 331–6 the last four wickets added 149 to gain a first-innings lead of exactly a hundred. Nobody made more than 68 but everyone got into double figures. It was a typical gutsy performance and the third day ended with Somerset in trouble at

104–5. There was a strong likelihood we would take the other five wickets and knock off the runs just after lunch on the last day. Unfortunately, Hampshire were not keeping their part of the bargain and they ended day three following on behind Warwickshire and had already collapsed to 43–3 in their second innings. Even if we won, so, it seemed, would Warwickshire and the Championship would again remain tantalisingly out of our grasp.

The last day of the county cricket season dawned bright and fair. On the run from Frome to Taunton the rolling Somerset landscape had never looked more beautiful – at least to someone who had never seen it before he had met Katherine. There was a hardy group of Lancashire supporters who cheered their team to the echo without the need to abuse the Somerset supporters, who roundly applauded their side's recovery from the depths of 130–7 to a worrying total of 310 all out. I never saw those last two wickets fall, having incarcerated myself in the Gents – recommended by Neville Cardus as the most reliable way he knew to take wickets for Lancashire – but I heard the roar and emerged to find that we needed 211 at a rate of more than six an over. This run rate doesn't sound much in the days of T20 cricket but in first-class cricket with wides down the leg-side frequently not given, as they are in one-day cricket, and with no field restrictions it would not be easy.

More to the point, as the late morning passed into lunch and the heart of the afternoon, the news from the Rose Bowl was that Neil McKenzie, who had defied us for so long at Aigburth, and Michael Carberry, who had only recently returned to the game after a serious illness, were both on their way to scarcely believable centuries. Far from wilting, Hampshire looked as though they were going to defy Warwickshire at the last. Stephen Moore and Paul Horton set out in pursuit of the victory total as if it were a one-day game and soon they had the run rate up beyond seven an over. Both passed their half centuries but then got out, leaving Lancashire on 135–2. The news from Southampton was that Hampshire were still batting out time and it seemed probable now that the match there would end in a draw. If Lancashire didn't collapse at this supreme moment we would do it. Young Karl Brown (appropriately from the small town of Atherton) and Steven Croft from Blackpool never looked troubled. Somerset strove mightily to prevent the victory charge but they couldn't do it. Around five o'clock, on a glorious Somerset afternoon in late September with the first nip of autumnal chill still an hour or so away, Croft drove Meschede for two and the title came back to Lancashire in a noisy, emotional, tear-filled celebration.

The tension of the four days dissipated entirely with news from the Rose Bowl that Hampshire's heroic resistance had successfully blunted the Warwickshire attack and Sky Sports packed up their cameras in the full knowledge that they had gone to the wrong match. As Croft and Brown leapt into each other's arms and were joined by the entire squad sprinting from the pavilion on to the pitch, a middle-aged man unashamedly wept. Tears filled his eyes as he thought of his uncle Laurence who had instilled a love of Lancashire cricket almost from birth, of his school friends whom he'd dragged on the bus to Old Trafford, of his older brother who bowled against the garage to encourage his cover drive and who is now the vice chairman of the club. Above all, he cried at the memory of the men he first saw wearing the red rose cresting the caps he was to know so well. Into his mind came the vision of his great hero Brian Statham running in to bowl from the Stretford End, the wind filling his open shirt like the breeze sweeping an Elizabethan galleon across the seas.

I had plenty of City heroes, too, who roused that kind of

emotional response in me – pre-eminently Bert Trautmann, Colin Bell and Mike Summerbee. Somehow Lancashire's triumph and, above all, the manner of their victory confirmed my belief that my disappointment at the way City had lost their romantic aura was a reasonable and genuine reaction. I hadn't changed. I was still the same sports-mad romantic I had always been and in today's world of sport, driven by money and the media, creating sports stars obsessed with their wealth and their celebrity, there was still room for a moment such as Lancashire had given me at Taunton. Manchester City can buy twenty-five new players and pay them £10 million a year each and it will have no effect on me comparable to that moment when Croft scored the runs for victory. All my years in the Hornby Stand behind the bowler's arm (no longer, of course, since the pitch has recently been turned ninety degrees) watching Statham and Washbrook, Pullar and Marner, Lloyd and Engineer, Fairbrother and Atherton seemed somehow raised to that of a religious dedication. How I longed for City to be able to do that for me again but I didn't see how that was ever going to be possible now.

Although I think we baby boomers who were born between 1945 and 1960 have probably had the best of times, a life spared the miseries of war and depression that our parents had known only too well, few of us have led lives into which no rain has fallen. I have been blessed in so many ways – a free education to Ph.D. level at Cambridge, parents who could afford to clothe, feed and house me, a beautiful young wife and a long marriage, two wonderful, loving and successful children, and now at more than sixty years of age the extraordinary good fortune of falling in love with a clever and attractive woman for the second time in my life.

Set against that has been the awareness of the fragility of human happiness that has stayed with me since September 1962 when I was thirteen years old and I came home from school to be told that my mother was dead. To lose my wife, struck down by a similar neurological tragedy, seemed insupportable, but so life has always proceeded – triumph and tragedy, two sides of the same ubiquitous coin. Just in case I entertained any ideas that tragedy had gone off on holiday to Antarctica and was stranded out there on the ice, the summer of 2011 showed once more just how close the two emotions remained. David's father-in-law Ralph, a truly delightful man, passed away at the age of sixty-three, cut down by leukaemia. Two days after he died, Susie gave birth to his first granddaughter, Roselynn Shindler, a most welcome sister for Oliver.

Lynn and I had met Ralph and his wife Ava in Boston shortly after David and Susie had moved there in 2001. Ralph had endeared himself to me immediately for David had told me that Ralph was deeply devoted to the New York Mets, so when I met him I said, 'David tells me you're a Mets fan.' 'Well yes,' demurred Ralph, 'but really I'm a Brooklyn Dodgers fan.' I knew exactly what he meant. Brooklyn was where he and Ava had been born and grown up. Brooklyn was thickly present in his accent and I have no doubt in his heart, even after he and Ava and their children moved out to Metuchen, New Jersey. In 1957 when Ralph was nine years old, the owner of the Brooklyn Dodgers, a man called Walter O'Malley and a name engraved in enmity on the heart of every Brooklyn Dodgers supporter, simply moved the team from Brooklyn to Los Angeles. In 2002 when Ralph and I discussed this monstrous betrayal he confessed openly that his heart was still with the boys of '55 – Jackie Robinson, Roy Campanella, Pee Wee Reese. He also told me how lucky I was to be able to support my home town team, which had just been promoted back to the Premier League with the best chairman in football, a charismatic

manager and a team that thrilled and excited me with the exhilarating football it played. I smiled and I said I knew I was fortunate
but really nothing like what had happened to the Dodgers could
ever happen in English football. So much for my smug complacency.
Goodbye Manchester City, hello Abu Dhabi United.

Afterword

I HOPE THIS BOOK HAS BEEN AN EASY ONE TO READ BECAUSE it's been extremely difficult to write. It isn't just the traditional anxieties associated with any autobiography. How much does the writer have to reveal to make the reader an interested friend? How much detail is too much information? How little leaves the reader frustrated and dissatisfied? Who, among his friends and family who are described within its pages, will be offended by what they read? The hurt of bereavement never disappears entirely and a masochistic splashing about in the tub of memories can be an extremely painful experience as old wounds are exposed to public view. Thus far, so predictable.

To celebrate one's devotion to a football team takes little courage. To admit to a lessening of that devotion, to confess to being embarrassed by the behaviour of that club and to do so in plain sight of a remorseless media and an unforgiving public could be construed as idiotic. The bile, the hatred, the venom that is poured upon the heads of those who dare to question the infallibility of the club would act as a deterrent to most. The fact that I have dared to reveal the extent of my disillusionment with the entity that Manchester City has become is evidence of the depth of my feeling both for the club as it was and about the club as it is now.

The publication of this book will see the launch of a number of rather pointless attacks on me, certainly if they are directed towards me on Facebook or Twitter since I don't have an account on any social networking site, I am very pleased to say. If an author with my name pops up, I am afraid it will be the entirely blameless Professor of Israeli Studies at the School of Oriental and African Studies in the University of London, whose knowledge of football is, he will happily admit, not worth abusing. I am sorry if people take offence at the genuine expression of a personal opinion but I find it extremely disturbing that anyone who expresses views on football that do not accord with a very vocal and unpleasantly aggressive minority is subject to tirades of abuse, bile and venom (a splendid firm of solicitors). It is a trend that is deeply to be deplored and it is facilitated by the recent growth in these social networking sites and, indeed, in the interactive nature of broadcasting companies and newspaper websites. It is part of an aspect of modern society with which I feel entirely out of sympathy. Ethnic minorities who are subjected to hate crimes have in theory the protection of the law. Football supporters, even those of us who express our opinions forcefully but in a reasoned manner, are simply sitting targets for the worst kind of mindless abuse. I therefore repeat for the edification of Manchester City supporters who do not share my views that I respect their right to hold whatever views about the club they wish to profess. I ask only that the same respect and courtesy is shown to me, someone who has great moral doubts about the path upon which the club is currently embarked.

If I needed proof that the club was in the hands of people whose sensibilities I did not respect, the embarrassing exit performed by the co-executive chairman furnished all the evidence that was necessary. In September 2011 Garry Cook was forced into a resignation he clearly did not wish to make. His end was both predictable and humiliating for all concerned. He had written an email to the Director of Football, another of the many executive figures at Manchester City who seem to live in the shadows, ridiculing the mother of Nedum Onuoha who was continuing to conduct the contractual affairs of her son while undergoing chemotherapy for cancer but had mistakenly sent his unpleasant message to the unfortunate Dr Onuoha. His immediate response to the revelation of his maladroit use of the keyboard was that someone had hacked into his email. It was the equivalent of the well-known schoolboy's defence that 'the dog ate my homework'. It is not necessary to have experienced the ravages of cancer oneself or even to have lost someone close to you because of the insidious evil of the disease to be utterly disgusted by this behaviour, a feeling that was only exacerbated by Cook's reprehensible attempt to lie his way out of trouble.

In the end the owners, presumably confronted by incontrovertible evidence, persuaded him to leave. However, instead of dissociating themselves from their disgraced chairman in the strongest possible terms, they chose instead to laud his alleged achievements. 'His judgment in this matter,' opined Mubarak, 'should in no way lead to his accomplishments being overlooked.' As a denunciation of appalling behaviour this mealy-mouthed statement left something to be desired but it was in keeping with the self-congratulatory tenor of the club's current administration. They, like so many other Premier League clubs, appear to live in a hermetically sealed fantasy world that does not permit them to perceive life as the rest of us do.

Early in 2012, with the club's former star player still in self-imposed exile in Argentina, the club's public relations department cranked into action, releasing the information that by walking out on the club, and taking into account his fines and suspension, Carlos Tévez had foregone something in the region of £9.3 million. Clearly the intention was to tell the fans that Tévez was a fool and that the club had taken a strong and principled stand against him. Perhaps it did not occur to anyone at the club that supporters who earned £30,000 a year before tax and National Insurance deductions might possibly wonder why the club was paying this man such inflated sums of money in the first place.

In February 2012 the club that had taken such a firm and principled stand against their player's childish and expensive tantrum started to worry that Manchester United were breathing down their necks. Mario Balotelli, another of their gifted strikers seemingly with a chronological age far in excess of his mental age, was serving yet another ban, this time for back-heeling Scott Parker in the face. Roberto Mancini, who had constantly reiterated his decision that Tévez would never kick a ball for the club again, was apparently prepared to accept the Argentine back into the squad if the errant forward apologised. Tévez then complained that Mancini had treated him 'like a dog'.

It was an odd sort of apology from someone who was desperate to play football again and whose January transfer hopes had all evaporated. City wouldn't sell him for less than what they considered his market value, which was already some £20 million less than the fee for which they had reportedly signed him. By their foolishness in spraying money about simply because they could and without a thought for the consequences of their actions, the owners had made a rod for their own backs. They couldn't take a major hit on the Tévez transfer fee because they might be penalised by UEFA's projected Financial Fair Play Rules. With one hand they castigated their errant star and with the other they offered him a way back into the club.

A week after Tévez had publicly complained that his manager had treated him like a dog, the player returned to England and issued another public statement through the Manchester City public relations department, this time apologising 'sincerely' for the terrible wrong he had committed, which up to that moment he had vigorously denied. Predictably, the players, pragmatists to a man, welcomed him back with open arms. I didn't hear too many complaints from the fans either. City's defeat at Swansea had sent United back to the top of the table, causing fans to contemplate the unpalatable prospect of losing out to their bitterest rivals. Even the fans who had been photographed burning a Tévez replica shirt shortly after his disappearance to South America were probably of the opinion that, if he could score the goals that would win the title, his previous appalling behaviour should just be glossed over.

Similarly, the club's moral and principled stand lasted just as long as it suited them; until the demands of greed, glory and capitalism issued their final demand. 'A plague on both your houses' was the only sane reaction to the sight of these two bald men fighting over a comb. It had been a thoroughly unedifying spectacle reflecting no credit on either party. The need to win, to parade a trophy of some description to justify the outlay of those vast sums of capital was so overwhelming that any kind of moral stance stood no chance of success in the face of such cynical pragmatism.

In 1966 Alan Ogley had rowed with Joe Mercer at half-time in the dressing room at Bramall Lane. Ogley had performed heroics in the City goal to keep Sheffield United down to a one-goal lead secured by a header from Mick Jones. Mercer thought Ogley should have got to the ball first and told his goalkeeper so in no uncertain terms. Ogley was incensed, took off his jersey, hurled it to the floor, and stamped off into the showers, refusing to go out in the second half. This was the era in which only one substitute was permitted and number 12 was never a goalkeeper. Malcolm Allison, in the unaccustomed position of pouring oil on troubled waters, persuaded the still visibly upset Ogley to pick up his jersey and go out for the second half. The match ended with no further score. On Monday morning, Mercer told the *Manchester Evening News* that Harry Dowd would be recalled for the sixth-round FA Cup tie against Leeds United at Elland Road the following Saturday. Ogley was devastated. He stormed into the manager's office but Mercer was unmoved. They never spoke again and Ogley never played for the first team again.

A few weeks into the following season Ogley was transferred against his wishes to Stockport County in a player exchange with Ken Mulhearn. That is how you deal with player dissent. The supporters knew nothing about it and I only learned the full story from Alan Ogley when I interviewed him while researching *George Best and 21 Others*. Today, Ogley bitterly regrets his actions, which were entirely out of keeping with his normally respectful character, and recognises that, even if Mercer was wrong to have yelled at him after he had personally kept Sheffield United at bay for 45 minutes, he was just a player and should not have spoken to the manager like that. Carlos Tévez is paid £198,000 a week compared to Alan Ogley's £40 a week but the relationship between player and manager should not have changed. Ogley would have been thrilled to have been allowed to apologise but he was never given the chance. The prospect that he might have stated publicly that Joe Mercer had treated him like a dog was non-existent. The prospect that Mercer would back down as a pragmatic response to a far more challenging title race in 1968 was also non-existent.

To emphasise the gulf between players now and players then it is enough to reveal the difference in basic salary levels because money is what drives football now and takes it on a journey inconceivable to 99% of its suppporters. In March 2012 Mario Balotelli visited a strip club in Liverpool, emerging in the early hours of Friday, the day before City were due to face Bolton Wanderers in a Premier League match. Faced with unquestionable evidence, Balotelli publicly confessed his breach of club rules and was, it was reported, subsequently fined two weeks' wages, a sum amounting to a quarter of a million pounds. If, for reasons I cannot even imagine, I were to be fined a quarter of a million pounds I would probably have to sell my house in order to pay it. For players who earn at this level a fine of that nature makes no significant impact. Mario will presumably still be able to afford his extra large box of fireworks when Guy Fawkes Night next approaches.

For most professional clubs it is the lack of money that is the problem. The huge debts incurred by clubs in their ruthless pursuit of glory and more money, frequently threaten the very existence of the club. Leeds United are the most visible example of the broken dreams of the foolish men who thought they could get to where they wanted to go by borrowing money they couldn't repay. Portsmouth have been in administration twice in two years. Glasgow Rangers, while on their way into administration, revealed that they had somehow 'lost' £24 million. The club owes HMRC £9 million. If you or I owe HMRC £311.76 the bailiffs are on the way round. A few days ago it was rumoured that Port Vale were on the verge of liquidation. It seems that scarcely a day passes when some poor supporters are suddenly confronted with the prospect that their team might shortly cease to exist.

At the other end of the spectrum there are the teams at the top of the Premier League, bankrolled by rich men seeking to become even richer, or at least more famous, for football has usually been the graveyard of financial ambitions. You only had to see Bernie Ecclestone staring at a case of bottled water in the QPR dressing room in BBC 2's eye-opening documentary film about the club's 'four year plan' and bemoaning this crazy extravagance to realise that football is rarely the passport to riches. My club has posted losses that would astonish Ecclestone and his eccentric partner Flavio Briatore. Few businesses could continue trading having sustained losses of over £120 million in the last financial year. Manchester City now can because the Royal Family of Abu Dhabi has decided it is the appropriate vehicle to advance their own ambitions. They may have incidental benefits for Manchester City but supporters should not mistake them for a twenty-first century version of Jack Walker. They will be there for just as long as Manchester City suits the purposes of Abu Dhabi.

That is why I cannot make the adjustment so many of my friends have made. There is no joy now for me in watching Manchester City because I do not believe I am looking at 'my' team any longer. I recognise that City now have under contract the best squad that most of us have ever known. Naturally, I admire the skills of players like Aguero and Silva and Yaya Touré but then I used to admire the skills of Zola and Bergkamp and Henry. 'Ownership' is what distinguishes City players from those of other clubs. I look at the array of talent now gathered at Eastlands and I genuinely admire it – but I don't 'own' it, so I don't love it. Love is what matters, just as it does in more conventional areas of life. I loved City when we had Barry Betts and Bill Leivers in the 1960s and when we had Gordon Smith and Graham Baker in the early 1980s; for heaven's sake, I even loved City when we had Gerry Creaney and Michael Frontzeck in the 1990s. Of course it was much easier to love Lee, Bell and Summerbee or Barnes, Tueart and Owen because they were all great players but that was incidental. If you boot out the players who really care about the club like Richard Dunne and Stephen Ireland, get rid of them so cursorily that they say bad things about the manner in which they were hustled out of the place, and you import Adebayor, Robinho and Carlos Tévez, because they roll off the tongue in Beijing then you are improving the quality of the squad while alienating at least one of your most dedicated and longest-serving supporters.

One of the reasons why I have so cordially disliked Manchester United for so long is because, for me, that club represented the nadir of bullying. They have, after all, a manager who might be the greatest manager in the history of the game if you judge by the number of trophies he has won, but whose public bullying and hypocritical attitudes have made him a justifiable object of widespread loathing. However many trophies he wins, he will never compare to his great predecessor, Matt Busby, because Busby knew how to behave with dignity and grace, two words rarely attributed to the current Manchester United manager. Even that wouldn't bother me if Garry Cook in his infinite wisdom hadn't decided that the club whose behaviour he wished to imitate was . . . Manchester United. As Mama and Velma sing in Kander and Ebb's *Chicago*, 'Nobody's got no class.'

When Manchester City win the Premier League they will have bought it, they won't have earned it. We live in an age of instant gratification, when it is so difficult to teach children about the pleasure that comes from deferred gratification – not being given everything you want as soon as you want it just because your parents can afford it. I was brought up in Manchester in the 1950s and 1960s and what I was taught by the older generation who had survived the Great Depression and a World War was that life was hard and success had to be earned. You couldn't buy success and you couldn't buy respect – either self-respect or the respect of others. You could only earn it. Earning it takes time. Good food needs slow cooking in an oven, not fast heating up in a microwave. It's an old-fashioned attitude, this belief in moral integrity, and it doesn't seem to fit into a world dominated by the greed of the Premier League.

It's sad that I can't enjoy Manchester City's current renaissance. As and when City tick off their trophy successes I shall be delighted for my friends who do not share my reservations. I shall be glad for my children who suffered merciless teasing during their schooldays but kept their faith in Manchester City to the great joy and thankful admiration of their father. For them and their contemporaries, who have known nothing but minor triumphs and major disappointments, I am glad that they will take pride in being the best team in the world, if that's what City become, even if I shrink from the label of 'the richest team in the world'.

My journey seems to have come to a sad and highly unpredicted finale but in the end I can only trust the feelings of my heart. I know what it is to be in love. I also know what it is to be disappointed in love. Manchester City in their current guise feel like the end of a love affair, a bereavement of a unique nature. Just like the end of a love affair I understand rationally why it had to end but emotionally I remain confused. I sit in the bath and I lie awake at night and I wonder, did it really have to end like this? Maybe the phone will ring tomorrow and when I pick up the receiver I shall hear the sound of her mellifluous voice again. Maybe the doorbell will ring and even as I dash down the stairs to answer it I will know that when I open the door there she will be on the doorstep, hair dishevelled, tears streaking her beautiful face as she hurls herself into my arms sobbing for forgiveness. Well, I can dream can't I? Isn't supporting your team all about dreams? My dream now is just to care again.